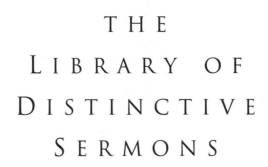

THE
LIBRARY OF
DISTINCTIVE
SERMONS

❧

VOLUME FIVE

GARY W. KLINGSPORN
General Editor

QUESTARS PUBLISHERS • SISTERS, OREGON

Executive Editor
Stephen E. Gibson, B.A.

General Editor
Gary W. Klingsporn, Ph.D.

Associate Editor
Mary Ruth Howes, M.A.

THE LIBRARY OF DISTINCTIVE SERMONS, VOLUME 5
published by Questar Publishing Direct
a part of the Questar publishing family
© 1997 by Questar Publishers

International Standard Book Number: 1-57673-158-8
Design by David Uttley
Printed in the United States of America

Scripture quotations are from:
The Holy Bible, New International Version (NIV) © 1973, 1984 by International Bible Society, used by permission of Zondervan Publishing House.

The New Revised Standard Version Bible (NRSV) © 1989 by the Division of Christian Education of the National Council of the Churches of Christ in the United States of America.

The Revised Standard Version (RSV) © 1946, 1952 by the Division of Christian Education of the National Council of the Churches of Christ in the United States of America.

The New Testament in Modern English, Revised Edition (PHILLIPS) © 1972 by J.B. Phillips.

The Message © 1993 by Eugene H. Peterson.

New American Standard Bible (NASB) © 1960, 1977 by the Lockman Foundation.

The Revised English Bible (REB) © 1989 by Oxford University Press and Cambridge University Press.

The Good News Bible: The Bible in Today's English Version (TEV) © 1976 by the American Bible Society.

Acknowledgement is made for "The Creation" excerpted from *God's Trombones*, by James Weldon Johnson. © Viking Press 1927; copyright renewed 1955 by Grace Nail Johnson. Reprinted by permission of Penguin USA. All rights reserved.

For information:
QUESTAR PUBLISHERS, INC.•POST OFFICE BOX 1720•SISTERS, OREGON 97759

Library of Congress Cataloging–in–Publication Data

The library of distinctive sermons/Gary W. Klingsporn, general editor. v. <4>:25 cm.
Includes bibliographical references. ISBN 1-57673-158-8 (v. 5) 1. Sermons, American.
2. Preaching. I. Klingsporn, Gary W.
BV4241.L47 1996 96-173243 252--DC20

97 98 99 00 01 02 03 — 10 9 8 7 6 5 4 3 2 1

TABLE OF CONTENTS

PREFACE 6

INTRODUCTION 8

CONTRIBUTING EDITORS 12

BRUISED REEDS AND DIMLY BURNING WICKS
Rev. Dr. Thomas G. Long 17

SIGHT FOR SORE EYES
Rev. Dr. David C. Fisher 33

TEMPLE CROSSING
Rev. Dr. Richard L. Eslinger 49

THE MAN JESUS
Rev. Dr. Buckner Fanning 63

BLESSED BY MENTORS
Rev. Dr. F. Dean Lueking 83

ON TAKING PAIN SERIOUSLY
Rev. Dr. John Killinger 99

ELLIPSIS AND ETERNITY
Rev. Dr. Michael P. Halcomb 111

MEANWHILE
Rev. Dr. William J. Ireland, Jr. 127

RISKY BUSINESS
Rev. Dr. Paul S. Wilson 139

THE VISIT OF THE MAGI
Rev. Dr. Gary A. Furr 151

WHAT ARE YOU DOING HERE?
Dr. Gary W. Klingsporn 167

PRACTICING FORGIVENESS
Rev. Dr. Curtis W. Freeman 183

LOST AND FOUND: CLIMBING THE WRONG LADDER

Rev. John F. Crosby 197

A DANGEROUS DISTURBANCE

Rev. Dr. Robert T. Snell 213

PRAYING IN THE DARKNESS AT NOON

Rev. Dr. Stephen Brachlow 227

THE LOVE THAT LIES BENEATH THE WOE

Rev. Dr. John Mark Jones 237

A SURPRISING UNCONVENTIONAL FRIEND

Rev. Dr. David L. Williamson 251

LIFE AS IT IS SUPPOSED TO BE LIVED

Rev. Dr. Gary Dennis 267

WHAT REALLY CHANGES PEOPLE?

Rev. Ronald W. Higdon 279

THE BEGETTING OF JESUS

Rev. Dr. Martin B. Copenhaver 291

TOPICAL INDEX 305

SCRIPTURE INDEX 309

For all who preach

How beautiful upon the mountains
are the feet of the messenger
who announces peace,
who brings good news,
who announces salvation,
who says to Zion, "Your God reigns."

ISAIAH 52:7, NRSV

The idea of *The Library of Distinctive Sermons* originated in painful practical circumstances rather than in an academic context. A pastor friend of mine went through a prolonged ordeal of tension and conflict with a congregation before he was terminated primarily "because his sermons were dry and hard to follow." As a new, young pastor, he was doing the best he could without the benefit of much experience in ministry. By and large, however, he was not connecting with the congregation in his preaching. The congregation became impatient and was less than compassionate in handling the situation. This led to a bitter parting of the ways.

As a lay person sitting in the pew and aware of the tension, I felt the pain on both sides of the issue. I began to ask myself what more might be done to assist ministers in learning and sharing the insights which contribute to effective preaching. *The Library of Distinctive Sermons* originated from that experience. It is a resource designed to promote vital and effective preaching through the sharing of sermons and insights on preaching by working pastors.

The Library of Distinctive Sermons brings together a collection of powerful contemporary sermons of diverse style and content, along with careful reflection as to what makes each sermon effective, and how each sermon relates to biblical, theological, and practical ministry issues facing pastors today.

It is important to note that we have chosen not to engage in an academic critique of each sermon. No sermon is flawless. We have chosen good sermons and have asked some simple questions: What makes each of these sermons good? What can we learn from the creative elements of style and content in each sermon to assist us in the art of preaching?

Discussion of these questions in the Comment section following each sermon makes *The Library of Distinctive Sermons* unique among sermon publications. We have enlisted only working pastors for the task of commenting on each sermon. While there are many excellent books on homiletics, we discovered that few are written by pastors for pastors. The Comment sections are a means of sharing practical ideas and insights from pastor to pastor in a way that is helpful to pastors of all backgrounds and levels of experience. Our desire is that *The Library of Distinctive Sermons* will enhance your own process of developing new sermons and contribute to the continual renewal of your preaching ministry.

Many people gave of their talents to this series. First, we are deeply grateful to all of the preachers whose sermons appear in this volume. Their commitment to the proclamation of the gospel and their willingness to share their sermons "out of context" with a wider audience beyond their local congregations, have made this series possible. Special thanks go also to those pastors who shared their wisdom, perspectives, and insights in the Comment sections. Appreciation goes as well to the General Editor, Dr. Gary W. Klingsporn, whose special gifts and talents in communication and publishing are reflected throughout the series. Special thanks to Mary Ruth Howes, who, as Associate Editor, kept us all in line with her wonderful editorial expertise in the written word.

In a rapidly changing consumer culture which is increasingly visually oriented, the sermon "competes" as never before with a multiplicity of media and voices vying for our attention. In a culture where the entertainment world sets the pace and celebrities are often the measure of "success," preaching today is subjected to intense scrutiny and is regarded by many as outmoded, especially if it does not "entertain." And yet, since the beginning of Christianity, followers of Jesus Christ in every age have found preaching the most powerful and effective form of communicating the gospel. Indeed, there is something about the gospel that seems to demand this particular expression, this form of communication, and none other. Through preaching, lives continue to be saved and transformed, liberated, healed and reconciled. We pray that *The Library of Distinctive Sermons* will encourage you and help you create new and effective ways of proclaiming the gospel of Jesus Christ in today's world.

Stephen E. Gibson
Executive Editor

INTRODUCTION

Welcome to Volume 5 of *The Library of Distinctive Sermons*. As we did in the first four volumes of this series, we are pleased to offer here another twenty outstanding sermons with comment.

Much has been written on the subject of preaching. Seldom, however, do we find good sermons brought together with commentary on why those sermons constitute effective proclamation of the gospel. Among the literature available today, we can read sermons. Or, we can read about preaching. But seldom do we have the opportunity to do both at the same time: to read good sermons, and to reflect on the art of preaching as it is embodied in those sermons.

The Library of Distinctive Sermons is designed to promote the enrichment of preaching through the sharing of good sermons and careful analysis of their style and content. The purpose is to read a sermon and ask, "What makes this sermon effective as the proclamation of God's Word?" The philosophy underlying this series is that, whether we are novices or seasoned preachers, we can always learn from others who preach. One of the best ways to do that is to "listen" to others, to observe how they preach, and pick up on some of the best of what they do in a way that is natural and appropriate in our own preaching.

Each of the sermons in this volume is accompanied by a Comment section. Here working pastors reflect on what makes each sermon distinctive and effective. To some extent, of course, this is a very subjective undertaking. What makes a sermon "good" or "effective" to one person is not always the same in the opinion of others. Given the subjectivity involved, it would be easy to avoid ever undertaking the task of serious reflection about our preaching. However, in the Comment sections in this volume, the writers have taken the risk of opening the dialogue about what constitutes effective preaching. There is much to be gained in this process: new ideas and techniques, new perspectives on texts, creative forms and structures, new stories and illustrations for preaching.

It is one thing to hear or read a good sermon and to have some sense of why we like it. But how often do we give serious analytical reflection, asking what we can learn from a sermon? *The Library of Distinctive Sermons* provides an opportunity for the enrichment of preaching through thoughtful consideration of why each sermon has been done in the way it is done.

In the Comment sections in this series the writers reflect on the style and content of each sermon. They look at such things as the genre and structure of the sermon, its use of biblical texts, illustrations, literary or rhetorical techniques, tone, and language. They also comment on how the content of each sermon proclaims biblical faith; remains true to the biblical text; reflects sound theology; deals with faith questions; addresses ethical and social issues; and shows the relevance of the gospel in today's world.

The Comments are presented in a fairly nontechnical way. The focus of this series is not on an academic analysis or critique of sermons, nor is the focus on theoretical aspects of communication and homiletics. The purpose of this series is to offer practical reflection aimed at stimulating our thoughts and improving our preaching in very practical ways.

The format of this volume is simple. Each sermon is presented as closely as possible to the original form in which it was preached. Obviously, in moving from the original oral medium of preaching to the written form represented here, some editing has been necessary to facilitate literary style, clarity, and comprehension.

The Comment following each sermon assumes that every effective sermon includes at least three basic elements. First, every sermon addresses questions relating to the problems and needs of the human condition. Second, every good sermon has a thesis and makes an assertion. It proclaims truth from the Scriptures using one or more biblical texts. Third, every good sermon invites people to respond or motivates them to think, act, or believe. These preaching elements can be described in many different ways using varieties of language. In their Comments the writers commonly use the terms Text, Problem, Proclamation, and Response (or Invitation) to refer to these elements of sermonic structure and content.

In the Comments, then, you will notice frequent discussion of the following items which are intended as helpful tools of reflection and analysis:

1) Text. How does the preacher interpret and apply the biblical text(s) in the sermon? What techniques are used? What insights into the text(s) are found in the sermon?

2) Problem. What human problem, need, question, or life situation does each sermon address? How is the problem of the human condition understood and presented in the sermon?

3) Proclamation. How does the sermon proclaim the good news of the Christian gospel? What is the truth or "kerygma" drawn from the Scriptures and applied to the human situation?

4) Response. How does the sermon invite us to respond? What does the preacher invite, urge, or encourage us to believe or to do? What motivation is there to act or to change, and how does this flow out of the interpretation of the biblical text(s), the human problem, and the proclamation of the gospel?

5) Suggestions. Each Comment section concludes with some practical suggestions for thought or discussion, for further reading, or for incorporating some of the insights from the sermon into one's own preaching.

The Library of Distinctive Sermons features a wide variety of sermon styles and subjects. This is important in a series designed for the enrichment of preaching. You will undoubtedly like some of the sermons more than others. You will react differently to different sermons. You may agree or disagree with some of the Comments. But all of these reactions can be learning experiences. So as you read, ask yourself: "What do I think about this sermon? Why do I feel as I do?" Interact with the material! Reflect on your own preaching and ministry as you enjoy this volume. Then the sermons and Comments will become a valuable resource for your own ministry.

It is important to remember that each of the sermons in this volume was preached in an original context, most of them in congregations on Sunday mornings. Each was spoken with the presence and guidance of the Holy Spirit to a particular people in a particular time and place. Each sermon had a life of its own as the Word of God in that specific moment.

While the sermons that appear here are removed from those original contexts, there is much we can learn from them. Whenever possible, the attempt has been made to acknowledge significant aspects of the original context. But now these sermons appear in a new context. God can use them in this context to speak home to our hearts and to create new understanding and possibilities for ministry.

The apostle Paul wrote, "So then faith comes from what is heard, and what is heard comes through the word of Christ" (Rom. 10:17, NRSV). It is in and through the preached word of Christ that God directs us to faith in Christ and imparts to us the gift of faith. In preaching, the wonderful work and mystery of God take place: the living Christ becomes present through the preached word. Bonhoeffer said, "The word of Scripture is certain, clear, and plain. The preacher should be assured that Christ enters the congregation through those words which he [or she] proclaims from the Scripture...."[1] Preaching is a holy calling filled with the mystery and promise of God. We do well to give all the careful time and attention we can to this holy task, while always giving ourselves to God. As Augustine said of preaching, "Lord, give me the gifts to make this gift to you."

Gary W. Klingsporn
General Editor

Note
1. Dietrich Bonhoeffer, *Worldly Preaching*, ed. Clyde E. Fant (Nashville and New York: Thomas Nelson, Inc., 1975), p. 130.

Donald K. Adickes is a retired minister of the Evangelical Lutheran Church in America. A graduate of Gettysburg College (B.A.), Lutheran Seminary in Philadelphia (M.Div.) and the University of Kansas (M.A.), he served twenty-five years as a chaplain in the United States Army and a number of years in parish ministry in Texas, where he continues to serve parishes on a part-time and interim basis.

Dixie Brachlow is a recent graduate of Louisville Presbyterian Theological Seminary (M.Div.) and a candidate for pastoral ministry in the Presbyterian Church (USA). Her professional experience includes college administration, grant writing, public speaking, program development and high school teaching. She is a graduate of the University of Minnesota (B.S.) and Augustana College (M.A.).

Richard A. Davis is Teaching Pastor of Hope Presbyterian Church in Richfield, Minnesota. A graduate of the University of Minnesota (B.A.), Luther Theological Seminary (M.A.), and San Francisco Theological Seminary (M.Div.), Davis has served Presbyterian churches in Minnesota and Belfast, Northern Ireland. He has contributed a number of articles to various publications and is author of *The Prism Project: A Survey of the Bible for Adults*.

Gary W. Downing is currently Evangelism Pastor of Faith Covenant Church in Burnsville, Minnesota. He has previously served as a seminary instructor, executive minister of Colonial Church, Edina, Minnesota, executive director of Youth Leadership, and area Young Life director. A graduate of Bethel College (B.A.), Bethel Theological Seminary (M.Div.) and Luther Theological Seminary (M.Div.), Downing is author of *One Man's Heart*, a book on male spirituality.

Gilbert R. Friend-Jones is Senior Minister of Central Congregational Church (UCC), Atlanta, Georgia. He previously served churches in Minneapolis, Minnesota; Reston, Virginia; and South Paris, Maine. A graduate of Princeton Theological Seminary (M.Div.) and Howard

University Divinity School (D.Min.), he has been active in ecumenical and urban ministries and initiatives against violence and racism. He has written articles for national publications on subjects as diverse as jazz, Chernobyl, philosophy, sexuality, theology, and urban violence.

Marianna Frost is Professor of Bible and Religion at Athens State College in Athens, Alabama. She is an ordained United Methodist minister who has served pastorates in Tennessee and Texas. An author and former newspaper editor, she received the Doctor of Ministry degree from Vanderbilt University.

Gary A. Furr is Pastor of Vestavia Hills Baptist Church in Birmingham, Alabama, and adjunct instructor in New Testament at Samford University. The author of numerous articles and book reviews, Furr is coeditor of *Ties That Bind: Life Together in the Baptist Vision.* He has served churches in Texas, Georgia and Alabama, and is a graduate of Carson-Newman College (B.A.), Southeastern Baptist Theological Seminary (M.Div.) and Baylor University (Ph.D.).

Greg Garrison is Religion Editor and staff writer for *The Birmingham News* in Birmingham, Alabama. A graduate of the University of Missouri School of Journalism (1985), he has written articles for the *National Catholic Reporter, Liberty,* and *Presbyterians Today,* and was a 1996 finalist for the Templeton Reporter of the Year Award sponsored by the Religion Newswriters Association.

William J. Ireland, Jr. is Pastor of Briarcliff Baptist Church, Atlanta, Georgia. A graduate of Mississippi College (B.A.) and Southern Baptist Theological Seminary (M.Div., Ph.D.), he has served churches in Louisiana, Kentucky and Georgia, has served as Moderator of the Atlanta Baptist Association and has written numerous articles for preaching and teaching publications.

Debra K. Klingsporn is an author and former public relations and marketing executive who has served as executive director of marketing for Word Publishing, and as a vice president of Carol DeChant & Associates, a public relations firm based in Chicago. A graduate of Texas A&M University with a bachelor's degree in journalism, she is the coauthor of

Shattering Our Assumptions: Breaking Free of Expectations—Others & Our Own; Soul Searching: Meditations for Your Spiritual Journey; and *I Can't, God Can, I Think I'll Let Him;* and coeditor of *The Quickening Heart* and *The Remembering Season.*

Gary W. Klingsporn is Teaching Minister of Colonial Church in Edina, Minnesota, and serves as General Editor of *The Library of Distinctive Sermons.* He has served churches in Texas and Minnesota and has taught religious studies at Baylor University and Metropolitan State University in Minneapolis. Formerly a writer and editor with Word Publishing, he is a graduate of St. Paul's Lutheran College (A.A.), Oral Roberts University (B.A.), and Baylor University (Ph.D.).

Paul D. Lowder is a retired United Methodist minister who has served North Carolina churches in Davidson, Greensboro, Eden, and Charlotte. Author of two books, *Let Us Pray* and *Feed Whose Sheep?,* he reviews books for the *North Carolina Christian Advocate* and has contributed articles to numerous magazines. He is a commentator on WUNC-FM and a graduate of Albion College (B.A.) and Candler School of Theology, Emory University (B.D.).

James J. H. Price is Professor of Religious Studies at Lynchburg College, Lynchburg, Virginia. An ordained minister in the Presbyterian Church (USA), he holds a Ph.D. from Vanderbilt University. For several years he has written exegetical/expository studies in the International Uniform Lessons in *The Presbyterian Outlook,* along with articles, book reviews, and exegetical studies in a variety of other publications. He is the coauthor with William R. Goodman, Jr., of *Jerry Falwell: An Unauthorized Profile* (Paris and Associates, 1981).

Peter J. Smith is Pastor of First Congregational Church of Thomaston, Connecticut. A graduate of Trinity College (B.A.) and Gordon-Conwell Theological Seminary (M.Div.), he has served United Church of Christ churches in Indiana and Minnesota and has been active in Habitat for Humanity, the United Church Board for World Ministries, and other ministry endeavors.

Peter G. St. Don is Founding Pastor of Harbour Community Church in Huntington Beach, California. A graduate of Fuller Theological Seminary (M.A.) and McCormick Theological Seminary (D.Min.), he has served a number of churches and is a leader in the National Association of Congregational Churches.

Karen Fisher Younger is Minister to Families and Youth at Faith United Methodist Church, Downers Grove, Illinois. A graduate of Trinity University (B.A.) and Gordon-Conwell Seminary (M.Div.), she won the Gordon-Conwell Seminary Preaching Award and has served as an intern at Park Street Church, Boston, Massachusetts.

BRUISED REEDS AND DIMLY BURNING WICKS

ISAIAH 42:1–9; MATTHEW 2:1–12

REV. DR. THOMAS G. LONG
FRANCIS LANDEY PATTON PROFESSOR OF PREACHING
PRINCETON THEOLOGICAL SEMINARY
PRINCETON, NEW JERSEY

REV. DR. THOMAS G. LONG

BRUISED REEDS
AND DIMLY
BURNING WICKS[1]

ISAIAH 42:1–9; MATTHEW 2:1–12

The Old Testament lesson from Isaiah 42 is taken from a section of the Hebrew Scriptures that biblical scholars today call "Second Isaiah." "First Isaiah" was addressed to the Israelites before they were taken into captivity in Babylon; "Second Isaiah" comes later, after decades of exile. It is a word for God's people just as they are about to be released from Babylon's grip and returned to their homeland. The prophet, convinced that their faithful memories may have faded over the long years of exile and that they may have forgotten the God of their forebears, reminds them of the identity and character of God, the God who is about to bring them home. The heart of the passage is this: Who is God? God is One who will not break a bruised reed; the kind of God who will not quench a dimly burning wick; the kind of God who will faithfully bring forth justice.

I.

When you get down to it, most of us, in our heart of hearts, have a quarrel with God. When I say we have a quarrel with God, I don't mean to imply that we are continually angry at God—although most of us, from time to time, do become angry at God. What I really mean is that we are puzzled and perplexed by the way God behaves in the world, by what God chooses to do, and how God chooses to do it. In other words, if we were God, if we had God's power, if we had God's majestic and comprehensive presence in the world, we are sure things would be different. We would be another kind of God; we would be God in a different way than the God we see in Scripture.

You may have read some years ago that wonderful book, *Children's Letters to God*. One of the letters was from a little girl named Norma. "Dear God, did you mean for giraffes to look that way; or was that an accident?"[2] Already beginning in her child's imagination was a kind of quarrel with God, a puzzlement about the ways of God in the world. Norma would not have made giraffes the way God made them—and neither would we. God's thoughts are not like our thoughts; God's ways are not like our ways.

Take the resurrection. When God raised Jesus from the dead, when Jesus stepped out of the tomb and shook off the powers of sin and death, the risen Jesus appeared only to the faithful, only to his little group, only to people who already believed in him. As a friend of mine said, "That's no way to run a resurrection. What he should have done was appear to the Sanhedrin. 'Would you fellows like to go another round?'" But no, the risen Christ appears only to a few women followers and to a few frightened disciples. We would not have done it that way. God's thoughts are not our thoughts, and God's ways are not our ways.

So, most of us have a quarrel with God, with the things God chooses to do and the way God chooses to do them. A physician in Atlanta says, "When I get to heaven, if I get to heaven, I'm going to stand before the throne of God with a cancer cell in my hand and say, 'Why, why?'"

Often, our quarrel with God becomes the occasion to redefine God. If God does not act like the kind of God we desire, we will simply fashion a God who will. As one systematic theologian, Cornelius Plantinga, has said,

> Why else do new revised versions of God keep appearing? Why else does God emerge as racist, sexist, chauvinist, politically cor-

rect, legalist, socialist, capitalist? If we are intellectuals, God is a cosmic Phi Beta Kappa; if we are laborers, God is a union organizer (remember, his Son was a carpenter); if we are entrepreneurs, God is for free enterprise (didn't his Son say, "I must be about my father's *business.*")[3]

We produce revised standard versions of God, theological amendments that express the way we wish God really were. This is, of course, the core meaning of idolatry, and our tendency toward idolatry is the principal reason the Bible keeps coming to us again and again to refresh our memory, to destroy the idols, to knock down the false images of God that we create, to regrind the narcissistically distorted lenses through which we view God, and to irrigate the fields of our religious imagination with the truth of the way God really is in the world. That's the purpose of this passage from Second Isaiah—to renew our understanding of the truth about God, of the way God really is in the world. But because this word from the prophet, like all true expressions of the living God, punctures our wishful thinking, we may not like what he says.

II.

The first truth Isaiah announces is that whatever agenda we may wish God to have, the main purpose of God in the world is to establish justice in the earth—which, in the vocabulary of the Old Testament, is simply another way of saying that God's primary will is to repair the creation, to make all things new, to restore humanity and all else that God has made into the way God intended at the beginning.

This divine intention to repair the creation—to make all things new—sounds like a good thing, of course, until we realize how much we have invested in the old, in the broken and decayed creation, in the way things are now instead of the way God intends the creation to be. That is why, in our New Testament lesson, Herod and all of Jerusalem shook when they heard that the Christ child had been born. Because if that baby is king, we can't be king. If that newborn child is God's intention for humanity, then I have to let go of a lot of things that are precious to me.

Every Christmas Eve there is a living nativity pageant on the front lawn of a church in a suburb of New York City. This church is right in the center of the town, and the pageant is a spectacle the whole town comes out to see. You know how these work: there are real people playing all of the parts in the Christmas story; there are live sheep and cows, a real donkey, and, if they get ambitious, a real live camel or two trotting across the church lawn. The characters in the pageant assemble in the fellowship hall of the church and wait for their cues before they head out across the lawn to the manger and to "Bethlehem."

One year, the wise men not only wore their silken robes and fancy turbans, but they also borrowed brass censers from the local Orthodox, so that as they headed out across the lawn, they could be shrouded in the mystery of smoke and the aroma of incense. Before they left the fellowship hall, they lit the censers and got the incense going. They then headed out to the manger, unaware that the smoke had set off the automatic fire alarms in the church. An electronic message flashed to the fire station, and the fire department, persuaded that the church was ablaze, responded.

Needless to say, it was a Christmas pageant the town will never forget. There on the front lawn of the church, heading toward Bethlehem, were not only shepherds and angels and wise men, but yellow-slickered firemen unrolling hoses, convinced they had a fire to extinguish. When the firemen finally figured out that this was a false alarm, the crowd on the lawn distinctly heard the fire chief say with irritation, "You wise men are setting off alarms all over town!"[4]

The original wise men would well have understood. They, too, set off alarms all over town, because they recognized that this Christ child was God's new thing in the world, God's intention to set things right, East and West, North and South. In this baby, God was repairing the creation, and the brokers of the status quo and the stockholders in the old order shivered and shook.

Indeed, all human sin can be understood as an attack on creation, and it is God's will to address human sin by mending the damage we have done, by repairing the creation. In Pierre Van Paassen's book about the rise of the Third Reich, he describes a day when a group of Nazi Brown Shirts captured a rabbi in his study as he was preparing his sabbath sermon. They mocked and humiliated him, then they stripped him and flogged him. As they did, they laughed and said, "This lash is for Abraham; this one is for Jacob; this one is for Isaac." When he was numbed with the whipping, they took out scissors, and they sheared his locks and his beard and mocked him.

"Say something in Hebrew," the S.A. Captain ordered.

"Thou shalt love the Lord thy God with all thy heart," the Rabbi slowly pronounced the Hebrew words. But one of the other officers interrupted him. "Were you not preparing your sermon this morning?" he asked him.

"Yes," said the Rabbi.

"Well, you can preach it here to us. You'll never again see your synagogue; we've just burned it. Go ahead, preach the sermon," he cried out. "All quiet now, everybody. Jacob is going to preach a sermon to us."

"Could I have my hat?" asked the Rabbi.

"Can't you preach without a hat?" the officer asked him.

"Give him his hat!" he commanded. Someone handed the Rabbi his hat, and he put it on his head. The sight made the S.A. men laugh the more. The man was naked and he was shivering. Then he spoke.

"God created man in his image and likeness," he said. "That was to have been my text for the coming Sabbath."[5]

All of this destruction that human beings wreak on each other is an attack on creation and on the image of God in humanity. Whatever we wish God would do and be, the true God wills to repair creation, and God will not rest until justice has been established.

III.

Sometimes, though, our argument with God is not with the truth *that* God is going to establish justice, but with the *when* of God's justice, with the divine sense of timing. There is a marvelous scene in August Wilson's play, *Ma Rainey*.[6] The play is about black jazz musicians who are rehearsing in a Chicago recording studio. At one point, they take a break from the rehearsal and begin to tell stories. One of them tells about a cousin of his, a minister whose sister in Atlanta was desperately ill. So this minister took a train to Atlanta to visit her.

The train stopped in a little south Georgia town to take on water, and the minister got off the train to visit the bathroom. He went into the station and was told "colored people" couldn't use the bathroom inside; they had to use the outhouse. So he went out back, and while he was there the train left the station. So this minister found himself standing on a south Georgia railroad platform—no train, no friends. Across the tracks there was a group of hostile-looking young white men, and not wanting trouble, the minister simply started walking up the track. But the men followed him. Catching up with him, they surrounded him and demanded to know who he was and what he was doing. "I am a minister," he told them, and showed them his Bible and his cross. He told them his sister in Atlanta was sick and that he'd been left by the train. No matter. "Dance for us," they demanded. "Why don't you dance for us?" Someone pulled out a pistol and began to fire at the ground, forcing him to dance.

The musician telling the story suddenly stops in midsentence and says, "Can you believe that? Can you believe they did that to a man of God?"

One of the other musicians says, "What I can't believe is that, if he was a man of God, why did God let them do that to him. If he was God's own man, why didn't God send fire from heaven and strike those crackers down? That's what I want to know."

Sometimes our argument with God is not with the truth *that* God is

going to establish justice but with God's timing. If God is going to establish justice, then why doesn't God send fire down from heaven and do it
now? God's ways are not our ways, and God's thoughts are not our
thoughts. We want a mighty, action-filled, fix-it-now God. But as the
prophet says, God comes not as a military conqueror but as a gentle gardener and a lamplighter. "A bruised reed he will not break, and a dimly
burning wick he will not quench" (Isa. 42:3).

Why is God this way? I do not know. God's thoughts are not my
thoughts; God's ways are not my ways. I do know this, though: When we
call down God's justice on the world, we usually assume that it is justice for
us and punishment for others. But the truth of the matter is that all of us
are bruised reeds and dimly burning wicks, and God, as an act of patient
mercy, chooses not to rain down wrath because it would fall upon all of us.

Instead, God comes into the world as a vulnerable baby, a baby who
did not grow up to be a military hero but a man who climbed up on a
cross for all of us, high and low, rich and poor, red and yellow, black and
white, who took on himself the wrath that belongs to us all. Why?
Because that is who God is. A bruised reed God will not break, and a
dimly burning wick God will not quench.

Early last spring, a former student came by my office for a cup of cof-
fee. We chatted about this and that, and then she said, "I have a secret to
tell you."

"What is it?" I said.

"I'm pregnant," she said.

I was overjoyed. She and her husband had a seven-year-old daughter,
and they had wanted another child. Now she was telling me that she was
pregnant.

"That's wonderful news," I said.

"We just got the test results, and we know two things about our
child. Our child will be a boy, and he will have Down's syndrome."

I wondered how she felt; I knew how I would have felt if I had been
in her place. Why is life this way? Why must there be such pain? Why
cannot God do something to fix this? If I were God....

"We will handle it," she said; "we are trusting in God to help us."
A few weeks ago I received a Christmas letter in which she wrote,

After nine long months of unmitigated discomfort, at four in the
morning on August 18, I knew the magic moment had come. At
last, at 10:55 A.M., Timothy Andrew took his first breath and let
out a hearty yell. He was whisked off to neonatal intensive care
where he spent the next three days before coming home. He's
strong, alert, beautiful. He has the sweetest disposition. Daily he
shatters our images of handicapped and special needs. He may
need special help, but already he is no slouch in giving us special love. We are blessed. Kate [their other child] is Tim's cham-
pion. Hearing our concerns about how well Tim might be
accepted by other kids, Kate informed the kids on our block,
"My brother has Down's syndrome and everybody's going to play
with him, or else!"
   One evening we overheard her talking to Tim. "I'm so glad
you're here, Timothy. I will always love you, I'll never leave you.
I'll always be nearby." Christ came to identify with us, especially
those most in need. We know miraculous blessings. We've experienced them firsthand.

God's thoughts are not our thoughts; God's ways are not our ways.
Thank God for that. For a bruised reed God will not break, and a dimly
burning wick God will not extinguish. Praise be to God.

Notes

1. This sermon was originally published in *The Princeton Seminary Bulletin*, New Series,
   Vol. 17 (July 1996), pp. 196–201.
2. Stuart Hample, et al., eds., *Children's Letters to God: The New Collection* (New York:
   Workman, 1991).
3. Cornelius Plantinga, *Not the Way It's Supposed to Be: A Breviary of Sin* (Grand Rapids:
   Eerdmans, 1995), p. 109.
4. I am grateful to P. C. Enniss for this story.
5. Pierre Van Paassen, *That Day Alone* (New York: Dial, 1941), p. 311; quoted by
   Plantinga, *Not the Way*, pp. 31–32.
6. August Wilson, *Ma Rainey's Black Bottom* (New York: New American Library, 1985),
   Act II, p. 98.

COMMENT

THEODICY, IDOLATRY AND INCARNATION

If Thomas Long truly means what I think he is saying in this sermon, he is here proclaiming a shift in theological perspective so extraordinary as to be breathtaking. This sermon, in the words of the fire chief, should be "setting off alarms all over town." It challenges the traditional theological enterprise, and offers the foundation for a new Christian spirituality. I can only hope that the listeners who heard this Advent sermon sat keenly forward in their pews, filled with appropriate dread and expectation.

"Bruised Reeds and Dimly Burning Wicks" begins, proceeds and ends with a profound question for would-be believers. This question sometimes takes the form of a quarrel, sometimes an angry inquiry, sometimes an intellectual exercise. Who is God? What can we know of the character of this One on whom we are expected to stake our salvation? Is God trustworthy? A great humility permeates Long's struggle to articulate here, not an answer, but a meaningful response.

Long affirms that our quarrels with and questions about God are appropriate and understandable. Why giraffes (to a child)? Why Nazis and racist "crackers"? Why cancer? But definitive answers elude us. God's ways are not our ways. God has a separate agenda, quite apart from our desires and preferences. Most of our answers are not only inadequate, but they lead us into idolatry. More than a century ago Ludwig Feuerbach called our attention to this phenomenon of projection. Our "revised standard versions" of God end up looking very much like us, or at least what we would like to be.

Yet to Long, God is neither completely mysterious nor wholly "other." Something of God's character is revealed in Christian Scripture. In these Advent lections we are given a penetrating glimpse into God's true nature and agenda. If his listeners were not "malled" into a pre-Christmas stupor, this glimpse must have knocked their holiday socks right off!

Most of us grow up praising "the Lord, mighty in battle." But who notices a lamplighter? More of us pray to "the Creator of the Universe" than to a gentle gardener. God's power, more than God's tenderness, has engaged our most serious attention through the centuries. After all, who would trifle with the One who slew Egypt's firstborn, or destroyed the whole world with floodwaters?

But this kind of limitless power, in the covenantal context of biblical faith, introduces a kind of limitless accountability. We can accept giraffes. We can explain Nazis and racist "crackers." But who is *responsible* for Down's syndrome or cancerous cells?

Our lifelong quarrel is classically theological. How can we affirm that (1) God is all good and (2) all powerful if (3) evil and suffering are real? Long's attempt to hold these traditional tenets together leads him to affirm (like so many before him) that "God's ways are not our ways." Right. But if "God's ways" include the horrible suffering of even one inno-cent child, argued Albert Camus, then God becomes the enemy of a morally superior humanity.

What are "God's ways"? To his credit, Long refuses to shroud this question in theological mystification. Instead, he is willing to declare "the *main purpose* of God in the world." Based on a consensus exegesis of Deutero-Isaiah, he flatly states that the purpose of God's activity is "to establish justice in the earth," and "to repair the creation." Restoration and renewal are what God is trying to do.

But how? When? Measured against these audacious intentions, doesn't Woody Allen's designation for God seem pertinent: the "Great Under-achiever"? Well, yes and no. Yes, if our limited expectations and impatient timelines prevail. No, if another and greater wisdom is unfolding.

"Love," said Goethe, "never dominates; it cultivates." Ironically, the explosiveness of this sermon lies here: "God comes not as a military con-queror but as a gentle gardener and a lamplighter." Not only do we *want* "a mighty, action-filled, fix-it-now God," but that is the God we *believe* in. That God is taught in our Sunday school classes, addressed in our prayers, and preached from most of our pulpits. That is the God we have chosen to placate, petition and adore.

God's intentions are being achieved through means unfathomable to us: militant gentleness, indiscriminate inclusiveness, radical respectfulness, a noninvasive regard for perpetrators and victims alike. God is very serious about neither breaking bruised reeds nor quenching dimly burning wicks. God's intention to repair creation includes *all* of it, and not just those parts we approve. This is good news for us; if the truth be told, all of us need repair.

Yet all this is merely preamble. Using well-chosen stories, Long establishes (1) that evil and suffering are aggressively real both in nature and in the world of human interaction; (2) that God compassionately regards all creation and is actively repairing it; and (3) that God's nature, unknown to us, precludes God's engagement in any activities or God's use of any means that carry within them divisive and destructive tendencies.

How then *does* God engage the world and repair creation? Through a vulnerable baby. Through one who "climbed up on a cross for all of us." After hearing this sermon, it still may be possible to talk about an all-powerful, conquering Creator, but each of these terms will be filled with new content—something akin to Lao-tzu's observation that water is mightier than the stone.

The strength of this sermon derives from its faithful reflection of Advent's (and Easter's) challenge to all traditional theologies of power. God does not intervene; God incarnates. More precisely, God intervenes *through* incarnation. Through an incognito presence in unexpected places. God is undermining both the immediate effects and the ultimate power of evil. Timothy Andrew, a Down's syndrome child, becomes the defining vehicle (incarnation) of God's love, grace and power. That really is a revolutionary notion.

STRUCTURE

The "alarming magi" story pleasantly relaxes the congregation even as it alerts us to what is coming. But the proliferation of illustrative material distracted me. The Van Paassen and Wilson stories together are overwhelming. Each is deeply moving, evocative and true. One could build a whole sermon around either one, and each deserves more "unpacking" than it receives. Add to that a child's charming letter, a doctor's poignant complaint, two biblical texts, some theological commentary and a Down's syndrome baby! This sermon reminds me of my grandmother's wonderful fruitcakes at Christmas; even she was heard to say, "Too much is not good."

I found jarring and too cerebral Long's off-hand remark, "Take the resurrection…etc.," wedged between Norma's complaint about giraffes and the doctor's heartfelt protest against cancer. One may argue that the resurrection is too BIG to be used as a mere illustration of how we and God might do things differently.

I wonder if the three-point format used in this sermon isn't counter-productive? The points are not sharply delineated, and one wonders what purpose is served by this division. I think it obscures the central point and diminishes the sermon's impact.

Finally, to quibble a bit, I would have begun the sermon with the second paragraph: "When you get down to it…" (I'd get right down to it.) The first paragraph, if used at all, would serve better as an introduction to the Isaiah passage when read as Scripture earlier in worship.

Well, Long's ways are not my ways. I also have a quarrel with Long about substantive matters. I particularly appreciate his caveats against idolatry and our tendencies to make God in our own image. But how else can we proceed? *Every* image of God contains projections. Every image of God is metaphorical. Most of our metaphors are anthropomorphic. It would have been interesting for Long to consider the question "When does a metaphor become an idol?" before he proclaimed, without quali-fication, "the *truth*…of the way God *really is* in the world." To state it baldly, why is "gardener" or "lamplighter" less wistful or more true than "conqueror"? How do *we* know what God's main purpose in the world really is? The biblical materials give us many and sometimes conflicting metaphors and purposes. If Isaiah's gardener is the same God who slew Egypt's children, an explanation is in order. If not, an explanation is also in order.

COMMENT

A related conundrum is the apparent contradiction within God. On the one hand Long refers to God's smoldering and lethal anger. (How else can we understand his phrase, "the wrath that belongs to us all"?) On the other is the lamplighter's absolutely tender concern. I suggest that this conundrum can be eliminated if we accept that we are merely mixing metaphors.

Having quibbled and quarreled a bit, I wholeheartedly endorse Long's conclusions. I welcome him as a comrade in the revolution of theological understanding. I especially appreciate his presentation on the way we "invest" in one or another image of God, and his caution to hold our images lightly and sometimes to let them go. When images become idols, they must be resisted because they block, distort or limit our ability to perceive and respond to God's self-revelation and grace. Idolatry is our way of validating our own projections. Idols "fix" in consciousness what is fluid, elusive and alive. With Long, I believe that Christian revelation leads us toward soft and nurturing metaphors, and away from hard and destructive ones. And with Long, I believe these metaphors help us to perceive aspects of God's activity in our lives that we would otherwise miss altogether.

The letter from Long's former student provides a fitting finale to this touching sermon. It is a personal testimony that illustrates the main thrust of the message. This sermon is not so much an "answer" as it is a response to the theodic question. It is purely incarnational. It invites us all to examine the images of the God whom we worship, and to witness God's activity in the midst of the most vulnerable among us.

SUGGESTIONS

- Distinguish between a metaphor, an image and an idol in your theological thinking and in your preaching. For a moment, assume that every sermon implicitly attacks one or another form of idolatry. Attempt to identify and describe the "idolatrous" understandings of God that are shaping your life and the life of your congregation. What is true about them? How are they helpful? How do they block access to the Living God and render God safe or harmless?

• Answer Norma's letter.

• Reread the story by Pierre Van Paassen. Imagine you have been asked to preach on this Isaiah text to two different congregations next weekend: the Jewish congregation (now meeting in an open field) and a Lutheran church in which some of the soldiers hold membership. How would you address each group? How would you begin? What would be your point(s)?

• Reread the story by August Wilson. If you think there is an error in the thinking of the musicians, describe it for them. How can you persuade them to have or to keep faith? What is their response to your remarks? What can you learn from this?

• Raise again in your own mind the question of theodicy. (Read, for example, the dialogue between the doctor and the priest in *The Plague* by Albert Camus for an excellent framing of the question.) How do you resolve the implicit tensions between God's power, God's goodness and our experiences of suffering and evil?

• Reread the Christmas letter from Long's former student. Imagine that Timothy Andrew, now age twelve, arrives in your office with his next door friend. They ask you why God has allowed Tim to have Down's syndrome and not his friend. How do you respond? Compare your response to this question with your answer to Norma's letter in the second suggestion above.

Gilbert Friend-Jones

Sight for Sore Eyes

JOHN 9:1–41

REV. DR. DAVID C. FISHER
COLONIAL CHURCH
EDINA, MINNESOTA

SIGHT FOR SORE EYES

JOHN 9:1–41, NRSV

I don't know much about being blind. I can scarcely imagine living in a world of darkness. But I've tried.

When I lived in Boston, we had a neighbor who was also a member of our church, who was legally blind. I often saw her on the streets and in church with a white walking stick. She lived a full life of work, recreation and church. I recall how amazed I was the first time I saw her jogging up Pinkney Street—without her stick! Yet she knew where she was and what was all around her. Later, she asked me if she could feel my face in order to "see" what I looked like.

The "sight" of so-called unsighted people is uncanny. A bit unnerving too! I couldn't fool my friend with appearances. I wondered what she saw.

Yet what greater gift is there in all the world than eyes that see? This time of year, starved by winter's brown and gray, my soul aches for the lush beauty of spring about to burst from the frozen earth, the wonderful colors in flowers, trees, fields and gardens. I'm so thankful I can see.

Like you, I've paused in worshipful wonder before mountain landscapes and the ocean's majestic beauty. Fields and streams, forests and meadows, even the backyard—all of nature is a sight for sore eyes.

But there's so much more to see. If only we had better vision or a better vantage point. My office in Boston was on the fourth floor overlooking the Granary Burial Ground. From my desk all I could see were treetops and the buildings on the other side of the cemetery. One day I saw a peregrine falcon (it lived atop an office building nearby) perched near the top of the huge chestnut tree that dominated the burial ground. Suddenly I was aware of how much that bird could see that I could not. God made its eyes so much more perceptive than mine. I wished I could see more clearly.

There's also spiritual and moral vision, the kind of vision that makes a Mother Teresa or Nelson Mandela. Some people have eyes in their souls that see what others cannot perceive.

I suppose that the greatest desire of a blind man would be to see. At least that's what one blind man told Jesus. When Jesus asked him what he could do for him, the man answered, "Let me see again" (Mark 10:51). We don't know, however, what the blind man in our Gospel lesson was thinking. He doesn't ask for help like that other blind man. In fact, this blind man doesn't say anything before he is healed.

Jesus doesn't say anything to him either. This is not your ordinary healing. Without a word or warning, Jesus spit on the ground, made mud of the spit and put the mud on the blind man's eyes. Then, and only then, he spoke. "Go, wash in the pool of Siloam," he told the man.

Strange isn't it? But it's not really, not in John's Gospel. In this Gospel nothing is what it seems to be. Everything that happens points to something else. In fact, this is no mere miracle. John calls it a sign, a symbol that points to a greater reality. In an ordinary story you'd expect some hint of this poor man's wonder at the new world that opens up before his eyes. But that's not John's point. He directs our attention beyond the man's eyes to his soul. The light that pours into the man's new eyes is nothing compared to the light that's dawning in his soul. The man is groping his way toward faith. He's beginning to see the light, the light of the world.

The trajectory of the story is ironic. At first the blind man barely knows Jesus' name. At the end of the story he says, "Lord, I believe" (v. 38). The beggar becomes a worshiper. Meanwhile, the religious leaders, custodians of God's truth and guides to God's people, grow increasingly unbelieving. They search for some theological flaw in Jesus' behavior, some mistake in this healing so they can overturn the obvious medical verdict.

The irony is tragic. The blind man sees with increasing clarity while the religious leaders grow increasingly blind. The blind man's spiritual vision becomes clearer and sharper while those who claim spiritual sight plunge into ever increasing darkness. As Paul Duke says of the Pharisees in this text, "An illusion of sight…has led them to a far deeper darkness than they know."[1]

This is a necessary word for our time—and for us. Barbara Brown Taylor suggests that if there were auditions for this play, "most of us would go after the part of the blind man. It's a hard part, but a great part. There he is just minding his own tin-cup business when the light of the world comes along and opens his eyes, shoving him into the spotlight…"[2]

But, in fact, we're not like him. As Taylor suggests, we're not naturals for the part. Most of us are not outsiders in the village, tin cups in hand, sitting outside the city gates begging. We've not been consigned to the margins for our sins, imagined or otherwise. We are consummate insiders, law-abiding, church going, pledge-paying, good folks. We are the ones who profess spiritual sight. We're not blind of eye or heart.

That's why we need to listen to this story very carefully. We insiders are the ones who end up acting the Pharisees in this story. Insiders have a tragic tendency to forget the darkness of their own souls. It's a human tendency actually. We tend to fool ourselves.

Several years ago the *Wall Street Journal* (12/21/92) published a fascinating article titled, "Why Smart People Do Dumb Things." We've all seen it in business, education, politics and life. Great men and women, leaders who should know better in fact, people with a great track record, make huge mistakes. They know better, but….

It's a theme as old as the human race. The Greeks wrote whole plays about *hubris,* the self-destructive pride that afflicts us all, especially the great among us. "It is the gods' custom to bring low all things of surpassing greatness," Herodotus wrote. The Greeks saw *hubris* as a kind of madness, and had a saying, "Whom the gods would destroy, they first make mad."[3] Peter Drucker paraphrased the quote to apply to business in our time: "Whom the gods would destroy, they give ten years of success."

Ken Olson, the founder of the Digital Equipment Corporation, is a deacon of Park Street Church in Boston. His company was one of the great success stories of the '70s and '80s. One year Ken was picked as one of *Fortune* magazine's entrepreneurs of the year. He told me that so much success was the worst thing that ever happened to Digital. It set them up for destruction. They didn't think they could do anything wrong and he included himself in the indictment.

The *Wall Street Journal* article says that the apparent end of long success is severe "feedback deafness." The great ones no longer pay attention. They think they are beyond the mistakes of ordinary mortals.

We've all seen this problem—in someone else! We just can't seem to see our own blind spots, and when we mess up we blame others. Dare any of us think that this kind of moral blindness bypasses people of faith? We do know better, because we can see the darkness in others; but it is very difficult to see it in ourselves.

Sadly, I've had too many conversations with young adults whose souls are deeply scarred by growing up in the church. They are seldom turned off by Jesus or faith, but they have little use for the church. They've seen too much that didn't ring true. The really frightening thing is that I know I'm one of the offenders. How many of my words have damaged fragile souls? How many young and tender souls have I wounded, even turned away from the faith? I'm afraid of the answer. But if I cannot admit that my own soul is dark, I am the blindest man of all.

If we are honest with God and ourselves, a story like this one confronts us with a sobering reality. Here, as elsewhere, Jesus puts us all on notice about the darkness in our souls. He forces us back to the center of our faith. We stand before God with empty hands—always.

I come today, however, not to tell you of the darkness, but to bring you good news. The good news is in the heart of this ninth chapter of John. Did you notice what Jesus said just before he spit on the ground to make mud? Did you hear it? He looked at that blind man and said, "I am the light of the world" (v. 5).

You see, God will not have a world full of darkness. This Gospel story powerfully directs us back to the beginning of creation, when darkness covered the face of the deep and the earth was a formless void. Dark chaos and emptiness reigned over all. Remember the first words from God's mouth in that first story in the Bible? "Let there be light." Can you see it?

I love the poetic power of James Weldon Johnson's poem "The Creation."[4] An African-American, who wrote in the early part of the twentieth century, Johnson patterned his poem after the imagery and rhythm of old-time black preaching:

> And God stepped out on space,
> And he looked around and said:
> I'm lonely—
> I'll make me a world.
>
> And far as the eye of God could see
> Darkness covered everything,
> Blacker than a hundred midnights
> Down in a cypress swamp.
>
> Then God smiled,
> And the light broke,
> And the darkness rolled up on one side,
> And the light stood shining on the other,
> And God said: That's good!
> Then God reached out and took the light in his hands,
> And God rolled the light around in his hands
> Until he made the sun;

And he set that sun a-blazing in the heavens.
And the light that was left from making the sun
God gathered it up in a shining ball
And flung it against the darkness,
Spangling the night with the moon and stars.
Then down between
The darkness and the light
He hurled the world;
And God said: That's good!

God will not permit a world without light. God turns back the darkness with light. It's there in the rhythm of the universe: day follows night, and in the darkness of night the stars and the moon remind us of daylight that will surely come. But "The Creation" goes on even more powerfully. The poet continues,

Then God walked around,
And God looked around
On all that he had made...
And God said: I'm lonely still.

Then God sat down—
On the side of a hill where he could think;
By a deep, wide river he sat down;
With his head in his hands,
God thought and thought,
Till he thought: I'll make me a man!

Up from the bed of the river
God scooped the clay;
And by the bank of the river
He kneeled him down;
And there the great God Almighty

Who lit the sun and fixed it in the sky,
Who flung the stars to the most far corner of the night,
Who rounded the earth in the middle of his hand;
This Great God
Like a mammy bending over her baby,
Kneeled down in the dust
Toiling over a lump of clay
Till he shaped it in his own image;

Then into it he blew the breath of life,
And man became a living soul.
Amen. Amen.

You see, God will not tolerate absolute darkness in his universe nor will God permit darkness to reign in the sons of Adam and the daughters of Eve. We humans are living souls, the beloved creation of a loving God, and God comes into the world to claim his own. Into the darkness God sends his Son, the light of the world.

In a scene reminiscent of the creation story, the One who is the light of the world bends down over the chaos and dark void of this shell of a man, makes some mud and with a creative word declares, "Let there be light." And there was light! In that divine moment God reached into the blind man's soul, opened the door and the light flooded in. "Lord, I believe," the man said. And nothing was ever the same. Now he had eyes in his soul.

That same God, the God who comes to us in Jesus Christ, knows the brooding darkness, the moral chaos of our world. God knows the deceptive darkness of our own souls. And know this: God has not and will not give up on what God loves.

If God can breathe the breath of life into the dust of the earth to create a living soul, God will shine the light of the world into folks like us when we bow before the Light and say, "Lord, I believe."

Here and now God is forming a new people, men and women of the

Light, people with a moral vision that is not shaped by the darkness of this tragic planet. This people, the church of Jesus Christ, is growing toward a moral and spiritual vision formed by values of eternity. Because we follow the One who is the Light, we see things from a new and trans-forming point of view.

God's people, folks formed by the Light, are by the very nature of things, *people of hope*. Despite the thickening darkness all around us, we refuse to be bad news people. The Light creates "good news people" who refuse to permit the growing darkness to darken their souls. For we know the Spirit of the living God hovers over the deep and God continues to speak the creative words, "Let there be light." And we know that here, there and everywhere, God's light reaches out to touch a man, a woman, a child, a church. And nothing is the same.

We know that the very character of faith is an indefatigable hope that despite all appearances to the contrary, God is Sovereign of the universe and, therefore, the good news ultimately triumphs.

Even in us it triumphs! The darkness cannot stand forever before the light. The words, "Lord, I believe," set in motion the very powers of the kingdom of God, and, wonder of wonders, the Light turns back the darkness. Slowly to be sure, too slowly, we think. But the darkness can-not turn back the light forever in the soul that declares, "Lord, I believe."

One of the ancient prayers of the church should be our prayer every day. The "Jesus prayer" is simple but profoundly powerful. "Lord Jesus Christ, have mercy upon me." There stands the foundational power of the moral universe.

People of the light who form the church of Christ are also *people of grace*. Our new moral vision permits us to see not only what is, but what can be. Our Old Testament lesson (1 Sam. 16:1–13) tells of the prophetic vision given to Samuel to see in the shepherd boy David what his father and brothers could not see: the man who would one day be the greatest king of Israel.

People of the Light, men and women with sight-lines formed by the kingdom of God, are people learning to see with prophetic vision. No longer bound by what is, we see what each other can be—because of the Light! That vision offers us the freedom to love each other with heaven's love. God isn't finished with any of us yet, thank God.

And God is not finished with this church yet. Can you see it? Can you see, not what is, but what can be? Will we give each other the grace God gives us? People of God: Lighten up!

The moral bottom line is, as always, the incomprehensible love of God. "God so loved the world that he gave his only Son." There is the moral vision that changes the universe—and you and me. Amen.

Notes
1. Paul D. Duke, *Irony in the Fourth Gospel* (Atlanta: John Knox Press, 1985), p. 124.
2. Barbara Brown Taylor, "Willing to believe," *The Christian Century,* March 6, 1996, p. 259.
3. This is Longfellow's version of a quotation from Euripides, "Those whom God would destroy, he first makes mad."
4. James Weldon Johnson, *God's Trombones* (New York: Viking Press, 1927; copyright renewed 1955 by Grace Nail Johnson).

COMMENT

Every Christian sermon faces the challenge of restating the message of the gospel, that God is love. By choosing themes and images, expanding upon biblical passages, adding contemporary elements and insights, every preacher stands in the sandals of the apostle Paul, weaving words together to reiterate the message of Christ's love. Every sermon becomes a synonym for the gospel. That responsibility often looms like Mt. Everest over the task of facing an empty page at the start of the sermon-writing process. David C. Fisher's sermon, "Sight for Sore Eyes," offers many clues to the sermon preparation process and a clear example of the fact that sermons are synonyms for a simple yet powerful message. Fisher has layered this sermon with image over image, phrase over phrase, all stacked upon the sight and light metaphors so heavily employed throughout the Bible.

THE BLIND MUST SEE

Fisher begins with the premise that we begin spiritually blind and must be made to see. The basic theme in the Gospel of John has been the subject of thousands of sermons, and it's difficult to bring a fresh perspective to it. Starting with a story remains the best way to bring attention to your text. A first-person anecdote, if it is a good story and naturally segues into the theme, cannot be topped. Fisher employs this technique by recounting his friendship with a blind woman who seemed to be able to see quite effectively without her eyes. Along with the pleasing novelty he achieves in presenting this relationship, Fisher enters his sermon with a high interest level, with the imagery set and the theme strongly suggested. This allows him to muse on the gift of sight and move nonchalantly to the text at hand, Jesus healing the blind beggar. Fisher can then frame our problem, the human condition of innate spiritual blindness, and state our solution, accepting the vision offered by Jesus.

SIGHT AND LIGHT

Notice that throughout this sermon, Fisher layers phrases that are essentially synonyms for the vision metaphor: sight, light, good news, grace and hope, versus blindness and darkness. The language has been carefully considered, along with the references to outside material. You can see how the skeleton of the sermon came together. He's not afraid to call on other sources that mesh with and buttress his theme. You can see the strings of a sermon being tied together. As he goes about writing the sermon, perhaps beside the computer in the study there is a clipping from the *Wall Street Journal,* a copy of *The Christian Century,* a book of poetry featuring James Weldon Johnson, a copy of Paul Duke's *Irony in the Fourth Gospel.* Having the references ready that meet the needs of the sermon can be like the baseball player going to the plate with a bat that fits his swing.

He also uses the device of repetition for effect, to reiterate the main themes of the sermon. For example, in quoting James Weldon Johnson, Fisher notes that "Johnson patterned his poem after the imagery and rhythm of old-time black preaching." Fisher himself, before and after quoting the poem, also employs some of the cadences and repetition characteristic of that style of preaching. During a portion of the sermon he adopts that style of preaching.

The repetition of key phrases can be very effective. Before quoting the poem, Fisher uses the phrase, "You see, God will not have a world full of darkness." During a pause in reading the poem, he reiterates: "God will not permit a world without light." And after the poem, he states, "You see, God will not tolerate absolute darkness in his universe nor will God permit darkness to reign in the sons of Adam and the daughters of Eve." Fisher also effectively repeats other key phrases in this sermon: "God's people, folks formed by the light" and "good news people," along with "people of the light" and "people of grace."

PROCLAIMING A VISION

"If only we had better vision or a better vantage point," Fisher writes. By alluding to the perceptive ability of a peregrine falcon and the moral vision exemplified by Mother Teresa or Nelson Mandela, Fisher appeals to the yearning for better physical and spiritual sight. He also refers to the kind of vision that allowed the prophet Samuel to foresee that David the shepherd would one day be the greatest king of Israel.

Fisher takes a broad view of vision and appeals for a constant striving for better spiritual vision. There is always, theologically speaking, a need for us to turn up the lights in our lives. It's not just a reference to an infusion of light in conversion moments, as when Paul was knocked down and made blind by a light from heaven. Fisher calls on those who have gone from being blind to seeing the light, but who may yet live dimly lit lives. He asks them to let in more light, to throw up the blinds on the windows and let the sun shine. He is not calling just for the blind to see, but for nearsighted people to get a better set of spiritual glasses. A declaration of belief is the cure for blindness and the prescription for the nearsighted. Fisher urges all to accept that empowerment by saying, "Lord, I believe."

CAN YOU SEE?

By introducing the story of the blind woman who insists on being able to live as if she can see, and by focusing on the blind man's willingness to have faith and gain sight, Fisher emphasizes that sight is something that can be chosen, that light can be embraced over darkness. By noting the Gospel of John's emphasis on the spiritual transformation of the blind, with blindness as a metaphor for the state of spiritual being which is more important than the physical handicap, Fisher conveys spiritual blindness as a widespread and pressing condition that can and must be changed. The unseeing must be made to see. He then rephrases and restates the theme, turning it into an emphatic call to the church for a vision check.

SUGGESTIONS

- Gather strings. Save articles and books that touch on themes you may preach about. Most newspapers now save their articles in computer libraries but they used to do it the old-fashioned way with a "morgue," a library of envelopes filled with clippings, with the name of the subject written on the outside, filed alphabetically in drawers. It may be helpful to the preacher to keep a personalized morgue—a drawer of envelopes in alphabetical order with magic marker subject names printed on the outside. If you see an article that relates to a possible sermon topic, you can keep it handy by clipping it out, writing the date on it, folding it up and putting it in an envelope labeled with a general subject heading. Then when you go to write about that subject, you've got good material at hand. This is an easy system and overcomes the problem of not being able to find that article you remember you read but now can't find.

- Try a dose of humility. Arrogance and pomposity, sometimes disguising insecurities, tend to reign from too many pulpits. But we have all sinned and fallen short of the glory of God. A little humility from the pulpit is more in line with Christ's example of washing the feet of his followers. Fisher brings a refreshing humility to this sermon. He ponders openly the scarring that the church can inflict on the flock and acknowledges "I'm one of the offenders. How many young and tender souls have I wounded, even turned away from the faith? I'm afraid of the answer." It's a sweet dessert for the congregation when the preacher offers up a slice of humble pie. Willingly exposing emotional vulnerability brings the clergy down off the pedestal on which they so often resent being placed. It makes the congregation more sympathetic, the sermon more user-friendly, and most importantly, calls the church to be a community of people living out their faith in honest humility, ready to recognize the church's own blindness. A church willing to see itself honestly is a sight for sore eyes.

Greg Garrison

TEMPLE CROSSING

LUKE 2:22–32

REV. DR. RICHARD L. ESLINGER
TRINITY UNITED METHODIST CHURCH
NILES, MICHIGAN

REV. DR. RICHARD L. ESLINGER

TEMPLE CROSSING

LUKE 2:22–32, NRSV

Things happen at intersections. People and events come together and then split apart. They converge, forming the intersection, and at "ground zero" they diverge, heading off in different directions. Intersections. We take them for granted. We need them to get from one place to another. We use them every day. But there are times when God is at the crossing, when our path intersects with the Divine. And doesn't a cross stand at the intersecting center of the whole universe— that intersection at Good Friday? Make no mistake about it, God surprises us at these crossing times, and we are never the same again.

The crossing we are looking at today happens earlier, long before Good Friday's cross. Luke locates this early "ground zero" in the temple. So in the court of the temple, moving along one trajectory through the crowd's noise and bustle, is the holy family, Mary, Joseph and the Christ Child. Their course is set toward the priest who will take their meager offering—a sacrifice according to the law of Moses. Not lavish, this sacrifice is only what is necessary—a pair of turtledoves or two young pigeons. The family moves through the crowd to accomplish this sacrifice. Also making his way through the sea of people, along another trajectory, is Simeon—righteous and devout Simeon, the one who "would not see death before he had seen the Lord's Messiah" (v. 26). The Holy

Spirit had revealed to old Simeon that it was time, the fullness of time for his hopes to be fulfilled. And guided by the Spirit, there in the temple court, the two courses converge—there is a meeting at this intersection, very much of God.

Simeon takes up the child in the crook of his arms, cradles him, praising God and singing his song, *Nunc Dimittis*.[1] "Master, now you are dismissing your servant in peace" (v. 29). Here, at this intersection, can you feel the weight of the tension? Old Simeon, the tug of the past, prayerfully waiting for God to complete things so he can be dismissed from his service. The infant Jesus, the power of God's future, brought to the temple, presented to God for service...but to all bystanders just a powerless child—whom T. S. Eliot referred to as "the Infant, the still unspeaking and unspoken Word."[2] This is the tension here in this temple at ground zero—the tug of the past and the power of the future, intersecting.

There is a logic to old Simeon's prayer. You wait for something long enough, pray for it, long for it, and when in God's time it is given, there is a deep sense of completion—a fulfillment, an ending. Some of us here have waited like Simeon. We have waited for work that is more than just a job, waiting and praying for that fitting place to use our gifts, for a real vocation, a calling. When it is given, in God's good time, there comes a sense of completion, and we want to sing a *Nunc Dimittis*, "Now let your servant depart in peace."

Others of us wait for a life partner, perhaps for years—pray and wait. Last month, we packed into this holy place, and at this intersection John and Ann covenanted together in a holy marriage. Did you notice a feeling of completion? We could have sung a *Nunc Dimittis* at their wedding! Finally, a time to depart in peaceful gratitude.

For this congregation, there have been long years of waiting, praying for renewal, for new life. At the end of this calendar year, with its awesome times of Advent and Christmas, with so many new faces and so much deepened faith, we too want to say with Simeon, *Nunc Dimittis!* "Let us depart this year in peace." Can you feel it—the tug of the past, the sense of things coming together, being completed, the sense of an ending? Then it is time to join with Simeon in his song.

Notice, though, that Simeon is cradling the Christ Child in his arms as he sings. He is holding the promise of God "now in flesh appearing." The power of God's future. At this intersection there is also birth. Good news—God's salvation. There is tension here—Simeon holding the Lord's Messiah. Completion, things coming together. Oh yes! Now, the Word spoken in the virgin's ear and Christ is born. Hope is born. Enough light for all the world! So the intersection—the tug of the past, and the power of God's future here in our midst.

For us, our calendar year is now coming to an end. But in our midst are all the new babes in Christ. What a roll call—our newly baptized brothers and sisters! Daniel, Dennie, Alex, Jody, Tim, Eddie, Hannah and Brennyn. Dennis and now Kelly Marie. Here is the power of God in Christ—forgiveness, gift of the Spirit, new birth, welcome into Christ's church, sharing in his death and resurrection. Haven't our eyes seen the salvation of the Lord's Messiah? Jesus has "come to give us second birth," a gift freely given to us all.

The world has a version of all this, a version of completion and new beginnings. It's a counterfeit. But for a lot of people it's the source of their hope. Remember earlier this week when you received your own very special letter from Publisher's Clearing House? The one that had your own distinctive press release already written so that when you won that ten million dollars next month, you wouldn't be at a loss for words? Did you notice the words that were put in your mouth? You said you were "stunned," and that "this was a dream of a lifetime." All served up for you in that press release for the big day. About the only thing they needed to add was the *Nunc Dimittis*. Now that would be a fine statement to the world by us new millionaires!

Here we are with Simeon this Lord's Day, at his intersection with the infant Christ. Tug of the past versus the power of God's future. But we don't stop there. The movement continues. The intersection opens out in two directions. The reason for this split in future directions is given in

Simeon's song. In the coming of Jesus, God strips away the disguises from all people. "The inner thoughts of many will be revealed" (v. 35), Simeon prophesies to Mary. God's revelation in Jesus will disclose our own hearts as well. The Lord's Messiah is now revealed and our own inner thoughts are uncovered.

From this intersection, two paths diverge. One—the course of the world, self-centered, resentful, playing it safe, indifferent to the needs of the poor. The way of the unjust. The other path—those who follow the Lord's Messiah from this place of meeting, humble, not afraid to take risks, filled with compassion, servants to those in need. The way of the just. Two movements from this place of meeting, all because the inner thoughts of many have been revealed.

There is also a personal prophecy for Mary: "A sword will pierce your own soul too" (v. 35). Simeon reveals that cross-shaped place. Through Mary's heart, but also through our world, this sword will pass—through Christ's church, and through our own souls. From this intersection there are only two ways into the future: the way of the just, whose hearts are open, and the way of the unjust, whose hearts are hardened. Now that our inner thoughts are revealed, the issue is forced. A decision needs to be made. Which way for us at this intersection? We cannot remain here at ground zero. Perhaps Simeon would agree that it is now a time for prayer, as once more we are confronted with the choice. The one that begins, "Almighty God, to you all hearts are open, all desires known, and from you no secrets are hid."[3]

Notes

1. *Nunc Dimittis,* the first words of Simeon's hymn in Latin from Luke 2:29–32, is used as the song's title when sung as a canticle in various liturgies within the Christian tradition.

2. T. S. Eliot, "A Song for Simeon," *The Complete Poems and Plays 1909–1950* (New York: Harcourt Brace, 1952), p. 70.

3. "The Holy Eucharist: Rite Two," *The Book of Common Prayer of the Episcopal Church* (New York: Seabury Press, 1979), p. 355.

COMMENT

The preacher's malaise on the first Sunday after Christmas is not a closely kept homiletical secret. The Sunday before, one was awaiting Christmas with eager anticipation. It was easy to preach. People did not need to be persuaded of the possibility that light does penetrate the darkness of our personal and social life; that peace and good will are manifest in an unfriendly world; that hope is possible in an uncertain time.

POST-CHRISTMAS SYNDROME

Then comes the first Sunday after Christmas when the wilting of both greenery and spirits is commonplace. The light, hope and good will celebrated in song and greetings may in retrospect seem almost an interlude of pretention. On the first Sunday after Christmas most people are thinking of the final days of a year that doubtless had some ragged edges. Painful experiences—changes, death of loved ones, disappointments—are permanently marked on the calendars we are throwing away.

This fresh sermon by Richard Eslinger was addressed to people who gathered as a congregation on the first Sunday after Christmas. Eslinger's opening words, "Things happen at intersections," should stir even the most distracted hearers. "Things happen at intersections." That phrase commands the attention of people caught in the "blues" or distress of "post-Christmas syndrome." Advent expectation ran high. The celebration of Christmas was full of joyous words and promises of hope and peace. But now Christmas is over. Life is back to the hard realities of darkness, suffering and unanswered questions. The post-Christmas syndrome sets in as an impairment of the spirit crushed by the burden of hopes not realized, promises not kept, good intentions not even partially expressed, and fears no longer concealed.

THE ANTIDOTE

What does a preacher do on the first Sunday after Christmas? One answer is to follow Eslinger's lead in this fresh, attractive, and insightful look at a Lukan infancy narrative that on the surface does not appear very "user-friendly." Eslinger offers an effective antidote to chronic "post-Christmas syndrome" from the opening to the concluding words of this sermon's twelve short paragraphs. The opening words remind us that "things happen at intersections." Before we know it, we have begun to move out of the post-Christmas malaise and depression. Eslinger reminds us that "our path intersects with the Divine" and that "God surprises us at these crossing times, and we are never the same again."

After gaining our attention in the first paragraph, the preacher in the second paragraph briefly runs through the Scripture passage for the day (Luke 2:22–35). Read through this biblical text and then reread Eslinger's second paragraph. It's evident that the preacher sketches the biblical story while avoiding a tedious retelling. The listener, knowing that the meeting of the holy family and old Simeon is "very much of God," wants to hear more about this intersection where God is encountered.

TUG OF THE PAST, POWER OF THE FUTURE

In the third paragraph Eslinger introduces the sermon's leitmotif: "tug of the past, power of the future." This is apparent in Simeon's waiting in his final days to see the completion of God's purpose in "the infant Jesus, power of God's future." The hearer knows that this odd story has to do with the "intersecting" of the "tug of the past" and the "power of the future."

By the fourth paragraph Eslinger has moved from the temple in Jerusalem where the aged Simeon sings the *Nunc Dimittis* to the variety of ways members of the congregation doubtless experience the waiting game: fulfillment of vocation, marriage, congregational renewal (fourth through sixth paragraphs). Eslinger appeals to fulfillment as "the sense of things coming together."

Note that Eslinger departs from a wooden, literal reading of the finely nuanced and well crafted literary and theological composition by the author of Luke-Acts. The passage in Luke presents Simeon as looking for the "consolation" or comfort of Israel (v. 25) and his seeing the salvation of God (v. 30). Eslinger elects to seize primarily on the fulfillment motif without attaching all the theological freight.

But the seventh and eighth paragraphs pick up those more sharply sketched theological themes of God's salvation while reintroducing the "tug of the past, power of God's future" leitmotif. By now the listener or reader of Eslinger's sermon knows that the preacher will not stay in Bible-land. He alludes to the end of the calendar year and the infants being baptized as a sign to the congregation of exactly what old Simeon saw—the salvation of God. Eslinger avoids any ponderous typology, but he presents the hearer with the dynamic analogy of temple and church and people at the end of the year ("the tug of the past") witnessing the "salvation of the Lord's Messiah" in the newly baptized infants now sharing in Christ's death and resurrection. It goes without saying, of course, that this part of the sermon will have little meaning for those traditions who do not accept the baptism of infants. But for those who do, this writer included, Eslinger shows us a way to link this old story with a congregation.

READING THE CONGREGATION'S MAIL AND THE CONGREGATION

In the ninth paragraph Eslinger knows what is in the mailboxes of his parishioners. Through gentle criticism of Publisher's Clearing House the preacher suggests a counterfeit understanding of completion ("fulfillment" in the biblical story) and new beginnings. Eslinger does not have to flog his hearers to make the important point that there is a lot of bogus salvation out there.

The tenth and eleventh paragraphs of the sermon concentrate again on the "tug of the past, power of God's future" leitmotif. Without developing in an arcane theological fashion the division theme that is central to Luke's narrative (vv. 33–35), Eslinger notes that the intersection where one meets the Lord's Messiah is the place "where the inner thoughts of many have been revealed."

The twelfth and final paragraph picks up that jarring announcement about the sword which will pierce Mary's soul (v. 35). The sword forces the decision of which way we will go from the intersection: the way of the just or the way of the unjust.

In this fresh and challenging sermon Eslinger intentionally does not offer an exposition of the passage or an exegetically driven theological reflection. But he shows a keen eye for exegetical nuances and the theological dimension of the passage in every paragraph of the sermon. Whatever his normal approach to preaching, one can recognize the value of this approach on the first Sunday after Christmas. On this Sunday most congregations are not prepared to listen to a recondite exegetical or literary analysis of a passage. One can only applaud Eslinger's fresh and creative encounter with the passage and his refusal to be captive to an arcane theological treatise.

This sermon, therefore, is an impressionistic encounter with the biblical text which forces the hearer/reader to move to the next step. Following the death of Willem de Kooning in March 1997, many observed that this American artist from Holland had a vision that kept dissolving and retreating so that he could not describe it in a matter-of-fact fashion in his art. De Kooning himself once described his vision as "a glimpse of something, an encounter, like a flash." In this sermon we are given glimpses of a reality of life intersecting with God. Eslinger does not attempt to explain everything. This kind of text from the Lukan nativity narratives cannot be repeated in discursive speech. Eslinger helps us to encounter the text.

OTHER DIRECTIONS

Some congregations, unaccustomed to following the lectionary readings and not having a grounding in the biblical narratives, may require more tutoring in a sermon based on the passage from Luke 2:22–35. The context of a congregation helps to guide one.

One of the guidelines for those writing comments on sermons in these volumes is to offer suggestions about different approaches to the text. One might take a more overtly exegetical and theological approach to the story of Simeon. Above I mentioned the dangers of a wooden use of the text in such an approach. To begin with, one notes that following the narrative of the birth of Jesus, Luke sets before his readers the ringing words of Simeon (Luke 2:29–32), known to the church as the *Nunc Dimittis*. In this song Simeon praises God for bringing his purposes to fulfillment in the birth of Jesus.

For Luke, the opening lines of Simeon's words are crucial: "My eyes have seen your [God's] salvation" (v. 30). The "seeing of salvation" motif is intentionally advanced by Luke in the next chapter when he has John the Baptist conclude his message to the people with words cited from the Book of Isaiah, that "all flesh shall see the salvation of God" (3:6). These words are omitted by all the other Gospels. They are important words in the Gospel of Luke. Seeing God's salvation is recognizing it and responding to it. God's salvation is for *all* people. These are key themes in Luke-Acts.

Do we really think that all flesh has seen the salvation of God? Does Simeon's robust confidence in the arrival of God's purposes of wholeness and renewal for the world connect with our world which knows Bosnia-Herzegovina, Saddam Hussein, conflict in Zaire, cancer which takes the life of a young child, violence in the Middle East, and various types of distress?

The church has treasured the glory and triumph of the *Nunc Dimittis* (vv. 29–32) and rightly so. Luke, however, does not make Simeon into a gullible cheerleader for Jesus. In a second oracle (vv. 34–35), he relates a special work to Mary: "This child is destined for the falling and the rising of many in Israel, and to be a sign that will be opposed" (v. 34). Or to put it more directly, "he is one who will be rejected." The salvation prepared for all people will meet resistance. It will not always be evident. This salvation will not always be seen by all flesh. It can be rejected by humans. Simeon's second oracle to Mary reminds readers of the complexity of God's way of achieving his purposes. This second oracle

C O M M E N T

denotes the ambiguity not only of human perception, but of the ways of divine grace. Yet both oracles speak to our uncertainty with a word of certainty: God's purpose will triumph. More often than not, the way by which God carries out that purpose will remain hidden. Simeon's oracle invites trust before all the evidence for God's promises is in.

Yet Luke does not draw back from a theological crisis which persists to our own day for every believer and community of faith. All flesh has not seen God's salvation, and yet that does not lead Luke to tone down Simeon's declaration that he has seen the salvation of God in the first (vv. 29–32) of his two oracles.

The second oracle (vv. 34–35), which accents human rejection of God's promised salvation, saved the church of Luke's day and saves the church of our day from despair by emphasizing that ambiguity, suffering, and rejection belong to Christian life and faith. The Christian gospel is not tied to a Gallup Poll. Moreover, Simeon's word to Mary speaks not only of the fall of Israel, but also the rising. There will be partial fulfillments which sustain believers. We render our faith and witness without total victory over every obstacle. But we do have sufficient hints of God's salvation to sustain us.

Is a congregation ready for a more overtly exegetical and theological treatment of the text as sketched above? It all depends on the context. I have offered an alternative way of treating the text simply to remind us that any text offers a variety of homiletical options.

I am certain that Richard Eslinger's approach sent people from church pondering those "crossing times" with God when "we are never the same again." It was a fortunate congregation which heard "Temple Crossing" on the first Sunday after Christmas.

SUGGESTIONS

- Reflect on my comments about the differing homiletical approaches to biblical texts. In your preaching, do you use both the "impressionistic encounter" with a text (as Eslinger uses here) and more intentionally exegetical/theological treatments? It is good to vary the approach. Many of us may tend to use only one kind of approach as our preaching style.

- Think about Eslinger's leitmotif, "tug of the past, power of the future." How can you let this theme come to prominence in your preaching of the biblical story?
- What other "intersections" do you find through the biblical story? Why not develop this theme over time in your preaching, whether you follow the lectionary or not.

James J. H. Price

COMMENT

THE MAN JESUS

LUKE 9:49–56; JOHN 6:1–15;
COLOSSIANS 1:15–20

REV. DR. BUCKNER FANNING
TRINITY BAPTIST CHURCH
SAN ANTONIO, TEXAS

THE MAN
JESUS

LUKE 9:49–56; JOHN 6:1–15; COLOSSIANS 1:15–20

M ost people find their ideal in this man Jesus. To the banker he's the hidden treasure. To the jeweler he's the pearl of great price. To the florist he's the rose of Sharon, the lily of the valley. To the geologist he's the rock of ages. To the physician he's the great physician. To the hungry he's the bread of life. To the thirsty he's the water of life. To the lost and lonely he's the Savior of the world.

Jesus is God in human flesh. If you want to know what God is really like, look at Jesus. When we turn that around, Jesus is not so much like God as God is like Jesus. If you want to know how God feels about things, look to how Jesus feels about things. If you want to know what God's attitude is to people who are having problems, study Jesus' attitude toward them. All the fullness of God dwells in Jesus Christ. "It pleased the Father," the Scripture says, "that in him should all fullness dwell" (Col. 1:19, KJV).

Jesus is the totality of God. That is why we've been emphasizing Jesus these last few Sundays. In reality we don't have any other message but this man. Last week I mentioned that in the four Gospels you find his name four or five hundred times; in the entire New Testament you read his name 905 times.

Many people get off track because they begin trying to define God somewhere else than with Jesus. George Buttrick, a marvelous preacher, teacher and pastor, was chaplain at Harvard for many years. One day a student said to him, "I don't believe in God."

"Come in and sit down," Dr. Buttrick said. "Let's talk about it. You know, I probably don't believe in that kind of God either. Tell me what kind of God you're talking about."

I've read a number of books by or about people who profess to be atheists. I've read the biography of Clarence Darrow, who was supposed to be an atheist. Darrow wrote a marvelous book called *Attorney for the Damned*. What a great title for the life of Jesus—attorney for the damned! I don't really believe Clarence Darrow was an atheist; I believe he just got the wrong idea of God along the way. As I read his story, I heard him saying things about God that, if he knew Jesus, I don't believe he would have felt. I've read the works of William Cowper Brand, the editor of the *Iconoclast* magazine in the last century. Brand was shot down by a person with a pistol on the streets of Waco, Texas, because of what he was saying about some churches. Some of the things he was saying about churches from the outside are things we are saying about us from the inside—we need to be more like Jesus. Brand was really writing about false ideas about God.

If we want to know what God is like, we must look at Jesus. And for a few moments this morning, let me put the magnifying glass upon him.

If you take a magnifying glass and look at one part of a beautiful painting to see how the artist did it, and to get more of the detail, you will find the part under the glass clearly magnified. But on the edges, on the circumference of the glass, things look blurred. That's why we want to focus on Jesus. Too often in the church, in our theology, in our teaching and preaching, we get focused on something else, and Jesus gets blurred in the process. We need to focus on Jesus.

Martin Luther said, "Flee the hidden God and run to Jesus." Flee the *hidden* God, the God who is not totally revealed in the Old Testament. In the history of Israel God is being progressively revealed—not because of

God's reticence, but because of human incapacity to understand the nature of God. So we don't find a full revelation of God in the Bible until we get to the New Testament and to the person of Jesus Christ. That is why Martin Luther also said, "The Bible is read forward, but it's understood backward." You'll not understand the Old Testament adequately unless you begin with Jesus. You will not understand the epistles and the remainder of the New Testament properly until you understand Jesus. That is why I urged you last week to spend at least 50 percent of your Bible-reading time in Matthew, Mark, Luke and John. The Gospels are the heart of the story. Jesus is the heart of God.

What kind of man was Jesus? Each of us has a mental picture of him, and that's proper. But there's no physical description of Jesus in the New Testament. I believe that's providential. The silence of the Bible is important. There are some things God doesn't want us to know. God wants us, with our own minds and thoughts, to sift through and fill in some of the blanks. Every person sees Jesus through the lens of their own experience.

Many years ago I visited a Christian mission school in Oklahoma. A Native American artist had painted a picture, his interpretation of Da Vinci's *The Last Supper.* Jesus and every one of the disciples were Indians. I have preached in East Africa, Kenya and Tanzania. In their art about Jesus, they picture him as black. Jesus is the universal Savior. The universality of his message and of his love means that he is the One for *all* persons, for all seasons.

What kind of person was he? Through the lens of my own experience I see him as a real man. I see him as a very physical man. I see him as a very energetic man. He had something about his personality which attracted people to him, and I don't believe it was just his physical strength—though I believe he had that. He cleansed the temple, as you know, overturned tables with his muscles straining, and drove the animals and moneychangers out of the temple. For most of his thirty-three years, he worked as a carpenter outdoors in the hot sun. He walked everywhere he went, never rode anywhere in his life except the last week, when he borrowed a donkey to ride. He was an outdoorsman, a man's man. You'll never convince me that a sailor by the name of Simon Peter would have followed some namby-pamby, apologetic, milquetoast kind of pusillanimous nonentity. I believe he was all man from the top of his head to the bottom of his feet. I think he could walk further and work harder than any man that ever lived. That's my perception of him.

I also believe he was a likable man. People liked him. True, the religious leaders had trouble with him. At first they had a kind of love-hate relationship with him. Some of these Pharisees, Sadducees and scribes disagreed with him and fought with him, but they couldn't let go of him or ignore him. They kept coming back to him again and again. He kept upsetting their apple carts and kicking their sacred cows. He kept trying to get them to see the truth behind all the tradition they had built up which had gotten in the way of a relationship with God. The *common* people, though, heard Jesus gladly, the Gospels tell us (Mark 12:37). What does that mean? That means folks who had ordinary problems, who knew it and were willing to admit it. People who feared, who had failed one way or another in their life. People with hurts and hates. Common folks with problems common to all of us. They heard him gladly. Why? Because he gave them hope. He gave them assurance that life could be better and could be changed. He never put down anybody.

He was a likable man. Children liked him, and that, probably, is one of the best compliments he could ever be paid. Children gathered around Jesus with their ringing laughter. Children are the best judges of character in the world. They can spot a phony quicker than anybody else, and that's because they haven't yet learned how to be phony. They're just so open and natural. Children loved Jesus. They crowded around him.

Jesus was often invited to have dinner in people's homes. Most of the invitations came from the nonchurchgoing crowd, the nonreligious crowd. And even when an invitation came from the religious crowd, who wanted to put him on the spot, Jesus accepted it. He never turned down an invitation to a meal. Doesn't that make Baptists feel better about all the eating we do? Jesus always went wherever he was invited, and I think he always had a good time. No one ever felt the presence of Jesus to be a cloud upon the company. No one ever laughed any less because Jesus was there. Jesus did not come as the world's great wet blanket. He didn't come to frost the earth, cut the flowers, kill the soil or turn out the lights and drape life in black. "I've come to give you life," he told his disciples, "and to give it to you abundantly" (John 10:10).

Jesus liked to go to parties. In fact, his first miracle was at the celebration of a wedding, not at a cemetery. They'd run out of refreshments at Cana of Galilee and there were no convenience stores open at that time of the night. Jesus turned the water to wine and saved the day for an embarrassed host. He had a good time.

I believe Jesus laughed. I believe he had a smile on his face. I believe he was a hugger. You read the Bible from Genesis to Revelation, and 826 times you will read the words *rejoice,* or *be glad,* or *rejoice and be glad.* Rejoice and be glad. Rejoice and be glad. If I were to start every sermon with that sentence, I would have to preach sixteen and a half years to cover all the separate "rejoice" and "be glad" texts that you find in the Bible. Jesus came to set the world singing. Jesus came to bring joy. He is the King of Joy. What a man! He was a happy man.

He was also a marvelous teacher. Little children can read his stories and get understanding out of them. Adults can read the same stories for fifty years, as some of us have done, and constantly see something new in them. Not because the story's changing, but because we are. We're understanding more about God in the process, and we're understanding more about ourselves as we understand more about life. These stories about Jesus, these parables from Jesus, are fathomless. A parable is a short story with a long meaning, and it can reach through eternity. What a teacher!

Let me point out two or three things about Jesus' teaching that apply to us as Christians—those teachings that he directed particularly toward his disciples. He had general teachings, that he gave in great crowds, but he had specific teachings that he gave to his disciples. Why did he do that? Well, there were times when he taught his disciples because they were to be models of what the church was meant to be. Jesus was endeavoring to inculcate values and ideas and principles into this inner group so that they would later be able not only to go into all the world to preach and perpetuate his teachings, not only to proclaim the good news of the kingdom, but also to live that good news in little cells or communities just like that first little group that began following Jesus. That little cell group became a church—in Antioch and in Ephesus and in Rome and in Athens and in Corinth—and in San Antonio. Jesus was teaching his disciples how the church was to be through the centuries.

Listen to some of the things Jesus taught. Jesus did not condemn obvious badness as much as he did obvious goodness. Jesus did not condemn obvious badness. He didn't approve of it; he came to change it and redeem it. But Jesus did not condemn obvious badness as much as he did obvious goodness—artificial piosity, goody-goody, phony, two-faced hypocrisy. Play acting. "You hypocrites," Jesus said, quoting Isaiah's prophecy, "'This people honors me with their lips, but their hearts are far from me; in vain do they worship me, teaching human precepts as doctrines'" (Mark 7:6–7, NRSV). Who shapes our theology? That's why we need to read the New Testament. We need to let Jesus shape our theology, not our culture. We must not let the predominant thoughts of the day shape our theology, even when those thoughts may be predominant in the minds of a majority of Christians.

Quickly now, three other very important things that Jesus was teaching the disciples, and consequently, teaching us who claim to be his followers. The apostle John, the beloved apostle, was I think, about sixteen or seventeen years old when he and his brother James started following Jesus. Jesus nicknamed them "sons of thunder" because they were so impetuous and so energetic. You catch that characteristic in some of the things John and James say in Luke 9: "Master," John says in verse 49, "we saw someone casting out demons in your name, and we tried to stop him, because he does not follow with us" (NRSV). Jesus said to him—and I believe he looked at him with loving eyes but a stern face—"Do not stop him; for whoever is not against you is for you" (v. 50, NRSV). Jesus is teaching his disciples a profound and powerful lesson that needs to be replicated in our lives and in our church. Jesus is saying to John, *"Don't limit me*. Don't you draw the parameters of what's acceptable; that's my business."

Some of you, perhaps, have visited Westminster Abbey. Near the main entrance is the grave of David Livingstone. On that grave are carved the words, "Other sheep I have which are not of this fold. It is proper that they, too, should come." Somebody on the other side of the mountain, serving God in a different place, a different way, a different language, a different order of worship you leave them alone. Pray for them, don't hinder them. "That's my business," says Jesus. "You tend to your business and do it right, but don't limit me, because I am the universal Savior. I've come to save the whole world. Red and yellow, black and white, they're all precious in my sight, and they're all going to be a part of my kingdom. From the east and the west, from the north and the south, they shall come and sit down in the kingdom of God. Don't limit me."

Another dramatic event occurs in Luke chapter 9.

When the days drew near for him to be taken up, he set his face to go to Jerusalem. And he sent messengers ahead of him. On their way they entered a village of the Samaritans to make ready for him (Luke 9:51–52, NRSV). Now you need to know, if you don't already, that the Samaritans were detested by the Jews and vice versa—not by Jesus, but by the Jews. The Jews would not even walk through Samaria. They called the Samaritans half-breed dogs because they had intermarried with their conquerors many years earlier. The Samaritans equally detested the Jews. But here was a Jew going through Samaria!

I spoke a couple of weeks ago on the Samaritan woman who had been married five times and was now living with a man to whom she was not married. Jesus changed her whole life. She went into town and told everybody in town about Jesus, and they all came out to meet him. The whole town asked Jesus to stay for a couple of days, and everybody in that town became a follower of Jesus (John 4:1–42). But this Samaritan village hadn't gotten that word. Jesus sent a couple of his disciples ahead, telling them, "Go on and get us some reservations; get us a place to stay."

But when the town found out that Jesus was headed toward Jerusalem, they said, "No vacancy. You're not allowed here."

What did that do to the disciples? Well, it still has a tendency to do the same thing to us today. Somebody tells us, "You stay out of here, we don't want your Jesus; leave and go somewhere else," and we say, "Lord, they're saying that about you and I love you; therefore they're saying that about me. I'm gonna get them. I am gonna get them." That's what James and John both wanted to do. Listen to this:

They did not receive him, because his face was set toward Jerusalem. When his disciples James and John saw it, they said, "Lord, do you want us to command fire to come down from heaven and consume them?" [They rejected us; drop a bomb on them. Line them up and shoot them.] But he turned and rebuked them, and said, "You do not know what spirit you are of"...Then they went to another village (Luke 9:53–56).

Well, what about that village? Were they judged? Let me ask you a question. If you resist Jesus, if you kick him out of your life (and you can), does God judge you? No. You judge yourself. The rejection of Jesus carries within itself the seeds of its own judgment. If I refuse food and starve to death when it's set on the table in front of me, is it God's fault? Is it the chef's fault? No. I didn't take and eat. So Jesus didn't judge them; they'd already judged themselves. What could be worse than leaving Jesus out of your life? What could be worse? No forgiveness for sin. No peace. No hope. No joy. What could be worse?

What I hear Jesus saying to his disciples is "don't use force." Don't use force. Jesus never forced anybody; he never coerced anyone. He came and invited the whole world, but he didn't coerce them. He didn't force them. He invited them.

Some years ago we used to have two services, one at 8:00 and the other at 11:00. One Sunday I was leaving home about 7:30. A neighbor who moved away many years ago was out in the yard picking up his paper. As I drove by I rolled down the window and said "Good morning" to him.

"Buckner, where in the world are you going so early in the morning?" he asked.

"I'm going to church," I told him. "We've got a service at 8:00."

He said, "Oh, that's right. This is Sunday."

"Yeah," I said, "it's Sunday, and I'm going on down for the 8:00 service. I'll see you later."

"Give 'em hell, Buckner," he said and waved at me.

Give 'em hell, give 'em hell! Wow, I thought as I drove along, *they've already got enough hell in their life—we all do!* We don't need to come to church to hear more of that. We need to come here to find out if there's some heaven available, that there's hope available, that there's help available—spiritual and mental. Don't use force. The most powerful force in the world is not force. The most powerful force in the world is love. Love. Don't use force.

And then one more point before I conclude. The only miracle that every one of the Gospel writers recorded is the feeding of the five thousand. There's a reason for that, because this is a critical turning point in the ministry of Jesus. A significant fulcrum. A real juncture. After he fed the five thousand, the people began to say, "Hey, if this man can multiply five loaves and two fishes and feed five thousand plus—if he can do that, and we've already heard that he can heal the sick and even raise the dead, wow, what a king he'll make! I mean, somebody gets wounded, he'll heal them. If we run out of supplies, he can multiply loaves and fishes. If somebody gets killed, he can raise them to life. Why, if we get him as our king, we can get rid of the Romans. We can set up an earthly kingdom." That's exactly what they planned to do, John's Gospel tells us. "When Jesus realized that they were about to come and take him by force to make him a king, he withdrew again to the mountain by himself" (John 6:15, NRSV).

The accounts in Matthew 14 and Mark 9 tell us something more. Before Jesus went to the mountain alone, he constrained (it's a very strong word) his disciples, his followers, his church, "us," to leave. "Get in a boat and cross the sea. Get out of here." Jesus was in effect telling them, "My kingdom is not of this world. You leave. We're not going to be a party to this." And he went up into the mountain by himself, alone.

How powerfully significant this is! Jesus is saying, *Don't use me for some personal desires.* Don't use me as a means to some other end. I'm not a means to some other end. I am an end within myself. Don't use me just to get materially wealthy. Don't use me to get fame. Fame or wealth may come to you. But don't use me as a means to these ends. If, in serving me, you are blessed in such a way that you materially prosper, that the world comes to acclaim you, then give me the glory for it and use it for my honor and glory. Don't use me for some political end. Don't use me to get rid of the Romans. You are more concerned about getting the Romans out of Israel than about letting me get God into your heart. Don't you drag me and my holy name into the mud of partisan politics. My kingdom is not of this world. Do not use me. Worship me, follow me, obey me, for I have come to save you. If I save you politically a thousand times, if I save you physically a thousand times, if I save you financially a thousand times, and your soul is lost, what does it profit you?

What does it profit anyone if he gains everything he wants—even using the name of Jesus—but never knows Jesus? What does it profit a person to gain the whole world but lose one's own soul? Jesus is not a means to some other end. He is an end within himself. Alpha and Omega, the beginning and the end.

Jesus did not come primarily to teach. And he did not come primarily to give us an example of what God is like in the everyday course of events. He came to save us. What a Savior! *No one else can save us.* We cannot save ourselves—we cannot save ourselves by good works.

You remember when Daniel was called out to interpret the handwriting on the wall at King Belshazzar's feast in Babylon. The handwriting said, "You are weighed in the balances and found wanting." Picture a balance here—a huge balance, big enough for me to stand on. I stand here, and this side of the balance goes down to the floor. And over on the other side, there's nothing. I am weighed in the balance and found wanting.

"All right," I say, "I am going to pile all of the sermons I have preached in nearly fifty years, pile all of them up on the other side. All of the hundreds of revival meetings I've conducted, I'm going to put them up there. All the books that I have read, all the visits that I have made, all the people that I've tried to talk to about Christ, all the works I have done in the church—all that I'm going to put it over there." But the scale does not move one quarter of an inch.

So I call my friend Billy Graham and say, "Billy, come get on this thing with me, will you?" And he gets on there and nothing happens. Then I'd get all the religious leaders that I know. I'd get everybody from every denomination that I know. And I'd put them on there, and I'd say, "Help me, because I'm in terrible straits. I have been weighed in the balances and I've been found wanting." But the scale doesn't move a bit. All those folks, all those works, all those deeds, are still up there and the scales haven't moved. And they won't move. Then all of them get off, and there I am standing flatfooted without hope.

Okay, Father, I'm going to put your Son over there. Just him. I'll put my faith and trust in him, and him alone. And if he can't save me, I can't save myself. If he can't forgive me, I can't forgive myself. If he can't help me, I can't help myself. Jesus puts one foot on that scale, and the second foot on that scale, and I tell you it's like a rocket taking off to go into outer space. That scale goes up and I go straight into the presence of the living God. Weighed in the balance, and found saved by Jesus Christ and his grace.

This past Friday afternoon I talked to Genna, a sweet, beautiful little nine-year-old girl and her father, Dick. A wonderful father. She's the granddaughter of Dorothy, whom many of you know. Genna had said she wanted to talk to me about becoming a Christian. So we talked about it Friday afternoon. I don't know when I've talked to a sharper nine-year-old. I talked about what it means to be a Christian, and what it means to trust the Lord. She said, "I've done that. I'm doing it. I've talked with Daddy and Grandma. I've asked Jesus into my heart."

I said, "That's wonderful. You know he's there forever, don't you?"

"Yes."

I said, "Now, Genna, is there anything you want to ask me?"

"Yessir, there is. What's the difference between Jesus and God?"

I said, "Genna, that's a powerful question."

Today, Genna, as you hear me tell this story, it's because of you that I have a word to say to all the people. Thanks to you, I have a new insight myself into the nature and character of God.

"Genna," I told her, "Jesus is God's first name. Jesus is all of God we will ever see, for God is spirit, whom we are to worship in spirit and in truth. The God we will see in eternity will be Jesus."

"But," I said, "Jesus is only one of the names for God. The same person, but just a different name. Genna, what's your full name?"

She said, "Genna Lynn Ander."

"That's wonderful," I said. "You've got three names. I've got three names. My three names, Charles Buckner Fanning, all describe the same person," I told Genna, "just as your three names describe the same person." (I'd never thought of this analogy until I was talking to her.) "Genna, do you realize God has three names?"

God does have three names: God the Father, God the Son, God the Spirit. Three in One: one God, the Father of us all. Accept him. Let God stand on the scale of your life. You've been thinking about it—some of you for a long time. You'll never be in an atmosphere of more congeniality, more prayerfulness, more affirmation than you will here in this place. Maybe you've come from another church somewhere and want to be a part of this fellowship, this little cell group that's trying to be, in our day, what Jesus' disciples were in his day. We're trying to learn from Jesus and from the early Christians what we ought to be, what we ought to think, what we ought to do. So you do us good by joining us. You help us, and we'd like to help you. Together, we'll help one another be more like Christ, for that's the desire of us all. This is God's invitation, not Buckner's. God's invitation. I invite you to hear the word of the Lord and respond to it.

COMMENT

Phillips Brooks once said that preaching is "truth through personality."
More recently, David Buttrick puts it less succinctly in his book *Homiletic*
when he says, "At the outset, let us admit that as preachers we are
human, citizens of a human world, and obviously members of what we
ourselves term a 'sinful humanity.'"[1]

Any effort to preach "above the fray" of humanity's stresses and
struggles is doomed to fail, for the result is not a pure sermon but a barren
one. This does not mean that the preacher is always to be out "doing
something" in the world, but that the mind and heart of the preacher
should connect with the real anguish and issues which individuals experience.

Buckner Fanning has carried out a long and successful ministry as the
pastor of Trinity Baptist Church in San Antonio, Texas. One of the hall-
marks of his preaching, as the many pastors who receive and listen to his
tapes know, is his deep humanity, a pastoral "ear" that shapes his message.

Preaching is much more than sympathy for human need. Preaching
is about conviction. Preaching is the proclamation of good news. A
preacher must possess convictions about the gospel as truth. Preaching
is personality, but it is also "truth."

One of the great dangers of preaching week in and week out is not
that we will run out of things to say, but that we will not know it when
we do. Preaching can degenerate into entertainment. It can turn into self-
help advice. It can turn into meeting one's own needs on a vast (and
captive) scale. Preaching also may develop primarily into artistic expression—with an emphasis on well-crafted, interesting, even informative
presentations. Preaching can consist of clever, moralistic "how-to's." But
without conviction, a sermon is only a speech. Conviction is a belief or
truth that informs a sermon. Such conviction will always tell the careful
listener about that on which the messenger bases his or her own life.

FAITH IN CHRIST AS THE ANSWER TO LIFE'S QUESTIONS

One of the dangers of preaching our convictions is that the convictions of the preacher might overwhelm the questions of the listener before those questions can even be asked. Fanning's sermon begins with a powerful set of assertions about Jesus:

> Jesus is God in human flesh.
> Jesus is not like God, God is like Jesus.
> Jesus is the totality of God.

Those three statements alone kept several early centuries of Christians embroiled in theological debates! Theological assertions are not the primary point of a sermon, however. And they are not the main point of Fanning's sermon. The main question is, "How can we know this Jesus?"

We are always at risk of importing our own limited views into our assertions about Jesus. When this happens, we might misunderstand who Jesus really is and why he came. Rather than condemn this blindly, however, Fanning acknowledges this as the inevitable result of human limitations. Of course we see Jesus through "the lens of our own experience."

Fanning does a wonderful thing in this sermon. He tells us how he himself sees Jesus. And he connects wonderfully with the humanity of Jesus. Here is where Jesus meets us most understandably—as a man who is likable, who resonates with common people, who laughs heartily, and who is loved by children.

This human Jesus is where we must begin before we can move on to eternal assertions about his person. Fanning has taken us inside his own experience of Jesus—whom he sees as a robust, fully human person who dislikes pretense and show, loves sincerity and prefers heartfelt faith to intellectual correctness. Jesus is one who is honest and direct. If a little examination were possible the hearer might find that Buckner Fanning probably has a lot of those same qualities, too.

Jesus is such a multi-faceted personality in the Gospels that most of us can find what draws us to him. That is part of the genius and attraction of Jesus. Caution is necessary, though, lest we build our whole theology or church on the parts we like best. There are also some things about Jesus that will seem strange and objectionable. Jesus can confront us and make us uncomfortable.

Our goal, says Fanning, is to keep growing in our understanding of Jesus. Lest we become too enamored with our own conceptions, Fanning reminds us we need to heed three simple but crucial warnings about our limitations in knowing Jesus.

Fanning's affirmation at the end of this sermon, however, embodies the same elevated conviction with which the sermon began: Jesus is who we in the church claim him to be, and more. We have made a journey through our limitations and objections, and have returned to the bedrock conviction where the sermon began: Christ the Lord.

TEXT

Fanning focuses on three particular aspects of the ninth chapter of Luke, but the sermon reflects the entire chapter and its central question: "Who is Jesus?" (Luke 9:18–21).

First, we might limit Jesus. The work of the kingdom stretches beyond the reach of any single human perspective. This invites humility.

Second, using the text about the Samaritans' rejection of Jesus and his disciples, we receive a second warning: "Don't use force." Love is the only "force" Jesus uses in the lives of people. This is especially timely today when so much Christian anger abounds in our society. Perhaps some of that anger is righteous indignation. Many Christians, however, react emotionally instead of in a principled way. What appears to be anti-Christian hostility may also simply be the loss of cultural privilege. Christians must decide whether to grieve or celebrate.

Finally, Fanning warns us not to use Jesus as a means to an end. Loving Jesus is the end of discipleship. Political ends, moral and cultural concerns, financial agendas, and personal agendas are important, but not ultimate.

The purpose of Christ, says Fanning, is purely and simply to save, without restriction, anyone who will come. In many ways, a Buckner Fanning sermon is not like being preached to, but more like listening in on a pastoral heart, concerned that all the hindrances fall away so we can see clearly the "one thing that is most needful"—Jesus Christ.

In many ways, Fanning's use of the text is very simple. He does not engage in elaborate exegesis, but aims instead to capture the spirit of the biblical text. While this can sometimes bypass rich and fruitful matters, it is important (and necessary) for us to return now and then to the simple, central affirmations of the Bible. Remember, though these central truths are familiar to many of us who have been around them for a long time, there is almost always someone in the congregation for whom this is all new.

RESPONSE

This is an evangelistic sermon. Fanning is, in effect, clearing away objections to faith in Christ when he identifies the ways in which we might distort Jesus. His intent is that the hearer might set aside his or her own "lens of experience" and try simply to see Jesus Christ for "who he is."

SUGGESTIONS

- Do you ever do summaries of the gospel for your congregation? I once heard Elizabeth Achtemeier challenge a seminary chapel to try to preach the whole story of the Bible to a congregation in one sermon. I had the audacity to try it on a Wednesday night and found it to be a daunting task. Once I started, though, it was fun. The congregation had a great time kidding about "how he's going to do it." We need to touch the broad, familiar themes of the faith and reinterpret them for new generations. Try it—in one sermon!
- Take a look at some of your recent sermons. Can you find any convictions of your own in them? Are they easily recognizable? It is

helpful to ask ourselves regarding every sermon: What statement about the faith underlies this sermon?

Gary A. Furr

Note

1. David Buttrick, *Homiletic: Moves and Structures* (Philadelphia: Fortress Press, 1987), p. 256.

BLESSED BY
MENTORS

1 SAMUEL 3:1–10

REV. DR. F. DEAN LUEKING
GRACE LUTHERAN CHURCH
RIVER FOREST, ILLINOIS

REV. DR. F. DEAN LUEKING

BLESSED BY
MENTORS

1 SAMUEL 3:1–10, NRSV

N ow the boy Samuel was ministering to the Lord under Eli. The word of the Lord was rare in those days; visions were not widespread.

At that time Eli, whose eyesight had begun to grow dim so that he could not see, was lying down in his room; the lamp of God had not yet gone out, and Samuel was lying down in the temple of the Lord, where the ark of God was. Then the Lord called, "Samuel! Samuel!" and he said, "Here I am!" and ran to Eli, and said, "Here I am, for you called me." But he said, "I did not call; lie down again." So he went and lay down. The Lord called again, "Samuel!" Samuel got up and went to Eli, and said, "Here I am, for you called me." But he said, "I did not call, my son; lie down again." Now Samuel did not yet know the Lord, and the word of the Lord had not yet been revealed to him. The Lord called Samuel again, a third time. And he got up and went to Eli, and said, "Here I am, for you called me." Then Eli perceived that the Lord was calling the boy. Therefore Eli said to Samuel, "Go, lie down; and if he calls you, you shall say, 'Speak, Lord, for your servant is listening.'" So Samuel went and lay down in his place.

Now the Lord came and stood there, calling as before, "Samuel! Samuel!" And Samuel said, "Speak, for your servant is listening."

This beautiful story offers many themes for preaching. The one I have chosen is this: God blesses us with mentors who help us hear God speaking.

In mentors we may find the many qualities we associate with good coaches, teachers, guides, counselors, therapists, role models. The word *mentor* has an interesting history. Homer tells us it was the name of the teacher in whose care Ulysses left his son Telemachus when he went off to Troy. We've taken that proper name into our vocabulary and made it a noun describing a person of salutary and lasting influence.

A MENTORED MOMENT

Mentors usually have an ongoing relationship with us, but not always. I'd like to tell you of a mentored moment, brief in duration but long-term in effect.

Last Monday I went to David Hardin's funeral at the Episcopal Cathedral of St. James in downtown Chicago. This Christian layperson was a mentor to many throughout his business career as founder and president of Market Facts. He influenced many more of us in recent years as a leader of Opportunity International and host on Channel 11 of the *Chicago Sunday Evening Club* program. His death touched huge numbers of people; the cathedral was filled to the doors with notable men and women. The service was formal and beautiful. All of us were uplifted by the power of the liturgy which has sustained so many sorrowing hearts across centuries. The sweep of hymn, prayer, and Scripture carried us to that point in the service when family members spoke fondly of David. First his wife, Paula. Then a daughter.

Third came Chuck, a son in the family. His appearance—shirt sleeves and ponytail there in the formal cathedral—signaled a different message coming. Unforgettably different. Chuck laid aside his prepared eulogy and chose to speak as though his father was there beside him in the pulpit. He told of being in jail while his father was in his final weeks of cancer. In fact, Chuck was just released from a heroin- and cocaine-related imprisonment in time to get to the funeral. He spoke of the ups and downs between father and son over the years. His candor about the difficulty of being the son of a high-achieving father was stunning in its honesty. But the deeper message from his heart was his sorrow over the grief he had caused his father. His main word was the hope that the same God who gave Dave Hardin such sterling gifts would give Chuck Hardin the singular gift of turning his life around, kicking the addiction, turning loss into the gain of a worthy life. His sermon was all of three minutes. Not the usual eulogy.

Chuck Hardin mentored me in those brief moments last Monday in ways he could not know, though I would like him to know. His dad had indeed been a mentor, but in this moment, Chuck was the one whose witness gathered up the power to point beyond himself to the wondrous word of the living God. Since Monday afternoon, some deafness in my own heart has begun to open up. Deep within my soul I have begun to listen and to hear in a new way. Changes are underway in my inner life and outer relationships. That's what happens when a "Speak, Lord, your servant is listening!" moment comes. Mentors are the channel for such grace.

About Mentors

Eli, the patron saint of befuddled servants of God, teaches us much about mentors. He lived over a thousand years before Christ, and carried out his priestly duties in the tabernacle at Shiloh during a bleak time in Israel's history: "The word of the Lord was rare in those days" (v. 1). The blood-spattered era of the judges was winding down. The dawn of the great prophets of Israel was approaching. Mentoring the child Samuel was a new grace for a broken old man. Eli's sons, Hophni and Phinehas, were prototypes of today's religious hucksters—profiteering on bogus religion, bedding down vulnerable women, shamelessly misusing holy ordinances. (Both were later killed in battle on the same day, and the news killed Eli, then nearing one hundred.) But in spite of the times, the *hesed*, the compassionate mercy of God, had not run out, symbolized by the still-burning tabernacle lamp alongside the Ark of the Covenant. Eli could still mentor Samuel.

Mentors are those who know something of the wounds of life. The wisdom they impart has been tested in the crucible of tears and heartache. Mentors are not self-appointed. Often they are from outside the family (though faithful parents are powerful mentors). They embody a grace that comes from beyond blood lines. They bridge the generation gap. They see the good in lives and affirm it, stir it up, nurture it toward a future that God has in mind. Mentors can pick out, above the drone of the ordinary, the cadences of God's speaking, which always means God's doing.

Eli was a hinge in Samuel's life. Samuel became the first of the great prophets of Israel. He was a judge, reformer, protector of Israel's covenant. Samuel chose and anointed David, Israel's greatest king. "Great David's greater son" was Jesus Christ our Lord. Mentors are links in the long chain of God's saving acts in history. Samuel's name is on the honor role found in Hebrews 11, where the great ones of Israel are listed.

BEHIND ALL MENTORS

Today's Gospel from John 1:43–51 gives us a glimpse of the One whose grace is behind and in and over all faithful mentoring.

Jesus came face to face with Nathanael, whom Philip had found and brought to him. He saw an integrity in Nathanael and declared it to this startled man who doubted if anything good could come from Nazareth. The beginning of discipleship occurred in this decisive moment. Nathanael was given a future beyond anything he could ask or desire.

The future for Nathanael, and for each of us with him, has a cross in the center of it. Christ Jesus carried the full weight of sin that stops our ears from hearing, or even wanting to hear, the word of the living God. Jesus suffered the full burden of our deafness to God's speaking and our defiance of God's will. Jesus gave his life for us! His resurrection is the mighty work of the Father that gives us hearing and sight, and opens us to the towering greatness of the Divine love with which we all have been loved. The gospel—God's yes!—to you and me again this day in Jesus Christ is what I heard the other afternoon in the Episcopal cathedral from a surprise preacher. The good news for your ears and mine today is that the light of grace never goes out for us. The same *hesed* that gave Eli a new start in mentoring Samuel gives us a future, graced by mentors and blessed to make us mentors as well.

THINK OF MENTORS

Think of the mentors in your life. They are the people who bring flesh and blood to Bible passages, who live the gospel within our sight and hearing, who teach us godly wisdom by lives of steady faith. More often than not, their leavening influence takes root when we are young and malleable.

Among many mentors in my life I think today of Jason Woodside. He was a building contractor who hired me during the summers of my late teens. To this day I know how to carry an extended ladder, mix mortar, and paint houses because of his mentoring. But above all I remember him as a man of the church, a singer in the choir, and the one who played the part of Christ in Easter sunrise services. Kids take note of such things. Such mentors are decisive in shaping our spiritual outlook in ways that bear fruit for a lifetime.

Who comes to your mind as your mentor? It is a good time not only to think about them and thank God for them, but to talk about them around your table.

Be grateful that you have mentors. How many people in prison today ever had anyone mentor them, see good in them, stay by them, come what may? Now that original sin has surfaced in the ugly events of Olympic figure skating, think of what a mentor could mean in a Tonya Harding's hardscrabble life. Or in the lives of the goons hired to batter Nancy Kerrigan out of competition. Be grateful and humble for the blessing of mentors. Where would we be without them?

HEARING THE UNWELCOME TRUTH

Mentors love us enough to tell us unwelcome truths at times. Robert Fulghum (remember his *All I Really Need to Know I Learned in Kindergarten?*) gives us this recollection in his more recent book, *Uh-Oh: Some Observations from Both Sides of the Refrigerator Door.* His first job out of college was as a part-time horse wrangler at a resort in the Sierra Nevada mountains. One night he was ranting against the hotel management that served the employees wieners and sauerkraut for lunch nine days in a row, and compounding the insult by deducting the cost from their paychecks. Fed up and furious, he went on and on until there was only one listener left, the night auditor. Sigmund Wolman had been a quiet friend, never saying much. Nonetheless he was a man of influence on young Fulghum. No one knew he was a survivor of Auschwitz. Sitting there on a stool, watching with sorrowful eyes, Wolman finally said, "Lissen, Fulchum. You know what's wrong with you?...You think you know everything, but you don't know the difference between an inconvenience and a problem. If you break your neck, if you have nothing to eat, if your house is on fire—then you got a problem. Everything else is inconvenience. Life *is* inconvenient. Life *is* lumpy. Learn to separate the inconveniences from the real problems. You will live longer. And will not annoy people like me so much. Good night."

Thirty years later Fulghum recalled that mentored moment. He writes how, in times of stress, when life has him backed against a wall, that voice and that sorrowful face return and inquire, "inconvenience or problem?" "Life is lumpy," Fulghum concludes. "A lump in the oatmeal, a lump in the throat, and a lump in a breast are not the same lump. One should learn the difference."[1]

A TWO-WAY STREET OF BLESSING

I close with a story of how the mentoring blessing can pass from young to old as well as the other way around. Robert Smith of Stroudsburg, Pennsylvania, remembers a childhood experience that adds another facet to the blessing of mentors. It's longer than I usually quote from the pulpit, but worth every word.

> I was just twelve at the time. The season's first blanket of snow magnified the excitement as I dressed to—what? Build a snowman? Slide down the hill? Or just throw flakes in the air and watch them flutter down?
>
> Our family's station wagon pulled into the driveway, and Mom called me over to help with the groceries. When we finished carrying in the bags, she said, "Bob, here are Mrs. Hildebrandt's groceries." No other instructions were necessary. As far back as I could remember, Mom shopped for Mrs. Hildebrandt's food and I delivered it. Our ninety-five-year-old neighbor lived alone, was crippled with arthritis and could take only a few steps with a cane. I liked Mrs. Hildebrandt. I enjoyed talking with her; more accurately, I enjoyed listening to her. She told me wonderful stories about her life—about a steepled church in the woods, horse and buggy rides on Sunday afternoons, and her family farm without electricity or running water.
>
> She always gave me a dime for bringing in her groceries. It got so that I would refuse only half-heartedly, knowing she would insist. Five minutes later, I'd be across the street in Beyer's candy store. As I headed over with the grocery bags, I decided this time would be different though. Her birthday was coming. This would be my birthday present to her. Impatiently, I rang the doorbell. "Come in, come in," she said cheerfully. "Put the bags on the table." I did so more hurriedly than usual because I could almost hear the snow calling me back outside.
>
> She sat at the table, picked the items out of the bag and told me where to set them on the shelves. I usually enjoyed doing this, but it was snowing. As we continued, I began to realize how lonely she was. Her husband had died more than twenty years before, she had no children, and her only living relative was a

nephew in Philadelphia who never visited her. Nobody ever called on her.

She offered me a cup of tea, which she did every time I brought the groceries. Well, maybe the snow could wait. We sat and talked about what it was like when she was a child. Together, we traveled back in time and an hour passed before I knew it. "Well, Bob, you must be wanting to play outside in the snow," she said as she reached for her purse, fumbling for the right coin. "No, Mrs. Hildebrandt, I can't take your money this time. You can use it for more important things," I resisted.

She looked at me and smiled. "What more important thing could I use this money for, if not to give it to a friend?" she asked and then placed a whole quarter in my hands. I tried to give it back, but she would have none of it. I hurried out the door and ran over to Beyer's candy store with my fortune. I had no idea what to buy—comic books, a chocolate soda, ice cream.... Then I spotted a birthday card with a lovely country scene on the cover. It was much like the place Mrs. Hildebrandt described to me and I knew I had to buy it.

I handed Mr. Beyer my quarter, and borrowed a pen to sign my name. "For your girlfriend?" Mr. Beyer asked. I started to say "no" but quickly changed my mind. "Well, yeah, I guess so." As I walked back across the street with my gift, I was so proud of myself, I felt like I had just hit a home run in the World Series. No, I felt a lot better than that! I rang Mrs. Hildebrandt's doorbell. "Hello, Mrs. Hildebrandt," I said as I handed her the card. "Happy Birthday!"

Her hands trembled as she slowly opened the envelope, studied the card and began to cry. "Thank you very much," was all she could say and she said it in a whisper.

On a cold and windy afternoon two weeks later an ambulance arrived next door. My mom said they found Mrs. Hildebrandt in bed. She had died peacefully in her sleep. Her night-table light was still on when they found her. It illuminated a solitary birthday card with a lovely country scene on the cover.[2]

Like Samuel of old, we never quite know, do we, when it's not just another humdrum happening on a humdrum day, but an epiphany moment when some blessed mentor helps us hear what really is at hand, and we offer up our own "Speak, Lord, your servant is listening"!

Notes
1. Robert Fulghum, *Uh-Oh: Some Observations from Both Sides of the Refrigerator Door* (New York: Villard Books, 1991), pp. 143–46, quoting p. 145.
2. I am indebted to a friend, Robert Smith, who related this story to me in a personal conversation.

COMMENT

God always provides people we need when we are ready to receive them. We may not always immediately recognize them, but "the mentored moment" is a gift from God who loves us and blesses us. This sermon by Dean Lueking is just such a "mentored moment" not only for those hearing it, but also for those reading it. Sermons are intended for the spoken word. Very good sermons may also provide good reading. This is a good example of a sermon that "reads well."

ANNOUNCE A STATEMENT OF PURPOSE

Lueking's sermon reminds us of our own mentors. With an easy conversational style, the preacher helps us remember those who have mentored us and reminds us that we are called to be mentors for other struggling souls. Following the sharing of the text of 1 Samuel 3:1–10, the sermon opens with a clear statement of purpose. "God blesses us with mentors who help us hear God speaking." Such an early introduction of the subject helps listeners know where the sermon is going. This is always a good method of opening. Let the person in the pew know the purpose of the sermon. Don't keep them guessing. Make it clear, make it concise, make it memorable.

USE PERSONAL EXPERIENCES

Lueking defines the term "mentor" by alluding to the story from Homer rather than using a simple dictionary definition. Now we know not only where the word comes from, but its meaning and its importance for us. A mentor is a teacher who has a lasting influence for good in our lives.

The contemporary illustrations in this sermon are well chosen and provide us with a "you-are-there" experience. Lueking uses visual images to help us see and feel the moment he shares from his personal experience. People in the pew love good illustrations from personal experience. Chuck Hardin now lives in my memory because Lueking shared his own mentored moment. I've prayed for Chuck Hardin, though there is little likelihood of my ever meeting him.

Don't hesitate to use personal experiences and illustrations in your preaching. A word of caution, however. Make sure you are not always the hero or heroine of the story. One of my mentors, John Killinger, cautioned me many years ago: "People don't want to hear (read) of your successes. They want to hear (read) of your failures." Those words stayed with me. Successive years of pastoring have proven the wisdom of his observation. People identify more with our failures, our weakness and vulnerability, than with our successes.

I wanted to know more about Chuck Hardin, because of good preaching technique in this sermon. Leave your people wanting more. Preach to the needs of your congregation. Give them enough for the present moment, but leave them wanting more.

How did Chuck Hardin mentor Lueking on the day of his father's funeral? I wanted more. The preacher might have been more specific. "Some deafness in my own heart has begun to open up. Deep within my soul I have begun to listen and to hear in a new way. Changes are underway in my inner life and outer relationships." What changes? How did he know? What happened that made this a mentored moment in his life? Even though my questions may not be answered, Lueking has driven home the main point with convincing clarity. God's grace often comes through unlikely channels. "Mentors are the channels for such grace."

MAKE GRACEFUL TRANSITIONS

Lueking has wonderful transitions in this sermon. He moves with grace from story to information to application. He informs, illustrates, and entertains in the process. He moves well, for example, from the illustration about Chuck Hardin back into the biblical text. The transitions flow gracefully. "Mentors are channels for God's grace." "Mentors are links in the long chain of God's saving acts in history."

In the course of the sermon Lueking brings us to the Gospel reading from John 1:43–51 concerning Jesus and Nathanael. After considering

C O M M E N T

Eli, we are brought face to face with our greatest mentor, Jesus Christ. We are reminded of God's boundless love and saving grace in our own relationship with God-in-Christ. This is the good news that we as preachers of the gospel must strive to embrace and to proclaim to the people we are sent to serve. "The good news for your ears and mine today is that the light of grace never goes out for us. The same *hesed* that gave Eli a new start in mentoring Samuel gives us a future, graced by mentors and blessed to make us mentors as well." What a well-stated reminder of what God is doing in our lives! Lueking has taken the biblical texts, personalized them, and proclaimed them in such a way as to help people in the pew and readers rejoice. That is good preaching. Contemporary Christians have more than enough blame and shame in their lives. Preach *hope*. Preach the *good news*. The sermon could have ended here. But there's more.

CHALLENGE THE PERSON IN THE PEW TO ACTION

We are invited to remember our own mentors. Lueking speaks of another of his mentors, then leads us to think of those people who have had special influence on our lives. We are asked to do something: "Thank God for them…talk about them around your table. Be grateful that you have mentors." The best sermons give us a plan of action. They don't simply tell us what to do. They guide us gently along a path we want to explore.

I was immediately drawn into this sermon and could see the faces and hear the voices of my own life mentors. College professors: John Killinger, Dan Jones, Curtis Coleman, Gerd Luedemonn, Walter Harelson, David White. High school teachers: Mary Trim Anderson, Jane Dora Scarbro, Bobby Gentry. Pastors: Jack Wolfe, James Underwood, Ben Alford. The grandmother I called Pretty Jones. Ken, my dear and beloved husband of forty-two years. There have been many others. What a blessing to be asked to remember and give thanks for them. When one does what the preacher suggests in a sermon, then the sermon "works." The goal of good preaching is to lead people not only to hear, but to respond with positive action. Lueking attains that goal.

LEAVE THEM WANTING MORE

As this sermon draws to a close, Lueking tells the congregation he is nearing the end, then shares one more story of mentoring from a man named Robert Smith. It is a good visual story worth every word. It draws attention to the spontaneous action of a child that reminds us of the lasting impact of small kindnesses. The story speaks to people of every age hearing or reading the sermon. We all have many opportunities for such small acts of kindness in our daily lives. Just think how often a kind thought, word or deed from another person has brightened your life. We are not always so fortunate to know the benefit our kindness brings to another. But we all need to learn to give and to receive as many kindnesses as we have opportunities.

It is true. As Lueking reminds us, we do not always know or recognize the mentors and mentored moments, the epiphany moments of our lives. But this sermon has led us to see, remember and act upon those mentored moments from our past and to watch for such moments in the future.

SUGGESTIONS

- Who have been your mentors in life? Do you ever speak of them in your preaching? How can you tell some of the significant stories of mentors in your life? As you do study, exegesis and preparation of biblical texts from week to week, keep your mentors in mind, and when a biblical text appropriately suggests it, tell of your mentored moments.

- I have one criticism. It appears to me from this sermon that only Christians can be good mentors. The preacher seems to limit a mentor to being a good and faithful Christian without specifying that one is being mentored in the Christian faith. While it is true that most of my own mentors have been thoroughly grounded Christian men and women, mentors are not limited to any specific faith. It seems to me that God uses all kinds of people in our lives. They may be from other religious traditions or persuasions. The question is whether we are watching and listening for the ways in which God speaks and acts.

- What other examples of mentoring occur in stories from the Bible? Consider a sermon or series of sermons on these characters and stories.
- Explore the role of Jesus' disciples in the Gospels. How do the Gospels as narratives "characterize" the disciples in terms of their commitment, their understanding and their misunderstanding of who Jesus was? How do narratives about the disciples relate to "mentoring"?
- What does the term "discipleship" mean to you? How would you define it? How do you understand it theologically within your theological tradition? Do you ever preach about this subject?

Marianna Frost

ON TAKING
PAIN SERIOUSLY

2 CORINTHIANS 12:7–10

REV. DR. JOHN KILLINGER
PROFESSOR OF RELIGION
SAMFORD UNIVERSITY
BIRMINGHAM, ALABAMA

ON TAKING
PAIN SERIOUSLY

2 CORINTHIANS 12:7–10, PHILLIPS

O ne night recently I awoke with a pain in my arm. Two months earlier, I had injured the muscles and ligaments of my right shoulder, and now the pain was cascading down the arm. I lay there in the dark, thinking about pain and how real and insistent it can be. Should I get up and take an aspirin, I wondered, or lie there and meditate about pain?

Our society doesn't like pain. I don't suppose people ever did. But we have come to have an absolute intolerance of it. Our drug counters are an eloquent witness to that intolerance—hundreds and hundreds of painkillers, their manufacturers all promising fast relief (or at least faster than the medications of their strongest competitors).

Is it possible, I pondered, that we often miss an important dimension of human reality by refusing to undergo pain? Many saints in former centuries, you remember, actually cultivated pain as a reminder of their humanity and dependence on God. Were they being merely strange and eccentric, or did they know something about life and pain and God that we have forgotten?

I thought of Aldous Huxley's incredibly perceptive novel *Brave New World*,[1] which was published more than half a century ago, yet saw with steely-eyed clarity the technological, drug-oriented culture of our own time. Life in this gleaming, passionless society was regulated by a master-drug called *soma,* which kept everyone in a state of mild euphoria. Each citizen got a daily ration of soma, and it virtually eliminated pain and anxiety from the populace. But into this carefully controlled society, which had its geographical center in the city of London, Huxley introduces a conflicted character, a neoprimitive Native American named John Savage. Savage is amazed at life in the brave new world. He cannot believe that people purposefully choose to lead such bland and antiseptic existences. He cannot understand why the Bible and Shakespeare are viewed as subversive and are locked in the world leader's safe. At last, after several months in this advanced society, Savage disappears into the wilderness. When someone finds him, he is flagellating himself in the manner of his *penitente* brothers in New Mexico. "I want suffering!" he says, "I want death! I want God!"

Huxley was not a great theist, but he understood that there is a profound and intimate relationship between suffering and God. Pain reminds us of finitude, limitations, mortality. Pain is humiliating, in the best sense; it is a reminder of our true humility. It announces, "You are not God. Only God is God. Fall down and worship!"

I think this is part of what our text is saying. Paul was talking to his Corinthian friends about his ministry and their self-pride in rejecting it. He spoke of some great affliction that had plagued his life and work. We don't know if it was physical or emotional in nature. Some scholars have suggested that it was malaria or epilepsy, others that it was a problem with his eyes. Still others have said it was a woman, perhaps a wife who would not follow him into Christianity. Whatever it was, Paul described it memorably as a "thorn in the flesh"—a spine of some kind hooked in the meaty part of the body, producing pain and aggravation.

Whatever Paul's thorn was, he said he had prayed to God on at least three occasions to remove it, to set him free from the pain and discomfort. He even called his torment "an angel of Satan" sent to afflict him. But God had said to him, "My grace is enough for you; my power is at its best in weakness" (v. 9).

That's an astounding message. "My grace is enough for you; my power is at its best in weakness." That's the theology of the cross: God's power at work in the most vulnerable places. The divine power being manifested in weakness, in pain, in humiliation, in mortality and death.

It's true in my experience, and I expect it's true in yours as well: we are most aware of God when we are in pain and unsettledness. When everything is going well—all our body parts functioning properly, the sun shining, stocks doing well, children behaving nicely, food on the table, not too hot, not too cold—we tend not to notice God. But let something go awry—a hip give way, a child's divorce, a job turn sour, a storm knocks out the power—and we're suddenly aware, aren't we? Pain is the hook that draws our attention to the holy, the eternal, the beyond.

I thought of this as I lay there in the dark, and gave thanks for the pain. We are creatures who feel pain. There is something abnormal when we can't. When someone gets drunk we say, "He's beyond all pain." That is, he's deprived of his essential qualities. I have a friend who has a little daughter who cannot feel pain in her body. There is a problem with her nervous system. Her parents must watch her continuously, for she can do herself great harm. She wears leg braces to protect her from running into things she can't feel. She is kept away from fire, for she doesn't feel it burning her. To feel pain is normal. It is an intrinsic part of our creature-liness, of our being human.

One of pain's greatest functions is that it reminds us of who we are, that we are mortal and not immortal, weak and not powerful, the children of God and not God.

A few days ago I was seated on an airplane by a doctor from Maine. We talked about philosophies of life and medicine and wellness. He told me that he had a medical degree from UCLA and had practiced in two or three major medical centers before he realized how unhappy he was with our health-care system. "We fill people with pills and run them through surgery," he said, "as if that will fix everything that's wrong with them. And the tragedy is that both doctors and patients get to thinking that's true."

Searching for other answers, he studied homeopathy and osteopathy, and decided that truth involves a lot more than living on drugs and repairing broken hips. He left the increasingly depersonalized world of the "system," as he called it, and moved to a small town in Maine, where he opened his own practice. "I don't have a nurse or a secretary," he said. "There's a bookkeeper who comes in at night and does the billing. Otherwise I run everything myself. It gives me a chance to really know my patients." He said he spends an hour and a half interviewing every new patient he treats, talking about medical history, family systems, and philosophical or religious views. "I try to treat the whole patient," he said, "and not some fictitious entity in an office filled with other patients all eager to take a pill and feel better.

"What people don't realize," he said, "is that pain often has its uses. It points us to deeper realities in our lives, things we've been out of touch with. Pain can help us to locate the real meaning of our existence."

The real meaning of existence. That's what we ought to be seeking. Pain is one of our best tutors. We can learn from it. We can discover life through it. "My power," said God to Paul, "works best in weakness." Oh, of course pain can be debilitating and destructive, and it would be foolish to wish anyone to suffer too deeply and too long—not even the worst criminals in our society. But pain can also befriend us, if we will not treat it too lightly and dismiss it too quickly. In the final analysis, it is part of the sacrament of living.

Reynolds Price's beautiful book *A Whole New Life*[2] is the account of his battle with cancer. I was at Duke University recently, where Price teaches, and heard from one of the professors what a special place this courageous man occupies in the affections of his community. A few years ago, Price began to have problems walking. The doctors found that he had a strange tumor growing in and out among the nerves of his spinal cord. They operated, but could remove only bits and pieces of the long, networking tumor. Confined to a wheelchair, and with no hope of recovery, Price was sent home to die. His pain was excruciating. On a scale of zero to ten, he said, it remained constantly a nine or ten.

Then one day Price, who was only a nominal Christian, had a vision. It was not a dream, he insists, for he was fully awake. It was early morning, and the mist was rising from a nearby lake. He saw a little band of men asleep on the grass. They were Jesus and the disciples, and the lake, he figured, must be Kinneret or Galilee. Jesus awoke, rose, and motioned for Price to follow. He followed down to the lakeshore, where Jesus indicated that he should remove his clothes. Then he followed Jesus into the water. Jesus cupped his hand and raised it, pouring water on him. Price had a long, purple oblong mark on his back where the X-ray technicians had marked him for his radiation therapy. He felt the water running over the mark, and over the scar he had from his operation.

This done, Jesus said, "Your sins are forgiven," and walked out of the water. Price followed, stammering, "But what about my cancer? Am I healed?" Jesus turned and looked at him for a moment, then answered, "That too."

Price told his vision to his doctors. They listened politely but didn't take it seriously. They knew he would die from the cancer. Not even the therapy would be able to kill it. But now Price lived in hope. Some days were better than others. He took lessons in living as a paraplegic—how to get in and out of cars, showers, bed, public toilets, all the things most of us never trouble to think about. Slowly the pain began to abate. It became a seven, a six, a five and some days even a three or a two on the pain scale. Eventually the MRIs revealed that the tumor was shrinking, retreating. The doctors were amazed, but rejoiced with him.

Price is still a paraplegic. He still has some pain. But he probably knows more about himself—who he is, what his life is about, where God is—than any of us here today. His pain, his thorn in the flesh, gave him awareness. Like Job, like Jesus, like Paul, he understands who we are and who God is. He may even bless his pain for what it has revealed to him.

"My grace is enough for you; my power is at its best in weakness."

By the way, I'm having therapy on my arm; but I don't intend to forget the pain.

Note

1. Aldous Huxley, *Brave New World* (Cutchogue, NY: Buccaneer Books, 1932), see pp. 156–63.
2. Reynolds Price, *A Whole New Life* (New York: Atheneum Publishers, 1994). See also Reynolds Price, "Vision of Healing," *Guideposts,* (August 1994), p. 25.

COMMENT

There is great danger in writing a book on preaching. First, it's a tough subject. John Killinger in his newly revised book, *Fundamentals of Preaching,* readily admits, "No book can be a final arbiter of what preaching is and how it should be done." But more than that, the author of a book on preaching opens the door to intense scrutiny of his or her own preaching. Does the author preach what he/she teaches?

In his sermon, "On Taking Pain Seriously," does Killinger follow his own advice on preaching given in *Fundamentals of Preaching?* In the introduction to his book Killinger writes, "We have entered a new time for Christianity…" It is a time characterized by fragmentation and transformation. We see ourselves and our world dramatically differently than just fifteen years ago. Most importantly, Killinger asserts, people hear and act upon sermons differently, and it is our duty as preachers to rediscover the meaning of the gospel for our time and learn how to preach it in a relevant way.[1]

Does the sermon "On Taking Pain Seriously" proclaim the gospel in a relevant way? Quite simply, yes. This sermon is a model for any person wanting to know how to communicate effectively to postmodern people.

OPENING

Every sermon is still a new experience for me, a chartless journey upon the seas of life and death. There are tricks of the trade, habits of mind, a residue of experience; but every sermon worth its salt is a fresh creation, an unrepeated—and unrepeatable—adventure (*Fundamentals,* p. 1).

The first three paragraphs of Killinger's sermon serve as a road map for our "journey" with Killinger. This is because the rest of the sermon will deal with the three ideas presented in these paragraphs. The first paragraph *addresses the life situation:* we have pain. It is part of life. Here,

Killinger uses himself as the example. Twice, he will come back to his personal experience with pain: once in the middle of the sermon to bring us back to his first thought (we all experience pain), and again at the end, tying the sermon into a neat whole.

The second paragraph *raises the problem:* we don't like pain. Killinger is a master at getting inside the skin of modern thinking. He knows our culture and appeals to our modern consciousness. He calls this "conspiratorial" preaching. Instead of "marching at [us] in a frontal assault," he sneaks up on us. He slips by our defenses by creating interest and raising concern (*Fundamentals,* p. 5).

The third paragraph alludes to *the solution* to our problem. We all have pain and we don't like it. But Killinger raises the possibility that pain might not be all bad. In fact, it may be useful. "Is it possible, I pondered, that we often miss an important dimension of human reality by refusing to undergo pain?" By raising such a question, Killinger indirectly attacks modern thinking and makes us reconsider the place of pain in our lives. He then spends the rest of the sermon expounding on what important dimension pain supplies to human reality.

TEXT & PROCLAMATION

There should be a sense of inevitability in the progression of the sermon. A good sermon marches inexorably toward its conclusion, molding sense and sound together until it has accomplished its mission (*Fundamentals,* p. 82).

Killinger is methodical and logical. The sermon has direction and is tightly packaged. But more than this, Killinger is an artist. This sermon seems to blossom, like a well-watered bulb in spring. The preacher is not interested in debate or argument, but instead he weaves a web of progression and growth. We feel surrounded, drawn in. But the sermon is effective for several other reasons as well.

PERSONAL

We should try whenever possible to join people where they
stand—in doubt and fear and confusion—and work our way
from there to a position of illumination and understanding
(*Fundamentals*, p. 34).

Throughout this sermon's tone, its personal examples and its stories,
there is a clear and certain feeling of intimacy. It is as if there is a dialogue
going on between Killinger and the congregation. The sermon is full of
rhetorical questions and statements like "I think" and "Is it possible?" and
"Do you remember?" Again and again, Killinger speaks to his listeners'
shared cares and concerns. He identifies with his listeners, saying for
example, "It's true in my experience, and I expect it's true in yours as well:
we are most aware of God when we are in pain and unsettledness."

Killinger works back and forth between human situations and the
gospel. He addresses real needs and real people. He is specific: his own
pain, the person whose hip gave way, the child caught in their parents'
divorce, a job turned sour, a storm that knocked out power. And then he
interprets our situation through the grid of the gospel. "It is normal to feel
pain...And one of its greatest functions is that it reminds us of who we
are, that we are mortal and not immortal, weak and not powerful, the
children of God and not God."

Killinger writes in the conclusion to *Fundamentals of Preaching*,
"What it all comes down to in the end is the total relationship of everything the minister is and does to what is said in the sermon" (p. 217).
This is good advice for all preachers. Preaching is an enormous responsibility. We are wise to bring everything in our lives to the preparation
and delivery of sermons. We must know ourselves, and give all that we
are and have to the shaping of our messages. But we must also know our
congregation—their identities and experiences—and allow them to
shape our messages. Preaching is a relationship.

Storytelling

One helpful way to conceive of preaching is in terms of the story-teller's art. The good storyteller knows human nature so well that he or she always tells stories that involve the listeners and become their stories (*Fundamentals*, p. 35).

Another reason this sermon is effective is its use of story. Killinger is a master of using story to illustrate or to "do" theology. This sermon is driven by three major stories. The first, Aldous Huxley's novel, *Brave New World*, comes just minutes into the sermon to answer the rhetorical question, "Is pain useful?" The summation after the illustration, "Huxley was not a great theist, but he understood that there is a profound and intimate relationship between suffering and God," is Killinger's way of letting Huxley answer Killinger's own question.

The second and third stories make up the last half of the sermon. The second story comes directly after Killinger summarizes where he has brought the listeners thus far: Pain is normal. Moreover, pain is useful because it reminds us of who we are and who God is. But Killinger has one more step for us to take on this journey. There is another purpose to pain, perhaps the most important, and both the second and third stories illustrate what it is. Killinger says, "Pain can help us to locate the real meaning of our existence...We can learn from it. We can discover life through it." Pain is useful because: 1) it reminds us who we are; and 2) it gives life. This is because real life is lived under God's power and God's power works best in weakness.

The final story about Reynolds Price is the conclusion and climax of the sermon. It is a powerful story that serves as a parable for the sermon's main idea. Here, we see a real person living out the theology of pain in real life. Killinger has masterfully woven an individual's story into the fabric of the gospel story. In the end, he has reinterpreted our world. He has exposed one of modernity's lies. Pain is not our enemy, it is our ally.

RESPONSE

What the preacher does, when he or she is being effective, is to lay hold of the individual's story and relate it to *the* story...in such a way that the individual discovers new resources for solving problems, renewing life, or enjoying the world (*Fundamentals,* p. 36).

Killinger's sermon challenges us as listeners to reconsider our modern presuppositions. It reveals our cultural biases and misunderstandings and at the same time invites us to live life to its fullest by embracing our humanness and God's otherness. The power of this sermon lies in its truthfulness. Killinger does not minimize the reality of pain. Life is full of tragedies and sorrows. As Christians we are not exempt from pain. Pain is real and it hurts. We all experience it. But pain is also one of our best teachers. "We can learn from it. We can discover life through it," says Killinger. "In the final analysis, it is part of the sacrament of living."

The sermon is powerful in its invitation to hope. Pain is confusing and frustrating for all people. Killinger does a fine job of joining the tension of life which is full of pain and sorrow with the truth of the gospel. In the end, we hope. "My grace is enough for you; my power is at its best in weakness."

SUGGESTIONS

- What can you do to listen better to the voices in your congregation? How can you address concerns and cares of your people? Where do you stand—with them or above them?
- Be "conspiratorial" with regard to your listeners. Ask yourself, "How can I get inside their defenses in order to interpret the gospel in ways that appeal to their modern ways of thinking and being?"
- Use stories to relate the gospel to human situations. Do you balance abstraction and imagery in your sermons?
- Read or reread John Killinger's book, *Fundamentals of Preaching.*

Karen F. Younger

Note

1. John Killinger, *Fundamentals of Preaching,* 2nd edition (Minneapolis: Augsburg Press 1996), pp. 2–5.

ELLIPSIS AND ETERNITY

2 KINGS 20:1–21

REV. DR. MICHAEL P. HALCOMB
NATIONAL ASSOCIATION OF
CONGREGATIONAL CHRISTIAN CHURCHES
OAK CREEK, WISCONSIN

REV. DR. MICHAEL P. HALCOMB

ELLIPSIS AND ETERNITY

2 KINGS 20:1–21, NIV

S omething of a somber spirit permeates our worship for me this morning. Many of you are aware that this is the week that our missionary Edsel Bodden was to have been with us. Reverend Bodden's faithful service with the Honduran Congregational Mission has been an inspiration to us all. It was with shock that we received word that this Christian friend died suddenly of heart failure a few weeks ago while saving a young girl from drowning in the ocean.

Death is one of the subjects that ministers are sometimes told they should avoid in preaching. A seminary professor once advised me to avoid the mention of death in my preaching because it has such a depressing effect upon an audience. But the Bible candidly addresses all of life's vital issues, including death. There have been so many brushes with death in our nation and even in our church family this year that I feel I cannot avoid the topic. In addition, I find myself both challenged and comforted by what the Scriptures have to say on the subject of death.

First, the Bible challenges us to face the fact of death squarely and with candor. Scripture does us a favor in reminding us that death is a certainty for each of us. The message that came to King Hezekiah is one that all of us must hear. "Put your house in order, because you will die…" (v. 1). Actually, we do not need to go to the Scripture to substantiate this point;

we need only to look in the mirror. The ravages of time upon our bodies tell us that life in this body will some day end.

Sociologists tell us, however, that we are a death-denying culture. We do not want to accept the reality of our own death. We turn to gyms, spas, and health foods, not just for healthy recreation, but with an unhealthy obsession with youth. Do we actually believe that if we exercise vigorously and eat enough health foods we will not age and die? The Bible counters the idea when it confronts us with the reality that we are "destined to die once, and after that to face judgment" (Heb. 9:27).

The Bible's candor about death enhances the value of life. The Bible's candor about death reminds us that life is a gift from God. Because life is limited in duration, it is of great value. Every day that we are given, each year of our life that passes, is a precious gift from our Creator. We should be able to say with the psalmist each morning,

> This is the day the Lord has made;
> let us rejoice and be glad in it (Psalm 118:24).

Recently I was reading a Bible commentary by a distinguished scholar and had come to the conclusion of the book in which the author was developing a very important point. As I reached the last page, with my peripheral vision I saw that the book concluded midpage with an ellipsis! An ellipsis is an inconclusive ending, indicated by three little dots in place of a period. A footnote to the page told of Professor Cassuto's sudden death at that very point. He had actually died with pen in hand, right in the middle of a sentence. The publisher chose to print his work exactly as they found it.[1] Cassuto's life, scholarship, and words assumed greater importance for me in light of his sudden death.

Death often comes like that, suddenly and unexpectedly. We may only catch a glimpse of its coming out of the corner of an eye. An ellipsis...and then eternity. None of us can predict how our life will end. Some may have a prolonged ellipsis, as did Hezekiah. God gave Hezekiah an additional fifteen years to adjust to the fact of his own dying. Others have only a second or two to recognize death approaching. The ellipsis of Edsel Bodden's life was brief. At forty-nine years of age he plunged into the surf to save a small girl, and suddenly his last words were "God is calling me." Our friend is no longer with us, but the suddenness of his death makes us value his life and our times together with him even more.

Your life or mine could end just as suddenly. As the old saying goes, "It's a short walk from the womb to the tomb!" While we should plan wisely for the future, life is unpredictable and we do not know how much more time we will be given in this life. The writer of Proverbs must have had this in mind when he wrote,

> Do not boast about tomorrow,
>   for you do not know what a day may bring forth (Prov. 27:1).

Because life may end at any time, it is to be cherished and appreciated. The brevity of life should add joy to every friendship. It should cause us to relish every experience and anticipate each opportunity because it is a gift from God.

The Bible's candor about death also emphasizes our responsibility to be good stewards of life. Because life may end at any time, we should use it wisely. The very brevity of life lends an increased importance to each decision, to every activity, to each priority that we propose.

Recently I saw a bumper sticker on a recreation vehicle which read: "He who has the most toys when he dies…wins!" Some may spend their lives pursuing pleasure or accumulating things. Others may choose to live for some lasting and redemptive purpose. But each of us must account for how we choose to spend this precious commodity called life. The unpredictability of death emphasizes the need for wisdom in our daily decisions.

In Psalm 90 the psalmist says,

> The length of our days is seventy years—
>   or eighty, if we have the strength;…
>   for they quickly pass, and we fly away.

And then, in light of this precious brevity of life, he prays,

> Teach us to number our days aright,
>   that we may gain a heart of wisdom (vv. 10, 12).

Life is a stewardship; and there is no greater issue for us to consider than the stewardship of our time. We may not control the duration of our life, but we may dedicate our life however we choose.

How did Hezekiah use those fifteen precious years of life? We see that he was greatly concerned with accumulating material possessions. With pride he displayed "the silver, the gold, the spices and the fine oil— his armory and everything found among his treasures" (2 Kings 20:13). When Isaiah came and told him that all of these material things would someday fall into the hands of foreign kings, surely Hezekiah realized how foolish he had been. Hezekiah would have been better advised to have spent the last years of his life with his son who was born during those fifteen extra years. Apparently, Hezekiah was so occupied with his treasure that he neglected the spiritual development of his son Manasseh. Manasseh, as you may read in chapter 21 of 2 Kings, grew up to be the most evil and sinister king in the history of Judah. How tragic!

Some time ago a Japanese Air Lines 747 flew out of control and crashed in the mountains of that island nation. The touching aspect of that story, however, is that the plane flew out of control for thirty minutes before crashing. All aboard knew that it was out of control. They knew it was only a matter of time before they would crash. What did they think about? Among the wreckage several hastily scribbled notes to loved ones were found. One gentleman wrote to his wife, "Machiko, take care of the kids." An employee of the airline wrote, "Scared, scared, scared, help, feel sick, don't want to die!" Another man had the presence of mind to write a seventeen-sentence letter that was alternately wistful and philosophical. It began, "I'm grateful for the truly happy life I have lived up until now." Five hundred and twenty people faced a brief ellipsis of thirty minutes, and then eternity.

If you had only thirty minutes to live, what message would you leave your loved ones? Each of us is writing a message that we will leave behind. We may not be writing it with pen and paper, but we are with the words we speak, the relationships we develop, and the conduct of our lives. What is the message of your life? Are you able to say with the apostle Paul, "For to me, to live is Christ and to die is gain" (Phil. 1:21)? Paul had no control over the duration of his life, but he was certain about the direction of his life. And Paul was certain about eternity.

Secondly, the message of the Bible in regard to death is one of consolation. The Bible speaks with assurance that there is eternal life beyond the brief ellipsis of this life. Some of the most resonant and triumphant passages in the Bible have to do with the victory over death that is ours when we trust in Christ, passages such as Romans 8:38–39: "For I am convinced that neither death nor life, neither angels nor demons, neither the present nor the future, nor any powers, neither height nor depth, nor anything else in all creation, will be able to separate us from the love of God that is in Christ Jesus our Lord."

The Bible is filled with images of eternity that speak to the longings of our hearts. It describes a new heaven and a new earth, where "an eternal house…not built by human hands" awaits God's people (2 Cor. 5:1). In that new home, those who are faithful will be given a crown of life (Rev. 2:10). There will be no night there; and no tears of sorrow. Heaven will be a place of reunion. There we will come face to face with Christ, with faithful friends, and with loved ones. The Right Reverend Scott Holland is the Canon of Winchester Cathedral in England. When we visited Winchester Cathedral recently, we picked up a pamphlet with this poem written by Henry Scott Holland:

Death is nothing at all. I have only slipped away in the next room.
I am I and you are you.
Whatever we were to each other, that we are still.
Call me by my old familiar name.

Speak to me in the easy way which you always used,
   put no difference into your tone.
Laugh as we always laughed at the little jokes we enjoyed
   together...
I am but waiting for you,
   for an interval, somewhere very near, just around the
   corner.
All is well. Turn towards the sun and let your shadows fall
   behind you.[2]

Christians can speak of death with that kind of relaxed confidence because they have faith that life continues beyond this world. And this faith can help us face death courageously. Thousands of Christians down through the centuries have known Christ's love so powerfully and his presence so personally that they have chosen to be martyred rather than deny Christ. A Romanian Christian, whom we know only as Sabas the Goth, was put to death in the fourth century for his faith. But he has left us a prayer that has kept his witness to Christ and his faith in eternal life ringing down through the centuries:

Blessed are you, Lord,
   and may your Son's name be blessed forevermore.
I can see what those who persecute me cannot;
   on the other side of this river is a multitude
Waiting to receive my soul and carry it to glory.[3]

Faith in the risen Christ gives us eyes of faith. With the martyrs we can see across the river. "We look not at what can be seen but at what cannot be seen; for what can be seen is temporary, but what cannot be seen is eternal" (2 Cor. 4:18, NRSV). And from that faith issues irrepressible hope and joy.

We do not need to feel depressed when we think of death. Someone has said that a good way out of depression is to sit down and write our own obituary as we would ideally like for it to appear at our death. When we have finished writing it, then we should begin living in such a way that it will come true.

What will we do with the ellipsis of our lives, however long we may live? I've been thinking about that question in my own life. I've also been thinking about the message I would most like to write to my loved ones, and to you my Christian family, if I were a passenger on that flight careening out of control with only minutes to live before a fiery crash.

I would want you and my family to be reminded of my love. We never affirm one another as much as we should. We do not speak often enough of our love for one another. At the same time, I would have to express some sadness. This is not unchristian. While my faith keeps me from fearing death, I still do not welcome the prospect of dying. I enjoy life, and it would be sad to think it must end soon. The thought that I would be separated from my family and my Christian friends brings real sadness, and I would want you to know that.

Hard on the heels of that sadness, however, would come a word of joy. Most of all, I would want you to know that I faced death with joy at the prospect of eternity with my Savior. Face to face with Jesus, at last! And I would also urge you to grow in your own faith, to trust Christ even in the valley of the shadow of death.

With that joy of Christ in my heart, I pray that I would have the time and the presence of mind to quickly scribble these last words in my message to you:

"Where, O death, is your victory?
    Where, O death is your sting?"

...But thanks be to God! He gives us the victory through our Lord Jesus Christ. Therefore, my dear [ones], stand firm. Let nothing move you. Always give yourselves fully to the work of the Lord, because you know that your labor in the Lord is not in vain (1 Cor. 15:55–58).

That would be my final message to you my Christian friends, because ours is not a death-denying faith, but a death-defying faith. Because Christ is a risen, victorious Savior, we do not go on grieving like the rest of mankind. Through Christ we have a living hope, in this life and beyond. In this Ellipsis and throughout eternity.

Notes

1. U. Cassuto, *A Commentary on the Book of Genesis, Vol. II*, trans. Abrahams Israel (Jerusalem: The Magnes Press, The Hebrew University, 1964), p. 369.
2. Words by Henry Scott Holland, poem uncopyrighted.
3. Sabas the Goth, from *Prayers of the Martyrs,* compiled by Duane W. H. Arnold (Grand Rapids: Zondervan).

COMMENT

Death is still a taboo subject unless you are at a funeral. Or, death is used as a tool to instill religious fear and thereby cause desired behavioral change. It is okay to talk about sex but not death. Michael Halcomb's sermon, however, models a different way to approach a difficult subject. Halcomb's message confronts our death-denying culture with a biblical alternative. Both the style and content of this sermon are helpful models for any preacher who is willing to take the risk of venturing into an issue most people would rather ignore—at their own peril!

QUESTION

"Death and taxes are the only two things you can count on in life." While taxes may infuriate, the end of life scares most people half to death. That may be the main concern that needs to be addressed when we talk about death. There is natural curiosity about the hereafter. But there is profound existential fear that is often repressed by adults who hush the child innocently asking, "Mommy, what happens when you die?"

Halcomb starts with the simple, practical question, "What happened to the guest speaker?" He acknowledges reality. He personalizes his response without expecting everyone to share his mood. He points to the challenge of dealing with the topic of death and immediately offers a reason to consider a biblical view. "Scripture does us a favor...."

In this sermon the preacher moves from the practical to the philosophical quickly without unnecessarily dwelling on his personal shock or grief. He approaches the ultimate question of the meaning of life by helping the audience see a way both to overcome the fear of death and to accept the value of biblical faith.

The Bible is quite candid and honest about death. But Halcomb reminds his hearers that this honesty is not morbid. Instead the Bible affirms and enhances the value of life. The preacher then gives three diverse examples to illustrate: a Bible commentator, a missing missionary, and the focus of the text, King Hezekiah.

TEXT

I appreciate the natural ways in which Halcomb incorporates Scripture throughout this sermon. He uses different short passages to underscore and set the stage for what he wants to say without calling much attention to them. It is easy to see that the foundation for this sermon is not pop psychology or the tabloid newspapers. The preacher does not sensationalize or sentimentalize death. In a blunt, countercultural message he begins by quoting from the text, "Put your house in order, because you will die" (2 Kings 20:1).

It seems to me that Halcomb might have elaborated and created more of a word picture about Hezekiah from the text. His may be an unusual congregation, but we need to recognize that many people today are biblical illiterates. I'm not sure the majority of folks know the story of Hezekiah or his place in the Bible. Had the textual stage been more elaborately set, hearers might better understand why the circumstances were so compelling. It's a powerful story worth the time to retell.

In the rest of the sermon Halcomb incorporates both Old and New Testament insights. Hebrew and Pauline principles are a basis for Halcomb's encouraging and challenging words of hope. By his masterful use of the biblical texts he helps us move from our human space-and-time framework to gain an eternal perspective on death and life.

PROCLAMATION

There is a "bad news, good news" approach to the issue of death in this sermon. The bad news is "you're all going to die—deal with it!" The good news is that we don't have to be afraid of death. Again integrating a variety of resources (the newspaper, a Bible commentary, a Christian classic and the Bible itself), Halcomb uses quotes to illustrate a practical way to understand the power of faith.

Faith in God is the antidote to fear. In Christ, death has lost its sting.

Halcomb encourages and models authentic, hope-filled grieving. But he doesn't fall prey to the temptation to exhort his congregation legalistically, "Clean up your act 'cause you're going to die—soon!" Instead he points to the biblical proclamation of consolation and hope through the power of God's love.

In my opinion, Halcomb almost slips into sentimentalism when he quotes Canon Holland as if eternity is only a room away. But he recovers by focusing our attention on faith. Because of our faith in the risen Christ we can have confidence even when we face the most difficult of life-threatening circumstances. We don't have to be depressed by death. We can celebrate life, both now and in eternity.

COMMENT

RESPONSE

Because our faith in Jesus gives us a capacity to face death without fear and embrace life with confidence, we can accept the reality and inevitability of death. But that is not enough. This sermon is also a call to good stewardship of life. Because of the unpredictability of life, we must have wisdom in the use of our time. Using both biblical and modern models, Halcomb calls us to some simple action steps.

Hezekiah was an example of wasting time instead of investing it in his son. The story of the JAL 747 airliner preparing for a crash is a compelling challenge to affirm our relationships and to plan the message we want to leave to those we love. Without becoming clinical or overly analytical, the people were given a universally needed and practical way to live out the death-defying perspective of eternal love.

Halcomb does a beautiful thing in his conclusion by expressing his love for his congregation. What a wonderful opportunity to share his love for his people in a memorable way. And what a call to experience true joy! I was moved reading his message—and I'm sure the people who heard him found their hearts warmed by his words of love.

As pastors, we can authentically call our congregations to meaningful expressions of love. For many people, the only time they communicate love is in the worship setting. Love for God, for family, and friends become natural messages that can help overcome people's hesitation to express the love they feel.

Theological truth and practical application come together in this sermon. This is really a sermon about life, if people take to heart the candor and the comfort with which the Bible speaks about death. Our death-denying faith gives us living hope if we choose to accept God's wonderful provision of a personal relationship. And contrary to our culture, death is not the end to be avoided at all costs because of the cost Jesus paid when he gave his life on the cross. We can better celebrate life because the sting of death has been taken away. What a privilege we have as preachers to be able to proclaim that good news!

SUGGESTIONS

- We can learn several things from the approach Halcomb takes in this sermon. First, we need to deal with our own denial of death. Sometimes our personal fear of death causes us to avoid the subject in our preaching. Or, we take a fearful approach that doesn't allow our congregations to hear the gospel of life. Take some time to reflect and to journal the way Halcomb encouraged his congregation to do. Write down some messages you want to communicate. Talk to some trusted colleagues about your own concerns. Anticipate the fact that it is not easy to bring up the topic of death without someone wondering if you are depressed or even suicidal.

- Don't wait for a funeral to preach about death. The subject is on people's minds. Address the issue in a biblical way. With all due respect, Kubler-Ross is not the final authority on death. Recognize that within the sound of your voice there are people who are considering taking their own lives because they have lost hope for this life. Others are grieving the loss of a loved one to death. Some may find the topic so fearful they will want to leave or not listen.

- We need to be sensitive in how we preach about death. One way to take the "sting" out of the topic is by personalizing your own struggle in dealing with death. I had the experience of repressing the grief over the loss of my younger sister to cancer when she was only thirteen. At the funeral I prided myself on my strength in not expressing any feeling. I know now that it was my way of avoiding my own mortality. Ten years later, that "stuffed" grief came out when I least expected or wanted it. I found myself weeping uncontrollably in a circle of esteemed clergy. They were too stunned to respond. No one said or did anything. I finally was able to leave—alone, humiliated and angry.

That night, when I told my wife what had happened, it happened again. She was not a trained counselor or therapist. But she did exactly what I needed. She took me in her lap and rocked me like a little boy. I wept again, but they were tears of a grief understood. Her loving response gave me a physical, human picture of what it will be like when God wipes away every tear, and there will be no more death.

We have the opportunity to help our congregations feel the arms of a loving God. We have a message that will help them overcome their fear of death and experience the abundance of life Jesus intends for all of us.

Gary W. Downing

MEANWHILE

GENESIS 37:1–4, 29–36

REV. DR. WILLIAM J. IRELAND, JR.
BRIARCLIFF BAPTIST CHURCH
ATLANTA, GEORGIA

REV. DR. WILLIAM J. IRELAND, JR.

MEANWHILE

GENESIS 37:1-4, 29-36, NRSV

M eanwhile the Midianites had sold him in Egypt...(Genesis 37:36). Joseph was a brat! His older brothers hated him—and with good reason. Joseph was his father Jacob's next to youngest son and his favorite. Jacob made no effort to hide his delight in Joseph. As a sign of Joseph's status, his father gave him an ornamental coat. It was a very special coat and not one of his brothers had anything to compare with it. Joseph was also a tattletale, ratting on his brothers whenever they did anything wrong. They couldn't get away with anything with him around.

What really made Joseph's brothers angry, though, were his dreams. Joseph, being younger and probably a good deal smaller, harbored dreams like every other little brother and sister in the world. If you have older brothers and sisters, you know how this works. You get tired of being picked on. You get tired of being little. You get tired of never being able to win a fight. So one day you spit it out: "You just wait! One of these days I'm going to get you! One day I'm going to be in charge, and boy will you be sorry!" You dream of the day when the tables will turn and you'll have the upper hand. Joseph had dreams like that. He dreamed that his brothers would one day bow down to him and that he would reign over them. He dreamed of the day when he would rule not only over his brothers but also over his entire family. Every time Joseph came around, he would tell his brothers these dreams. They didn't like it—not one bit.

The day came when the brothers couldn't stand it any longer. They'd had enough of their father's pet. They burned with resentment every time they looked at his coat. They were mad because Joseph squealed on them. And they just couldn't stomach his crazy dreams. They were tending the flocks quite a distance from home, and saw Joseph coming to report on them—all alone. Now they could do whatever they wanted to him. "Let's kill him," they said. "Enough of his stupid dreams!" When Joseph reached them, they grabbed him, stripped him naked and tore off the coat his father had given him. Then they thought better of killing him and decided just to throw him into an empty cistern. While they were eating lunch, they spied a caravan making its way to Egypt. They flagged the caravan down and made a deal. They sold their brother to the Midianites for twenty pieces of silver. They all agreed it was better that way. They would be rid of Joseph without being guilty of killing him.

The only problem they had then was figuring out what to tell their father. They decided to take Joseph's coat and dip it in goat's blood. They agreed they would tell their father they had found the coat and assumed that Joseph had been attacked and killed by a wild animal. When they came to Jacob, bloody coat and tall tale in hand, he believed them and immediately went prostrate with grief. He cried and cried. No one could comfort him. He was so torn up over Joseph's disappearance he vowed he would go to the grave mourning.

Except for their father's intense grief, the brothers' plan came off without a hitch, and they secretly congratulated themselves on how well everything had worked. Their brat brother was long gone. They were sure they would never hear from him again. Chances were, he wouldn't live long as a slave. They were delighted. No more father playing favorites. No more tattletale. And best of all, no more crazy dreams. Joseph was gone—end of story.

Not quite. Tacked on to the end of this chapter is a verse that insists that the story may not be as over as we think. "Meanwhile the Midianites had sold him in Egypt to Potiphar, one of Pharaoh's officials, the captain of the guard" (Gen. 37:36). Focus on that word *meanwhile*.[1]

What does the word suggest to you? For some, *meanwhile* means that life just goes on as normal. It brings to mind the line from some of those grade-B westerns: "Meanwhile, back at the ranch." No change. Nothing exciting. The word suggests the dog days of summer when you can recite each day's forecast from memory: hot, humid, with a chance of afternoon or evening thundershowers. *Meanwhile* means nothing is going on. It suggests to us the closed universe of the ordinary. What you see is what you get; nothing more, nothing less.

But here in Genesis the word *meanwhile* serves an entirely different purpose. It leaves the door cracked, echoing the time-worn cliché, "It ain't over till it's over." It suggests that there's more to come. Above all else, it reminds us that God's ways are hidden, that God's purposes are worked out in secret and unnoticed ways. Despite what we see, God is working. Despite what each day's events might suggest, God is fulfilling his purpose.[2]

That's what takes place with Joseph. Certainly, his brothers believe that he is long gone. Their brother and his dreams have been silenced. But this *meanwhile* hints otherwise. You know the rest of the story. In Egypt, despite numerous setbacks, Joseph ascends to a place of prominence and power. Eventually, he is reunited with his family and his dreams are fulfilled. His entire family bows before him. All of this takes place in unexpected ways. *Meanwhile* affirms the hidden hand of God in human affairs.

If we take that word *meanwhile* seriously, if we take seriously God's hidden agenda in this world, we will be able to respond creatively to any number of situations.

For instance, the times when nothing is going on, when we labor hard and have nothing to show for it. A long time passed between Joseph's dreams and their fulfillment during which it seemed as though his dreams had no chance of being fulfilled. But scattered throughout Joseph's story is the refrain, "The Lord was with him." In other words while it seemed nothing was going on, God was there, working. Time wasn't being wasted. The Southern preacher Carlyle Marney once said,

"Unless we learn to live in the meantime, we won't amount to much."[3] That's the biggest challenge we face, isn't it? Living in the meantime. Living in between events. Keeping on when the landscape is barren. We can manage the *meantime* if we hold fast to *meanwhile*. We need to hold on dearly to the fact that God is at work right alongside us. If we take this word seriously, we will be able to say that no matter what, "Something is going on." We can live and work believing that nothing is wasted. *Meanwhile* means that something is always going on.

Certainly this word applies to the detours we have to take from time to time. We know the geometry axiom that the shortest distance between two points is a straight line. Most of us would like to make our journeys in just that way. We would like to get what we want and where we want in the shortest time possible. But we also know from experience that we rarely make our trip in the express lane. We usually have to take a number of detours before our dreams are fulfilled. That's the way it was for Joseph. If you chart the path his life took toward the fulfillment of his dreams, you see that the line goes up and down. Yet, those detours in every instance made possible the next phase of his journey. May I remind you that God works in exactly the same way with us. The interruptions, the inconveniences, the intrusions into our lives may be occasions for God to do his best work with us. God most often uses the side roads rather than the expressways. We are often frustrated when our plans do not proceed as we think they ought, and we are forced to stop somewhere along the way instead of taking the direct route to our destination. We view such reroutings as delays, when in fact they may be our best opportunities. *Meanwhile* means that this side trip is not a wasted trip. The side road we've ventured down won't come to a dead end.

I also believe this word speaks to the evil we see and experience in our daily lives. *Meanwhile* insists that the evil perpetrated by others can be bent to serve God's good purposes. In the concluding chapter of Genesis, Joseph voices the way in which the hidden purposes of God work themselves out: "You meant evil against me; but God meant it for good" (Gen. 50:20, RSV). You sold me into slavery; meanwhile, God used that to bring about his purposes. There is no better expression of the power of God than this. Whatever is evil in the hands of others becomes good in the hands of God. The ultimate illustration of this truth is Jesus' death on the cross.

I certainly don't want to leave the impression that everything that happens is good or even desirable. But to say "meanwhile" is to say that God can use whatever life brings our way—good or bad—to accomplish his purpose.

I have an idea that many of you today imagine that your dreams are long dead. Your life has taken a sharp turn, and for the life of you, you can't figure out what's next. Some of you feel that the door has been shut for good over something that means a great deal to you. Perhaps you're in the doldrums, and nothing is happening. God is nowhere to be found. If so, I have a word for you: "Meanwhile...."

Notes

1. Most versions of Scripture preserve the temporal note in their translations of this verse. Thus, the NASB reads, "Meanwhile, the Midianites...." The REB renders the verse as "The Midianites, meanwhile...." The KJV does not preserve the temporal sense, "And the Midianites...."
2. For an insightful discussion of this aspect of the Joseph narrative, see Walter Brueggemann, Genesis, Interpretation (Atlanta: John Knox Press, 1982), pp. 293–96.
3. Charles Foster Johnson, in The Second Page newsletter (February 15, 1991), p. 4.

COMMENT

This sermon opens at a fast clip. The introduction immediately pulls the listener into the story. "Joseph was a brat! His older brothers hated him—and with good reason." You sense that this preacher understands where the older brothers were coming from. You even wonder if the preacher were himself an older brother with a younger sibling—a brat always interfering with his life.

As soon as Ireland finishes relating the first part of the story from the perspective of the older brothers, he makes a quick shift. He turns to Joseph's side of the story: the dreamer, the father's favorite, the one who is stripped, beaten, thrown into an empty cistern, and sold into slavery. The tattletale is gone. Now we can get back to the older brothers who can get on with their lives. But what about Joseph? Here the sermon gets down to business. "Meanwhile the Midianites had sold him in Egypt to Potiphar, one of Pharaoh's officials, the captain of the guard." What do we do with the *meanwhiles* in life? How do we deal with the journeys in life that we have neither anticipated nor desired?

I loved this sermon from the beginning. It drew me in, captured my imagination, and made me eager to move on to the *meanwhile*. Ireland draws his audience into the hearts of these very human characters, weaving a tapestry rich with insight. This sermon exemplifies preaching that effectively captures our attention and holds it to the end of the story.

A MOMENT OF BROKENNESS, A MOMENT OF NEED

Brought to the breaking point of intense frustration and anger, Joseph's brothers can stand it no more. In a fit of rage they strip Joseph, beat him, and sell him into slavery rather than kill him. Everywhere we turn, similar stories break our hearts. People in severe circumstances—their hopes and dreams lost—become overwhelmed. To be sure, they are in our churches. They need to hear a word from the Lord.

Meanwhile, Joseph's life was shattered. His heart was broken and his dreams were gone. Joseph's despair reflects the agony of our time. But Ireland sees something we too easily miss. Ireland sees good news in a dark and tragic moment. In Joseph's story, and in ours too, we find this word *meanwhile*. "Meanwhile," proclaims the preacher, "…leaves the door cracked, echoing the time-worn cliché, 'It ain't over till it's over.' It suggests there's more to come."

The first part of this sermon paints a picture, showing us the circumstances that led to Joseph's difficulty. Ireland portrays this familiar story from the older brothers' perspective.

The second part of the sermon shifts from the picture to a mirror, inviting us as listeners to search for the hidden meaning in our own lives in times of brokenness.

The third part of the sermon is a window, helping us to see that God is present in the *meanwhiles* of life. "You meant evil against me," said a wiser Joseph to his brothers many years later, "but God meant it for good" (Genesis 50:20, RSV).

TEXT & PROCLAMATION

"The Midianites meanwhile had sold Joseph in Egypt" (Gen. 37:36). Although the text is a short phrase in a long biblical narrative, these few words become powerful in this sermon. Ireland spends a few minutes bringing the listener into the story of Joseph's conflict with his brothers. Then he becomes a teacher and advocate for the word *meanwhile*. The preacher makes an important distinction between the use of the word in the Joseph story and the meaning of the word in much of our contemporary usage. Today's listener might hear the text and think that "meanwhile" indicates nothing of significance is happening. But here in Genesis, the word serves an entirely different purpose. Hidden within a very simple word lies the profound reality that God is at work, no matter how things appear on the surface.

Ireland's description of *meanwhile* provides a wonderful insight to help us understand that evil, even when perpetrated by others, can be redeemed by God to serve a higher purpose. He weaves into this sermon a reminder for us to remain open to God's transforming Spirit—even when our dreams are shattered.

The good news proclaimed here is an alternative to despair. When we encounter detours, when our plans are frustrated, when we experience brokenness and loss, God continues to work with us as God did with Joseph. "God can use whatever life brings our way, good or bad—to accomplish his purpose," says the preacher.

Biblical faith challenges us to trust in the goodness of God even during times of hardship. Encouraged by the promise of God's help, we are called to trust that God's goodness and grace will ultimately prevail.

A WORD ABOUT STYLE

Stories capture our imagination. They hold our attention. They provide us with maps for the journey of faith. Joseph's sojourn invites us to embrace the detours and side roads of life. When our plans and dreams are frustrated by unforeseen events, God is still there. Ireland's style punctuates the journey with signposts reminding the listener that:

> *Meanwhile* affirms the hidden hand of God.
> *Meanwhile* means something is always going on.
> *Meanwhile* means the side trips are not wasted trips.
> *Meanwhile* insists that the evil perpetrated by others can be
>   molded to serve God's purposes.

In short, *meanwhile* says that God can use whatever life brings our way—good or bad—to accomplish the divine purpose.

The tone of this sermon is one of authenticity and pastoral encouragement. It is spoken from the heart. Ireland invites us to place our trust in God's goodness rather than to give way to doubt and fear. He provides the listener with a creative alternative in managing hardship. The closing thought offers comfort and hope for all of us: "Perhaps you're in the doldrums, and nothing is happening. God is nowhere to be found. If so, I have a word for you: 'Meanwhile.'"

SUGGESTIONS

- Try taking a seemingly insignificant statement or word from the Scripture and mining it for gold. As Ireland demonstrates, creative and meaningful insights can come when we pay attention to detail.
- Consider developing a sermon by unfolding both sides of the story, using good judgment, and avoiding judgmentalism. Note the balance and insight in the introduction to this sermon. Ireland helps us to understand how the older brothers might have felt before he moves on to Joseph's story.
- Preach from the heart. Throughout this sermon, one has the sense that Ireland is preaching from experience. People long for authenticity in the pulpit.

Peter G. St. Don

RISKY BUSINESS

MATTHEW 25:14–30

REV. DR. PAUL S. WILSON
PROFESSOR OF HOMILETICS
EMMANUEL COLLEGE
TORONTO, ONTARIO, CANADA

RISKY BUSINESS

MATTHEW 25:14–30

When I was growing up in Edmonton, our fifth grade Sunday school teacher for a short while was a young man in his final year of high school. He frequently seemed tired, and when the sunlight struck his face it showed dark patches under his eyes. He took great pleasure in telling us the details of his Saturday night dates—and we took great pleasure in hearing them. He seemed to do this with greater ease and delight than he was able to muster in articulating the fundamentals of Christian faith! When he came to the parable of the talents, he seemed to have found his element.

"You see," he said, with a slight swagger in his voice, "everyone has a talent. Some people are good with dating and others aren't. I happen to have a talent for it. So that is what I am supposed to do. You have a talent for something else. And you are supposed to use it. Use it or lose it."

There were some weaknesses in the character of my Sunday school teacher that he had not yet found a way of addressing. Yet his overall interpretation of the parable was not bad: "Use it or lose it." The status quo is not an option. Yet today so many people feel they have lost whatever talent they had and they need some word of hope.

Jesus spoke of a master who is going away on a long journey and entrusts three servants with great sums of money. There are no textual variants on this. All the sources agree, the number of servants is three—not five, not two. In spite of that knowledge, even as I heard the story again just now, I caught a glimpse of a fourth servant in the parable. I am wondering if any of you also saw that servant.

We have all met the three servants. The first servant is given a whopping five million dollars by the departing master. Things come easily to her. She is a sure bet—voted by her graduating class at Servant School as "The Most Likely Servant to Succeed." The master needed no recently published study to prove that women are better administrators than men. She has a mind for numbers. She previously ran the master's affairs when he was away on business. Now, the departing master with his luggage and servant are a mere speck topping the distant ridge on his way to the Mediterranean port. Yet she has already decided to diversify her investment in real estate, livestock and olives. When the master returns after some years, she has doubled his money to ten million dollars. Her reward—she is given more responsibility and invited to share in the Master's joy.

The second servant we know as well. She did not have a head for numbers. But she was a gifted grape-grower and vintner. The master gave her two million dollars. Within a month she had purchased a neglected vineyard and was pruning vines. When the master returned and found his investment doubled to four million dollars, she was also given more responsibility and invited to share in the master's joy.

The third servant felt he had never excelled at anything in particular. Although he was a capable miller, and could have set up a mill, he was most conscious of what he was not. He was not the other servants. He had no head for numbers. He could not make excellent wine.

Did he mind that the master had given him only one million dollars when other servants had been given ten million and two million? "Gracious no!" he exclaimed. "I wish he hadn't given me any. Why didn't he leave me alone and let me do what I want with my life?"

After several months of worry that someone might steal the money, he ended up burying it by moonlight in a safe place. When the master returned, every cent of the original money was still there, and not one cent more. This unambitious servant had not even given it to bankers to earn some interest. He was condemned, was not invited to the banquet, and lost what rank he had.

Fortune magazine has just rated Toronto as the number one city in the world in which to live and do business—and they knew about our weather! Last year we ranked only eighth, but this year, when they considered lifestyle, education, safety, health care and cultural opportunities, we shot up to first place. Still, even in Toronto not everyone is successful by the world's standards. Most of us know what it means to feel like a loser, at least at points in our lives. With downsizing so prevalent, we may be walking down the street next to an unemployed executive, or a GM worker whose job will end in three year's time, or a nurse who has already lost her job, or a teenager who holds little hope of finding one.

Right now five hundred thousand refugees—mothers, fathers and children in Zaire—are again running for their lives, carrying what few possessions they own. Who can these people identify with in Jesus' parable? They are not wealthy. They don't have ten million, two or one million dollars. They have nothing. They are certainly not idle; they did not bury the gifts God gave them—they are the victims of sin and tragedy, poverty and hunger.

That is why, when Jesus speaks about three servants, I see four. I see the servant who lost everything and has nothing. This fourth was in charge of the departing master's bags and accompanied him down to his ship. When the master said farewell at dockside, he gave this personal servant the largest amount of money. He had journeyed with his master on trading trips and had learned how to bargain and barter. Before the sails of his master's departing ship dipped over the cloudless western horizon, he was already buying jade, spices and silk from caravans from the East. He chartered boats and shipped his goods to market in Rome. Then he returned to his master's estate. Some weeks later a messenger informed him that the boats with his cargo had sunk. All was lost. Thus, when the master returns, this servant holds back, waiting to confess his great loss. He hears how the master deals with the other servants, punishing the one who buried the money to keep it safe. When the others are gone, he approaches. Before he confesses anything, the master says, "I heard that your boats sank and you lost everything. It was a worthy venture. I am sorry for your loss. But you dared to risk. You dared to risk everything in my service. You did well. Well done, my servant. Tonight you will share my table of honor. I give you oversight of my entire estate."

I think this is close to what Jesus meant. His parable was not about making money. It was about taking chances, using what God gives us to accomplish more. Jesus is saying, "My followers, do not be content with what you did yesterday or last week, for each day God offers fresh duties with opportunities. In God's economy there is no downsizing. There is work to be done. There are souls to be won. There is work for everyone caring for one another and sharing what we have." The sums are fantastic in Jesus' parable because what God has given us is fantastic and beyond price: life, love, joy, meaning, value, purpose. Whatever you have been given—health, money or talents—God will use for great things.

Even our losses God can use. That is the importance of the fourth servant. God can work all things for good. God is not satisfied with the status quo. God is not satisfied with injustice or pain—yours or anyone else's.

A woman in a nursing home was lonely, feeling as though she had lost her health, her friends, her home. Then one day one of the nursing care workers told her about the troubles of her daughter who was unmarried and pregnant. "Will you pray for me and my daughter?" she asked as she left the woman's room. That was the beginning of God's using what little she felt she had left to give, her ability to pray. Her church then began to pass prayer concerns to her. "I was ready to give up," she said, "but God wasn't through with me."

Preachers are supposed to preach the text and not mess around with it. "Don't put in a fourth servant who risked and lost, if Jesus didn't put him in," you might be saying. It is a risky business to mess with the text. And yet the fourth servant *is* in the original. Jesus, the teller of the parable, is the fourth servant—the one who risked all and lost all. He is the one who invested everything in us and was crucified for it. God in Christ became the loser, for our gain. In losing, he did far more than can be done with all of the money in the world. In Christ, and with the power of the Holy Spirit, no one can call themselves a loser again. All who have risked for God have a place of honor at God's eternal table.

A day is coming when all people will use their gifts for God. On that day, guns on tanks will fall silent, and all will live in peace. Until that day, keep risking. God will use your life to accomplish great things, for with Christ we cannot lose but only win.

COMMENT

He got me! The preacher got me. There I was, reading along, rather surprised to find myself enjoying this sermon in light of my far-too-critical attitude. "Aha!" I exclaimed to myself, delighted to have discovered the telltale flaw in Paul Wilson's sermon. That flaw is this: He constructed his message around what a particular Scripture *does not* say rather than what it *does* say. This is one of my pet peeves. So I felt the surge of secret delight in knowing I had the handle on how to critique this sermon. I thought I had him. But then the sermon took an unexpected turn, and Wilson got the last laugh. Clever fellow, this one.

THE UNEXPECTED TURN

The art of preaching, like storytelling, is based on drawing in the listeners, affecting them with a truth, and then sending them away changed in some fashion. By this measure, I'd say Paul Wilson's sermon is successful. But he does it in an unorthodox way. The emphasis of the sermon centers more on what the Bible does not say than on what it does say.

The text Wilson has chosen is the parable of the talents in Matthew 25:14–30. To most churchgoers, this is a familiar story. Perhaps that is why Wilson's handling of it works so well. It's easy to snore our way through stories we've heard countless times before. The preacher doesn't allow us to do that here. He begins by paraphrasing the parable, taking some liberties to update the story for a twentieth-century crowd. Each of the three servants in Jesus' original version is described with economy and creativity. But then comes the *real* creativity! Wilson veers away from the parable long enough to set up a totally different context: a world inhabited by wealthy people in Toronto and suffering people in Zaire. The hook is baited. How is the preacher going to relate the servant people to a scenario pitting rich Westerners against African refugees?

Wilson's rather unorthodox solution to the problem is to add a fourth servant to Jesus' parable. How dare he! Isn't that going a bit too far with the Holy Scriptures? This is where I thought I'd found the sermon's shortcoming. Don't tell me what the Bible "might" or "should" or "could" have said; tell me what it *really* says. I wasn't sure where he was going with this fourth servant, but I didn't like the looks of it.

Then came the unexpected turn. It didn't come until the next-to-the-last paragraph of the message. "Preachers are supposed to preach the text and not mess around with it. 'Don't put in a fourth servant who risked and lost, if Jesus didn't put him in,' you might be saying." Shucks. He got me! Just when I thought I had the upper hand, Wilson turns the tables, as if he had known all along what I was thinking, which, of course, he had. Not only does he escape the hold I thought I'd had him in, but he snatches me up into a hold of his own.

"The fourth servant is in the original." Okay. I'm all ears. Where is he? "Jesus, the teller of the parable, is the fourth servant—the one who risked all and lost all. He is the one who invested everything in us and was crucified for it." Brilliant. Every criticism I had prepared was deflated by this one statement. Preacher one, commentator zero. Game, set, match.

STYLE & CONTENT

Any creative preacher takes the risk of having his or her personal flair overpower the content of God's word. There's nothing noble in sending away a congregation wowed by a dynamic gimmick or a flamboyant personality. It's like cotton candy; it tastes incredibly sweet for a brief moment but quickly dissipates, giving no nutritional substance. The church is full of "cotton candy preachers" who do little more than entertain, adding nothing of real worth to the faith-lives of the congregants. Wilson is not among these, and this message proves it. He exercised his own creative style in a way that compliments the biblical text and implants it in the mind of the listener. We come away moved more by the challenge of the parable than by the flash of the preacher.

Why is this? How is Wilson able to stay on the safe side of this thin line of creative license? First, his message is faithful to the original parable told by Jesus. Even though he tweaks the characters and puts a modern spin on the servant motif, he never violates the truth of the parable. Second, he looks beyond the obvious. Isn't this why Jesus occasionally became frustrated with his disciples—because they were unable to get beneath the obvious in his parables? Wilson does his interpretation adeptly enough to uncover the importance of the storyteller himself. Jesus is the fourth servant. There he is, right in front of us telling the parable, and we miss him. How many times I have read this story or preached on it, and I never saw it! Jesus is the ultimate servant-model. Third, Wilson moves with economic dexterity to bring us to the parable's call on our lives. Are we willing to risk? And, if so, *what* are we willing to risk? Whether we are thriving Toronto entrepreneurs or starving refugees in Zaire, there is a place on God's servant roster for us. And it is left to us to find that place and live up to it. In submitting to God, even the world's losers become winners for the kingdom.

One further stylistic technique is worth noting here. Wilson begins with the anecdote of an adolescent Sunday school teacher who believes he's God's gift to women. Although this amuses us, we may wonder what this has to do with the message to follow? I found this opening worthwhile because it grabbed me with some humor, but also because it illustrated the superficiality within all of us when it comes to understanding the profundity of the gospel. Based on the "Use it or lose it" approach to God's gifts, the anecdote leads us to wonder what we are to do when we feel we have no "it" to use? This becomes the segue into the body of the sermon. As Wilson says: "Today so many people feel they have lost whatever talent they had and they need some word of hope." Taking that as a cue, we should be able to find, later in the sermon, what the word of hope might be. Thankfully, it surfaces in Wilson's closing words. "In Christ, no one can call themselves a loser again. All who have risked for God have a place of honor at his eternal table. A day is coming when all people will use their gifts for God. On that day, guns on tanks will fall silent, and all will live in peace."

Without hope, the gospel can sound like warmed-over law. With hope, it empowers us to strive for higher ground and reach out in risk. "Keep risking," Wilson exhorts his congregation. "God will use your life to accomplish great things, for with Christ we cannot lose but only win."

SUGGESTIONS

- Follow Wilson's example regarding sermon length. This is a comparatively brief message. It would lose something if it had been padded to make it longer. Most of us who preach today are lousy editors, and our listeners pay for it. Even Jesus taught with *short* stories. More often than not, brevity works best for both the preacher and the audience.
- Although this sermon appears at first to be constructed as a supplement to Scripture, it is actually almost entirely biblical in its content. The parable of the talents is not only the glue that holds the narrative together, it is the actual narrative itself. Creative preachers are not so much "bound" by the Scriptures as they are ignited and inspired by them.
- A strength in Wilson's approach is that he has anticipated what critical listeners like me will be thinking during his message. This is being self-critical in the most constructive ways. We need to be constructively self-critical and anticipatory in the preparation of our messages. Prior to preaching them, we need to get in touch with how our sermons will be received by the audience. This requires of us the ability to stand outside the material and assess the message with an objective ear. Had Wilson not done this, his message would not have worked for me. As it is, it worked well.

Richard A. Davis

THE VISIT OF THE MAGI

MATTHEW 2:1–12

REV. DR. GARY A. FURR
VESTAVIA HILLS BAPTIST CHURCH
BIRMINGHAM, ALABAMA

REV. DR. GARY A. FURR

THE VISIT OF
THE MAGI

MATTHEW 2:1–12, NRSV

I

t's no wonder Luke's account is hands down the favorite story of Jesus' birth. It is full of singing angels and gentle shepherds and a bright night sky! We have a devil of a time (oops, unfortunate terminology!) reconciling the birth accounts in Matthew and Luke, for Luke seems to tell us of a blissful scene, a presentation at the temple and a return to Nazareth. Nothing about Herod, Egypt or these disturbing dreams.

But we try to blend the narratives anyway. I've watched a lot of Christmas pageants in my time. According to my digest version, the story of Jesus runs something like this:

In those days a decree went out from Caesar Augustus that all the world should be enrolled. And all went to be enrolled, each to their spot on the stage as previously marked. And Joseph also came in along with Mary, his betrothed, who was with pillow. And while they were there, the time came for her to be delivered. She gave birth to her firstborn son and wrapped him in swaddling cloths, and laid him in a plywood cradle, because there was no place for them behind the scenery.

In that region there were also a lot of little shepherds out in the field, wearing their towels and bathrobes pretty tight. And the church spotlight shone on them and they reacted [some late] with facial expressions of practiced fear.

Then came [in the more upscale pageants] Wise Persons [these are modern times, you know] dressed in the borrowed worthy potentate costumes from the Masons, bearing two jars and a box.

A voice quoted Scripture over the loudspeaker with the good news. The choir sang. And the people watching in the folding chairs all joined in and sang, "Joy to the World." And the program ended. Then they took all the borrowed animals home.

And in the church office, there was peace among all, for no one was bitten and the lights stayed on. And everyone returned to their homes, promising to call their neighbors and invite them to the second performance tomorrow night....

That's the generic church version. We take two narratives from Luke and Matthew and press them together sandwichlike, and out pops a pageant, full of sweetness and light. If it happened again, you and I would see it, wouldn't we? Look for the star on the rooftop. And if that doesn't tell you, just listen for cattle lowing and a baby awake but not crying.

Matthew's account is different from Luke's. Of course, the wise men didn't show up at the manger at the same time as the shepherds. And the manger was likely not the wooden structure cheerfully constructed by volunteer carpenters that we see in today's pageants. The manger was probably in a dank, dark cave, a hole in the rocks where animals stayed at night. Matthew also tells us that Joseph and Mary were staying in a house in Bethlehem—whose we do not know. The wise men came much later than the shepherds. Nor do we know how many there were. They were not really kings but astrologers, primitive scientists who studied dreams and natural phenomena.

According to the biblical scholar Raymond Brown, these Magi probably came in the year 6 B.C., which we now think was the actual year of Jesus' birth. In the sixth century A.D. a monk, Dionysius, erred in correlating Jesus' birth with the Roman calendar. The Magi were drawn by a natural phenomenon. Some have speculated that it was a supernova or a comet. But perhaps the most likely candidate was an unusual conjunction of the planets Jupiter, Saturn and Mars. The great astronomer Kepler saw such a conjunction in 1604 and calculated that it only happened every 805 years. Thus it would have happened—surprise, surprise!—in 7–6 B.C. This phenomenon even appears to be mentioned in ancient cuneiform texts.[1]

This rare event set these seekers seeking. Something was afoot in the universe. When all you have is primitive science to go on, you go for it. So the Magi set out. Since the great conjunction of these planets occurred in and around the constellation Pisces, which they associated with the Jews and with the last days, they headed for Palestine to look for the coming world ruler who would appear in the last days.

The appearance of the Magi caused a stir in Jerusalem, a downtrodden and depressed place under Roman rule. Taxes being high and hopes pretty low, people were on the lookout for entertainment. And here came three strangers in flashy clothes—religious mystics asking about a star and a king.

Now this got King Herod's attention. Let me say a few things about Herod. It is not fair to say that only Jesus was a king without a country. So was Herod. Herod the Great never felt secure about his power.

Herod's father, Antipater, was not a Jew but an Idumaean (Edomite) who had been forcibly converted to Judaism under the Hasmoneans, the priestly line that ruled Judea in the second and first centuries B.C. Herod was the second son who rose to power by siding with Octavian, later Augustus Caesar, after Julius Caesar's murder and the subsequent struggle for power.

Herod's shrewdness saw him rewarded by the Romans. He was named king of the Jews by the Roman state. But he was a man without a country, because the Jews ultimately refused to recognize him as king.

They themselves considered him illegitimate. His ruthlessness made him no friends among his people. Despite his building program which produced the magnificent rebuilding of the temple, (a rather Baptistlike way to divert their attention from the moral and spiritual rot within), the people despised Herod. This was the most glorious version of the temple ever built, yet it could not overcome the Jews' antipathy for Herod or the king's inner decay.

In order to legitimate himself, Herod married a woman named Mariamne, who came from the old royal family of the Hasmoneans. When his remaining rival from his wife's family, his brother-in-law Aristobulus, was forcibly drowned in his own bathtub, it was commonly known that Herod had hired the killers. Yet Herod attended the funeral and feigned grief over Aristobulus' death.

Herod's fear, obsession and jealousy became so great that he murdered his favorite wife Mariamne, her mother and grandfather, and three of his own sons. Antipater, his firstborn son by another wife, was put to death just before Herod's own death. A second wife joined the hall of suspicious deaths at his hands. This inspired the Emperor Augustus to say that it was safer to be Herod's pig than to be Herod's son!

The historian Josephus tells us that Herod had no fewer than ten wives, and at least fifteen children, and his family life was a constant disaster of plots and backstabbing. When he was about to die, he ordered that the leading Jews of Jericho, where he was living, should be imprisoned, and decreed that when he died they were to be slaughtered, so there would be grief at his death. Fortunately, they were set free. Herod did all this as he feigned allegiance to the Jewish faith.

This, then, was the man Herod who "secretly called for the wise men and learned from them the exact time when the star had appeared" (Matt. 2:7). This was the ruthless, paranoid king who feigned devotion: "Go and search diligently for the child; and when you have found him, bring me word so that I may also go and pay him homage" (v. 8). Knowing all this about Herod, we can imagine that when the wise men finally arrived at the house where the baby Jesus was, there was some agitated conversation. E. Frank Tupper, in his marvelous book, *A Scandalous Providence,* suggests that Joseph and Mary reacted something like the following:

"You stopped where? You asked who? You promised what?"[2]

It is not the baby Jesus who is the pretender to the throne; it is Herod and every Herod the world has known. Herods seek to exterminate the king who said to turn the other cheek. Herods believe that if they kill enough babies, terrify enough old people, intimidate and control people, the kingdom will be theirs.

But these tyrants are like a small man trying to clamp down the lid of a boiling pot—the tighter the lid is pressed closed, the greater the force underneath. The power of the King of kings cannot be suppressed. Herod was maniacal in his fears, and now as an old man near his death, every threat was cosmic. So he put all the little innocent baby boys in Bethlehem to the sword.

This was the real world into which the wise men came. So if *we* want to look at the true face of Christmas, let us find the most desperate dumps where poor men forage for food, or let us go to Central American tyrannies where poor campesinos are killed for asking questions about their leaders. The tyrants of the world are not just fighting their enemies, they are always arrayed against God and his kingdom.

Today many of us sit around our television sets at news time and shake our heads about the dark, sad condition of the world. We get up and adjust our thermostats and get well-preserved food of our choice out of our refrigerators, heat it in our microwaves and lament the decline of civilization.

I want you to consider this: Three astrologers came from Persia without knowing anything about the person they were dealing with in Herod. The salvation of the world lay innocently in the arms of his mother, with nothing to protect him from the power of the state. His fate depended on these strangers and what they were to make of a dream that likely awakened one of them in the middle of the night with an uneasy feeling. "And having been warned in a dream not to return to Herod, they left for their own country by another road" (v. 12). "Having been warned in a dream" is all Matthew says, but it was a critical moment in the story—a critical moment in human history—just a dream in the middle of the night.

The fate of the whole world turned exactly upon that tenuous moment—a stranger with a dream who listened to his instinct. Had the wise men trudged that five or ten short miles to Jerusalem and told Herod about Jesus, it would have been a short story indeed—another dead child, another pretender to the throne eradicated.

What kind of God is this who would risk everything in such a vulnerable enterprise as a human infant? And please, none of that superbaby stuff! The light of the world lay there helpless—for the taking.

The world has certainly seen tough times. Yes, I know, children are still dying in the streets, dying from a lack of concern, dying from those who would make money off their drug habits or their broken families, dying from neglect, from rejection, from nearly everything. And in many places, still at the hands of Herods. But it's been that way before. And everything was changed by one dream. Powerful thing, a dream—it can shake us awake and get our attention. Watch out! Listen up!

So the wise men listened. They came, with outlandish methods and partial knowledge, but they were right and Herod the king was wrong. It is not the person with all the power who finally finds Jesus. It is those who, however imperfectly, seek God with their whole heart who find Jesus. Herod sought and slaughtered and turned Bethlehem into mayhem. But his little rival escaped his grasp. It always looks as though evil will win the day. Evil has all the cards. Goodness looks so tiny and so outmanned. But evil never has the last word.

In the still of the night, in a seeking heart, in a gentle prayer, in the anxious cry of faith to a listening God, there is a power which will never be overcome. One simple dream is enough to foil an evil tyrant and save the day.

And one young teacher on a cross turned the tide of history more than any cruel tyrant with his bloodbaths—more than all the economic powers and their treasure chests. That little babe in a fleeing mother's arms would prevail.

So the wise men returned, a little wiser. They had walked into the living room of evil and sat down to deal with the devil. And in the end, when the decision had to be made and the fate of the world hung in the balance, they listened, ever so surely, to the voice within, and they knew the truth.

There are so many voices, clamoring, demanding, threatening us all. But there is a wisdom in each of our hearts. Wisdom enough to listen to the vulnerable truth that will not be put away or diminished. Wisdom enough to see evil and walk away. Wisdom enough to push us to be the one who finally breaks the cycle of brokenness in our family tree. Wisdom enough to find the One whom we have always, in our deepest and truest hearts, been seeking with all our might.

Notes

1. See the discussion in Raymond E. Brown, *The Birth of the Messiah* (Garden City, NY: Doubleday & Company, Inc., 1977), pp. 166–77.
2. E. Frank Tupper, *A Scandalous Providence: The Jesus Story of the Compassion of God* (Macon, GA: Mercer University Press, 1995), p. 99.

COMMENT

"Lead with humor, end with heart," says Ray Johnston, a specialist in youth ministries. Johnston contends that a speaker has to grab the attention of a teen audience in the first half-minute. Then, for a talk to be of lasting effect, the conclusion must give the listener a heart-felt illustration or a poignant insight which will leave the listener reflective and thoughtful.[1] If Johnston is correct, this sermon by Gary Furr will appeal both to teenagers brought up in the TV/video/computer age and to older adults alike.

From the outset, Furr's conversation style and humor engage the listener and set a casual and intimate tone. The humor in a "slip of the tongue" in the first paragraph is a sign that the sermon will poke fun at an enjoyable and familiar event. The Christmas pageant whose Mary is "with pillow" and who lays the firstborn Son in a "plywood cradle" is playful banter about a scene to which we can all relate. But this sweet stage production contrasts with a vivid presentation of the danger surrounding the first nativity. Furr's humor-filled sermon drives home its point by giving the listener the hard facts of the oppressive political context into which Jesus was born. Jesus' miraculous survival becomes clear as the preacher leads us into an exegetical exploration of the historical context of Jesus' birth.

This sermon gives the listener a new appreciation for the faithful following of an intuitive response on the part of the Magi who came to find the divine child at his birth. Furr presents to the listener the wonder that God's purposes prevailed because the wise men attended to their dreams. Furr's conclusion is a time for reflection which affirms that each listener has "wisdom enough" to know truth, "wisdom enough" to be significant in history, "wisdom enough" to make a difference.

PROBLEM

Furr begins by pointing out the problem of the church's idealization of the first Christmas and our "sanitizing" of the nativity with sweet productions and images which avoid the real vulnerability and powerlessness of Jesus at his birth. A scholarly investigation of historical reality points to the risks involved for the baby Jesus even surviving his first year on earth. Furr provides historical information about Herod to allow the listeners to draw their own conclusions about Herod's ruthlessness. We are shown Herod's vindictive reactions to any power that might threaten his own. We come to understand more clearly the oppressive Roman forces dominating Jews in Palestine. Furr places before us the wonder of the child's survival and leads us to a new appreciation that Jesus was not destroyed as an infant and the whole Christian faith aborted before it even began. The sermon challenges our naïve, romanticized notions about the first Christmas.

The more significant problem Furr confronts, however, is our common inability to believe that God can do anything significant through us. The wise men, astrologers who were quite imperfect, provide models for us who are also imperfect, blundering human beings. Furr calls the Magi "primitive scientists" and "religious mystics" whose intuition to follow a warning in a dream was destined to preserve the vulnerable and fragile Christ child. Their seemingly unimportant action in failing to report back to Herod because of a dream—only a line in the biblical narrative—changed the course of history and was part of fulfilling God's plan for salvation for humankind.

Furr suggests that those of us who attend to that same inner voice may positively and significantly affect others in ways we cannot know or predict. In this way God's purposes are carried out in the world around us. It is always so. God's ends require our attentiveness and response to the ways in which God reaches us—whether it be through small inklings about events, intuition about a person's character, or through dreams that ring of truth. The problem is our inattentiveness to the ways God speaks and our failure to believe we can do anything significant for good. This sermon asks us to reflect on how God can use us to accomplish divine purposes—if we are listening to God.

TEXT

Furr's treatment of the visit of the Magi is both scholarly and refreshing. His clever use of transitions within the sermon leads naturally from the pageant to the star and wise men. Descriptions of the wise men who come to Herod lead to a natural exploration of Herod's character. After examining the tyrant, we imagine Mary's and Joseph's reaction to the wise men who had told Herod of the newborn Messiah. The sermon flows out of the biblical text by exploring the lives of the people who surrounded Jesus at his birth in order to find a word for us today.

The sermon never loses its ultimate focus on the wonder of Jesus' survival in the situation into which the Magi walked and from which they safely slipped away. The description of the strangers "in the flashy clothes, religious mystics," helps us to see the Magi through the eyes of a ruthless king. This leads us to consider who Herod really was. Herod starkly contrasts with the peaceable Son of God who was being born to a poor and powerless couple. The homiletical imagination allows us to imagine Joseph's and Mary's reaction to the wise men's disclosure. The sermon reveals their sense of fear and heightens our own: "You stopped where? You asked who? You promised what?" The players in the pageant are center stage, and the contrast between the church's generic version of the nativity and the more authentic historical version comes into focus.

Furr plants vivid images in the description of Herod. He quotes the Emperor Augustus who said "it was safer to be Herod's pig than to be Herod's son!" Lively metaphors enhance our understanding throughout the sermon. Tyrants are "like a small man trying to clamp down the lid of a boiling pot." The wise men were strangers who "had walked into the living room of evil and sat down to deal with the devil." Such metaphors engage our visual imagination and bring the narrative to life.

Furr has done the exegetical work of digging through the historical and sociological records to illumine the text so that we see it from new perspectives. Our sense of outrage at political oppression deepens as our wonder increases that the vulnerable Son of God was preserved by the

Magi. Our old assumptions are replaced with a deepened sense of awe and renewed affirmation that God's purposes will prevail, despite the incredible odds against them.

PROCLAMATION

Princeton Seminary preaching professor Thomas Long notes that, while attending to the text, the preacher must be asking questions creatively, imaginatively: "What about those people in the congregation who are hanging onto their church life by a thread, people who approach worship and the Christian faith warily, wondering if there is anything here for them?"[2] Furr attends to this segment of the congregation, aware that most of us have doubts about our own significance. "The Visit of the Magi" reaffirms faith in God's power to use all people for good, ushering the kingdom into the world through response borne from our intuition and inner wisdom. This sermon proclaims that "those disturbing dreams" of the Magi, recorded only in Matthew, are indeed significant for a deeper understanding of how God works within people.

Furr effectively ties the first-century situation to today's leaders who continue to wield power unjustly in areas throughout the world. The preacher reminds us of places where today the power of darkness and evil dominate innocent and vulnerable people. The sermon enters our living room as Furr gives a more personal critique of our position of abundance and complacency: we turn up thermostats, eat food from refrigerators and watch on television the news of violence from safe places of comfort. The sermon softly chides us for our lack of involvement, our apathy, our insulation from the harsh realities and our failure to do anything to change things.

The proclamation that God has worked through the Magi who simply followed a star to find the gift at the end, who believed in the warning of their dream and obeyed it, provides evidence that God can work through the least of us. Even in the worst of situations, when we doubt our own ability to effect change, we hear the message that we are used of

God as we are faithful to the Spirit planted by God within us. The sermon names the theological dimensions of the biblical experience of the Magi who followed their dream's warning and so conveys an immediate experience of the affirmation that we matter to God. The preacher announces, "Today this Scripture has been fulfilled in your hearing."

RESPONSE

Furr concludes the sermon with a thoughtful phrase repeated five times. God gives each one of us "wisdom enough" for being significant agents of God's purposes. By acting on that wisdom we can change the status quo in small ways, do good when we could do evil, or break out of destructive patterns in which we formerly were powerless. We are called to believe that we matter to God.

Furr has effectively described the parallels of the social and political situation of first-century Palestine to our own. "Taxes being high and hopes pretty low, the people were on the lookout for entertainment." Today there is a massive fascination with video lottery and casino gambling and we tend to become couch potatoes waiting to be entertained. People seem to be comfortable sitting back and taking little initiative to work or selflessly give of themselves to one another. The Magi came into just such a social scene with their own blundering actions and a seemingly naïve consultation with Herod. Yet they are models of people God used. Like the Magi, we are challenged to reevaluate our personal lifestyles, to dare to be different from the society around us, for God's purposes.

"The Visit of the Magi" continually engages the listener, challenges our thinking, and calls us to act faithfully upon those almost imperceptible whispers of truth within us, trusting that God can work through the least of us to bring about great good. We are encouraged to believe that we have "wisdom enough" to make a difference—no matter how insignificant and imperfect we may feel. The good news is that God is at work among us and within us. We need only listen and respond.

SUGGESTIONS

- Some churches often dramatize a biblical story for a congregation prior to the sermon. While it may be interesting to reenact a biblical story, a contemporary drama about the sermon's application to us today may be more relevant. For instance, a drama dealing with apathy and disbelief that we can do anything significant to prevent evil just outside our house, could dramatize Furr's point that we can attend to the inner voice to change things.

- Consider the use of humor near the beginning of a sermon, especially to draw in younger listeners. Furr's description of a Christmas pageant and his continual comic relief and lightness come through descriptive images, such as the wise men appearing "flashy" in dress. When dealing with very serious issues, such as oppression and evil, use colorful visual images and metaphors to provide both fuller understanding and some relief and contrast to the weighty matters. And end with heart, something for a person to ponder.

Dixie Brachlow

Notes

1. Ray Johnston (Pastor of Lakehills Community Church in Folsom, California, and Youth Conference Speaker), quoted in North American Baptist Seminary course, "Developing Student Leaders," January 24, 1997.
2. Thomas G. Long, *The Witness of Preaching* (Louisville, KY: Westminster/John Knox Press, 1989), p. 67.

WHAT ARE YOU DOING HERE?

1 KINGS 19:1–18

DR. GARY W. KLINGSPORN
COLONIAL CHURCH
EDINA, MINNESOTA

DR. GARY W. KLINGSPORN

WHAT ARE YOU DOING HERE?

1 KINGS 19:1–18, NRSV

I n the Klingsporn household, this summer will be remembered as the summer we "did the Dells."

If you haven't been to the Wisconsin Dells, or haven't been there in a while, let me tell you—it's an experience! T-shirt, souvenir, and fudge shops everywhere! Water slides, putt-putt golf, go-karts, and roller coasters one after another as far as the eye can see! For two days I went around asking, "So where's the river? Where are the dells?"

It's Las Vegas for kids. But don't take your Visa. Take cash! Twenty-dollar bills at a time. You can do the Kowabunga water slide at Noah's Ark Water Park and ride one of the many ducks! Tommy Bartlett's Thrill Show is still there after all these years. We did it all. Our girls had a great time, and it was fun—until the last night when we got to the bungee jump!

Our friend Mike, a fine father of two girls our girls' age, was ready to do it without a moment's hesitation. He scrambled up those stairs with disgusting eagerness, while I sat far below—watching. He jumped and lived to tell about it.

It was just as he quit senselessly boinging up and down that it happened. Our nine-year-old daughter, Katy, came running to me, screaming with excitement, "Daddy, Daddy, will you try it?" (Can you see your teaching minister bouncing up and down headfirst like a wet noodle on a forty-foot rope?)

No way! I don't mind heights, and I don't mind speed, but never the two together!

"Daddy, will you try it?"

I spoke with more truth than I knew when I said to Katy, "No, honey. It's not for me. That's not who I am!"

But in all seriousness, I need to tell you that in that moment, my spirit sank deep into the darkness of the abyss. As I looked into the bright, eager eyes of my daughter and said "No," part of me wanted to crawl into a hole and die. In that moment, without knowing it, she tapped into every fear, failure, and insecurity I have. Kids have a way of nailing you, don't they?

Walking back to the hotel that night I was one quiet guy. I was down in the darkness all alone with "Failed Dad" written all over me! Oh, it wasn't really the bungee jump. It was a lot of issues that go back into my childhood—issues that I suspect most of us wrestle with all our lives. My heart wanted to say, "I give up. I resign fatherhood and humanhood. I just want to go away and be alone and read."

Then out of the darkness a voice came to me: "What are you doing here?" Yeah, I thought, what am I doing here in glitz city? I need to get back to my books—to my safe, familiar world of study and writing.

"No," the voice said. "What are you doing *here*—feeling sorry for yourself, in the pit of self-pity, nursing your fragile spirit, blaming the world?"

What are you doing here? Roberta Bondi has heard that voice. She's a professor of church history at Emory University's Candler School of Theology in Atlanta. An Oxford-trained church historian and theologian, she's heard the question, too. It happened to her on a Friday afternoon before Easter, while she was cleaning her house, getting ready for a wedding anniversary and an Easter celebration.

Well into her career, in her late forties, and worried about her kids, on that afternoon the heaviness of her life weighed in upon her, and she sank down into the darkness. In her book *Memories of God*, she writes: "As I struggled with the vacuum cleaner and thought of my inability to keep either of my children safe and happy, I found myself pressed down by the weight not only of my failure as a mother, but of all my failures, of my inability not only to have been the mother I had wanted to be, but the wife, daughter, friend, niece, historian, and teacher I had intended to be as well. The memory of all my unmet obligations, all the people I had hurt, all the suffering I had done, my dirty refrigerator, my unfinished research, my unanswered correspondence [weighed in upon me]."[1]

She dragged herself into her study, sat down across from her desk in the tall red chair in which she always voiced her prayers, and she cried out to God: "I have failed in everything you have given me to do. I have tried so hard to be a good mother. With my whole heart I have wanted to love my children enough to keep them safe and happy.... But the harder I try the more I worry. There must be something...I am missing, something I can't see. I give up. If there is something you want me to know, you must find me yourself to tell me. I can try no longer, and I can look no longer. I give up. I absolutely give up."

There in her familiar chair on that green April afternoon, the light of her life went out. Her head fell to her chest, and her breathing slowed. All the unmet and conflicting expectations, the good intentions, and the desires to please she had ever had caught up with her. "I didn't care [anymore].... Emptied, at last, of everything, I finally felt nothing. I simply sank like a dead body into darkness."[2]

In time, out of the darkness, that same voice came to Roberta Bondi: "What are you doing *here?*" For the voice always comes.

My wife, Debra, has heard it, too. Ten years ago, Debra suddenly lost her dad during heart-bypass surgery. Within three days the family went from the initial diagnosis of a problem to his death. Three months pregnant with our daughter Katy at the time, Debra struggled with the reality that her dad would never see or know our kids. It seemed so unfair that our kids would never know this man of so much warmth, humor, and goodness. A few days after her dad's death, Debra wrote in her journal:

"I'm struggling, discouraged, doubting. Tired of feeling like I'm losing the struggle. I can't muster my usual optimism or proactive problem solving anymore. Yesterday I just gave up, came home from work, and buried my head in my pillow. But Lord, I can't run away every day. And I don't know what to pray or where to turn. Lord, I feel like a stranger with you. Open your arms and bring me in close to your heart. Let me know you again."

Eventually, out of the darkness, the voice came to Debra, too.

I suspect we've all been there. Or we will be there. Or we know someone who is there right now. It doesn't take a silly bungee jump or a struggle with depression or the loss of a parent or spouse. It can happen to us anytime, anywhere, in the day-to-day struggle of too much to do and not enough time, or the sheer weight and stress of our jobs, our health, our families, or just living in a dark and violent world.

Your job is stressing you out. The finances aren't working. A child goes off to college. A marriage breaks up. You lose your job: they come in at 10:00 and you're gone by 11:00. You have to move and leave your closest friends behind. The doctor calls you with bad news. You worry about your kids or grandkids. Yet another friend learns she has cancer. Someone hurts you. The church isn't the perfect group of loving human beings you had hoped it was.

We've all been there or will be there or know someone who is there right now. Most of us know what it is to feel like a "Failed Dad" or "Failed Mom," to sit in a chair or bury our face in a pillow and want to give up.

But out of the darkness, the voice comes, as it came to that crusty old prophet Elijah centuries ago: *"What are you doing here?"* For the voice always comes out of the darkness if we're willing to hear.

Whether we're sitting under a bungee jump, sinking into a tall red chair, burying our face in a pillow, or, like Elijah, hiding in a cave—the voice always comes.

Elijah was on the run. He was afraid, confused, burned out, exhausted. He ended up hiding in a cave in the dark, all alone, full of self-pity, blaming the world. "I give up," he said. "You can take this job and shove it, Lord. I give up."

What's remarkable is that just before this, Elijah had won a great victory in a confrontation with the prophets of Baal on Mount Carmel. With macho bravado, Elijah had taunted the prophets of Baal to prove that their god was real. They ranted and raved, trying to incite Baal to act. But nothing happened. So Elijah mocked their god, saying, "Maybe he has wandered away, or he is on a journey, or perhaps he is asleep and must be awakened" (1 Kings 18:27). But nothing happened, because Elijah knew that Baal was no god.

Then Elijah built an altar and prepared a sacrifice, put water all over it and all around it, and gathered the people of Israel together and prayed: "O Lord, God of Abraham, Isaac and Israel, let it be known this day that you are God in Israel, that I am your servant, and that I have done all these things at your bidding. Answer me, O Lord, so that this people may know that you, O Lord, are God" (18:36–37). And immediately the fire fell and consumed everything. And when all the people saw it, they fell on their faces and shouted, "Yahweh, Yahweh indeed is God!" (18:39).

On that day in the ninth century B.C. in the Northern Kingdom of Israel there was a great victory against idolatry. The 450 prophets of Baal were overcome. Elijah had won the day, and he raced down Mount Carmel with his Olympic gold medal in his hand.

But when evil Queen Jezebel heard what had happened, she said, "I want your life, Elijah, and I'm going to have it within twenty-four hours!"

So he was afraid. He ran for his life. He fled south to Beersheba in southernmost Judah. Leaving his servant behind, he went on farther alone—a day's journey into the wilderness of the Negeb.

After running long and hard, he finally sat down under a solitary broom tree in the middle of nowhere and prayed that he might die. He was a stressed-out, burned-out prophet. "I've had enough. I'm done. I'm outta here," he said. "It's enough; now, O Lord, take away my life" (19:4).

Elijah, who had been so strong, was now weak in resignation, cowering before Jezebel, fleeing into the desert, wanting to abandon life itself. One day the victory of the gold. The next day all was lost. There is no logic to the darkness of our lives.

Elijah fell asleep under the broom tree. But then twice, an angel, a divine messenger, touched him, awakened him, and said, "Get up and eat; you'll need this food for the journey." So he ate hotcakes and drank water. Then he began a long journey southwest into the wilderness, all the way to Horeb, or Mount Sinai—"the mount of God." There, at the end of his long journey, Elijah hid in a cave, in the dark, alone.

It was then that the voice came, as it often does, out of the darkness, if we're willing to listen at all. In the cave, at the lowest point in Elijah's life—the text comes to the heart of it—"Then the word of the Lord came to him saying, 'What are you doing here, Elijah?'" (v. 9).

Most of us in this room know something about that cave and what it is to sink into the darkness. Some of us have brought our darkness with us this morning. And we know what it is to say, as Roberta Bondi did: "I give up. I can't see it, God. If there's something you want me to know, you must find me yourself to tell me."

And that's exactly what happened in the story of Elijah. God found Elijah and asked him a question.

Elijah's answer was filled with self-centered pity and blame. He dumped on God: "I have been very zealous for the Lord, the God of hosts; for the Israelites have forsaken your covenant, thrown down your altars, and killed your prophets with the sword. I alone am left, and they are seeking my life, to take it away" (v. 10). So there, God, I'm done, I'm outta here! I want to die!

The tension at the heart of this story is whether Elijah would be allowed to give up and die, as he wished, or whether he would continue as God's person.

Isn't that the issue at the heart of all our lives, as people of faith? When we sit under the bungee jump or in the red chair or when we bury our face in the pillow, will we be allowed to give up, or will we go on as God's people in the face of difficult challenges or overwhelming odds?

Sure enough. God comes—with that persistent question: What are you doing *here?* Not a distant or aloof voice saying, What are you doing "down there"? Instead, the voice is nearby: What are you doing "here"?

The adverb "here" (v. 9) is important. It's as if God slips up beside Elijah and whispers in his ear: "What are you doing *here* so far from home, from the place to which I called you and sent you, far from Palestine, the Northern Kingdom, from the people of God, from your calling, and yes, from Ahab and Jezebel?

"Elijah, get out of your cave! Go stand on the mountain." Then there came a great wind, then an earthquake, and then a fire. But the Lord was not in the wind or the earthquake or the fire. And when the pyrotechnics were over, Elijah was still hiding. Finally there was "a sound of sheer silence. When Elijah heard it, he wrapped his face in his mantle and went out and stood at the entrance of the cave" (vv. 11–13).

Then out of the darkness the voice came a second time with the same question: "What are you doing here, Elijah?" (v. 13b).

Elijah's answer was the same as before—more self-pity (v. 14).

"Then the Lord said to him, 'Go, return...anoint Hazael...anoint Jehu...anoint Elisha.'" And oh, by the way, "I will leave seven thousand [faithful] in Israel" (vv. 15–18). So Elijah set out from there and found Elisha (v. 19).

Now what are we to make of all this? What's the point?

The good news I bring you this morning is that Elijah is never alone after all. What began for Elijah as a desperate flight for his life turned into a spiritual journey—a pilgrimage. He ran. But we soon come to understand that God was caring for him and directing his journey. God provided the angel and the food. God led Elijah on the journey to Sinai—the mountain of God where Moses once received his prophetic call. Elijah was never alone in this story. Nor are we.

There's that voice that comes in the darkest moments if we're willing to hear it. "What are you doing here?" With that persistent question, God refused to accept Elijah's resignation. Instead, God took Elijah's fear, exhaustion, and self-pity and turned it into a pilgrimage with a purpose. God gave Elijah a new call and set him on his way again with a new journey and a new task and renewed strength to carry on.

God would not let go of Elijah. The good news of this text is that in those moments when we sit where Elijah sat, God will not let us go. Rather, God comes out of the darkness with the question, "What are you doing here?" That question judges us in our self-centered sin and brokenness. But it's also always finally a question of grace. It's an expression of the deep and abiding love of God that refuses to let us go—if we're at all willing to listen.

Hymn writer George Matheson knew about that:

O Love, that wilt not let me go,
    I rest my weary soul in Thee,
I give Thee back the life I owe,
That in Thine ocean depths its flow
    May richer, fuller be.

O Light, that followest all my way,
    I yield my flickering torch to Thee;
My heart restores its borrowed ray,
That in Thy sunshine's blaze its day
    May brighter, fairer be.

This story of Elijah is a church text. The church in the late twentieth century, in the post-Constantinian era, finds itself no longer dominant in the culture. As Christians, we are increasingly a minority in a largely secular, pluralistic world. For decades now, the tendency among many in the church has been to lament our woes. "Where have all the people gone?" Sometimes we blame each other and create further divisions. Sometimes we create new initiatives to purify the church and take back control of the culture. Sometimes we seek to make the church more user-friendly in the hope that we can somehow reestablish the triumph of Christendom.

It's easy to forget in these times that at the center of the Christian faith stands the cross, the way of suffering and darkness. To be a disciple community following our Lord is to follow the way of the cross, to embrace the darkness, and to be a faithful people whom God shapes and molds to *God's* task and calling—not our own. God is always asking the church, "What are you doing here?" and then saying, "Go, and I will go with you."

You see, the crisis in Elijah's life had become the occasion for a new call, a recommissioning that gave Elijah back his life.

So the question, "What are you doing here?" is not just "What are you doing here this morning in this pew?" but "What is the core of your being all about? To what does God call you?"

Why are we here as the people of God? Where does God call us?

In the midst of our pain, darkness, and questioning, God comes and offers a new experience of his grace and presence. We hear a new call— if we're listening!

As Roberta Bondi did. We left her sitting in a red chair on an April afternoon, empty, giving up.

"How long I sat there in that state, I have no idea. Perhaps it was a long time that passed; perhaps it was simply a moment. I only know that, all of a sudden and without warning, I woke up. I heard my own voice repeating in my mind the words from the Roman Catholic eucharistic prayers for Easter, 'The joy of the Resurrection renews the whole world.' Every cell of my body heard them and for the first time I knew that the words were absolutely true, and that they were true for me. 'The joy of the Resurrection renews the whole world.'"[3]

The good news from this story of Elijah is that we are never alone after all. God is there. The presence of One who is bigger than the dark.

So you and I can trust in the dark. We can listen through it. Because finally, when we least expect it, the voice will come out of the sheer sound of silence, and it will say: "What are you doing here? Go, and I will go with you."

This is the same promise of God of which Isaiah spoke:

Do not fear, for I have redeemed you;
I have called you by name; you are mine.

When you pass through the waters, I will be with you;
   and through the rivers, they shall not overwhelm you;
When you walk through the fire you shall not be burned,
   and the flame shall not consume you.
For I am the Lord your God,
   the Holy One of Israel, your Savior (Isa. 43:1–3, NRSV).

This is a love that will not let us go, that refuses to give up on us. We call it grace. God's grace sets us on new journeys with new tasks and with the promise of divine strength along the way.

So, what are we doing here—wherever we are this morning? Are we listening? The voice will surely come. It always does. And it will say, "Now go, and I will go with you."

Lord, help us to listen and to hear your grace. Amen.

Notes

1. Roberta Bondi, *Memories of God: Theological Reflections on a Life* (Nashville: Abingdon Press), p. 168.
2. Ibid., p. 169.
3. Ibid., pp. 169–70.

COMMENT

I was there the Sunday this sermon was preached. I heard the laughter as members of the congregation imagined their proper, refined, academically inclined teaching minister "dangling from a forty-foot rope." I'll give you a clue—I know this particular minister and nearly every person sitting in the pews that morning knew it would never happen!

Not only was I there the morning this sermon was preached, I was there that day at the Dells. I watched my friend's husband bounce up and down headfirst like a "wet noodle on a forty-foot rope." I walked alongside my husband that evening as he plunged into a quiet, withdrawn melancholy. As we walked back to the hotel, our girls ran and skipped around us like excited puppies, laughing and chattering with little-girl adoration about Mike's daring jump. I knew the bungee jump and Katy's innocent question were not as fun for Gary as they were for us. The look on his face was transparent—a pained sort of grimace.

I've also read Roberta Bondi's book, *Memories of God.* I know the exact passage Gary quotes in this sermon, what precedes it, and what leads up to those moments in the red prayer chair.

And of course, I'm painfully familiar with the words Gary quoted from my journal, with my permission. My father's sudden, unexpected death had a profound impact on my life.

None of these illustrations came as a surprise to me; after all, I was personally involved with most of these experiences. What did surprise me was the pairing of these diverse experiences with the story of Elijah cowering in a cave.

PREACHING FROM UNIVERSAL, HUMAN EXPERIENCE

This sermon hits everyone. No matter where you are in life, you hear your own story in these stories.

A summer vacation, good friends, good times—life was good, until a bungee jump became the grinch that stole the fun. A happily married woman, an academically accomplished professional, the mother of well-adjusted, healthy kids—life was good for Roberta Bondi, but underneath it lurked depression, and finally exhaustion and despair. A young married woman, pregnant with her first child, a great husband, much to look forward to—life was good, until the unexpected death of a parent. And a prophet at the peak of his career, a moment of triumph, until he offended the wrong leader. Each of these stories is the same story: the experience of our lives coming to a complete standstill. These are the moments when the bottom drops out. "One day the victory.... The next day all is lost."

We've all been there. Elijah was there. But the sermon goes beyond proclaiming the good news that God will be with us. This sermon offers a message that is both grace-filled and unique: God doesn't shame us for dark thoughts in the midst of blessedness. Rather, the stories of a dad, a mom, a daughter, and a prophet honor the work of God in our lives—no matter when God manages to get our attention.

TEXT & PROCLAMATION

Most professors of homiletics have favorite maxims that help define the style of preaching they advocate. "Begin with the biblical text." "Don't let anything get in the way of the text." "Let the text speak for itself." You've no doubt heard some of these axioms.

One could easily question Gary's use of three illustrative stories before introducing the biblical narrative. In looking at this sermon, one has to ask, "What was gained by opening with the stories of a bungee jump, a red prayer chair, and a journal entry?" Gary *could* have begun this sermon directly with the Elijah story. It's a long, rich narrative filled with drama and pathos. The Elijah story is itself more than enough to occupy the whole sermon. So why begin with some other story—not to mention *three* stories? If the point of preaching is to lead your listeners into the text, why didn't he lead *with* the text?

This sermon is a good example of some issues in preaching. How does one best get into a biblical text? What functions do different kinds of introductions play? When do illustrations lead us as hearers into a text, and when do they run the risk of interfering with a text. I know that the structural sequence of illustrative material in this sermon is more a matter of style. Leading with stories of a bungee jump, a red prayer chair, and a journal entry is more than a matter of personal preference for this preacher. They are part of his conviction about the importance of establishing communication with an audience.

My background is communications—not homiletics or theology. And axioms of homiletics aside, this one thing I know: *We pay more attention to the unexpected than we do to the familiar.* These opening stories serve to establish a point of contact with listeners. The preacher sets the stage for hearing the text by enfolding the listeners in a universal, human experience which then leads us into the text.

Countless times church members have said to me, "I never know where your husband is going when he starts telling one of those stories— but I can't wait to see what he's going to do with it." Many strong, effective sermons begin with the text, but sometimes proclaiming the gospel is accomplished by keeping your listeners guessing.

EFFECTIVE USE OF REPETITION

I come to the task of writing this comment from a unique vantage point. I've known this preacher for nearly two decades and have now heard him preach more than three hundred sermons. A technique he consistently uses is the repetition of a key phrase throughout a sermon. It's usually a phrase drawn from the biblical text. If you look back over this sermon, one particular phrase appears more than once on nearly every page: "What are you doing here?" These five words, "What are you doing here? appear twice at critical moments in the Elijah text (vv. 9, 13). The words also appear sixteen times throughout this sermon.

Repetition of a key phrase has the same effect for listeners that boldface italics have for readers. It calls attention to the words. It helps us focus on the point of the sermon. It helps us remember. The repetition uses of these simple words connects our lives with the life of the prophet and the faithfulness of a God who always comes into our darkness.

The good news of this text and of this sermon is that this God cares about us and, in grace, will not let go of us. This sermon uses stories out of our own universal, human experience to lead us into Elijah's story and then out of that story with the good news of God's care and God's call in our lives.

SUGGESTIONS

- This sermon focuses on a key question in a biblical narrative. What are some other great questions in Scripture which could form important texts for preaching? If you preach following a lectionary, pay special attention to questions in the weekly texts. Consider doing a series of sermons on questions used in the Bible.

- How do you preach narrative texts? Do you use other stories to illustrate them or to lead the listener into a biblical narrative? Think about how you retell biblical stories in your preaching. Work creatively at retelling the stories in ways that will engage your listeners.

- Many sermons in the past have focused on the wind, earthquake, fire, and "still small voice" (v. 12, KJV) in this story. Do a thorough exegetical study of vv. 11–13 of this text to determine the proper translation and meaning of these elements in the narrative. What is the meaning of "a sound of sheer silence" (v. 12, NRSV), and what role does it play in the story?

- Read Roberta Bondi's book, *Memories of God,* as part of your general reading.

- Do you use the careful repetition of a phrase or sentence throughout a sermon to provide focus and reinforce a theme or point?

Debra K. Klingsporn

PRACTICING FORGIVENESS

MATTHEW 18:21–35

REV. DR. CURTIS W. FREEMAN
WEST END BAPTIST CHURCH
HOUSTON, TEXAS

REV. DR. CURTIS W. FREEMAN

PRACTICING
FORGIVENESS

MATTHEW 18:21-35, NRSV

S imon Wiesenthal was a young Jew who spent time as an inmate
in a Polish concentration camp during World War II. He was sent
to the camp as part of a cleanup operation to create a hospital for
German soldiers in a building that once housed the school that he had
attended. One day Wiesenthal was ordered by a nurse (a Catholic nun
no less) into the room of a dying Nazi SS trooper. The young German
pleaded, "I have to talk to a Jew. I have to tell a Jew some of the terrible
things I have done. I have to be forgiven by a Jew." Wiesenthal listened
silently as the young man confessed, covering his blinded and bandaged
eyes in shame while he told his horrific tale. As he listened, Wiesenthal
had no doubt that he was hearing a confession of true contrition and
repentance. Yet, in the end, he found the distance between them too great.
Without a word of absolution or condemnation, Wiesenthal left the room.

Haunted by the remembrance of that event, Wiesenthal later wrote
in his book, *The Sunflower,* that we can only judge his action by putting
ourselves in his place and asking, "What would I have done?"[1]

For those who have been forgiven by God in Jesus Christ and who
listen to the Gospel lesson today, there is a more determinative question
to be asked. We must ask ourselves what we as Christians would have
had the courage to do. Can we practice forgiveness? The Gospel for today

not only confronts us with the demand that we must forgive but it shows us exactly what it might mean for us to practice forgiveness.

I.

We are on the way to practicing forgiveness when we understand that forgiveness is the work of God. The Gospel reading begins with a brief exchange between Peter and Jesus about the extent of forgiveness (vv. 21–22): "Lord, if another member of the church sins against me, how often should I forgive? As many as seven times?" In other words, where do we draw the line and say, "No more"?

Jesus' answer is jarring: "Not seven times, but, I tell you, seventy-seven times." The literalists may hear this the wrong way. "When Jesus said seventy-seven times, he meant seventy-seven, not seventy-eight." But, of course, this grossly misses the point. Seventy-seven times can't quantify forgiveness. Forgiveness is limitless. It is infinite. The language of numbers and mathematics is both inadequate and inappropriate for expressing forgiveness.

The Gospel does not give us Peter's reply, but it evokes a puzzling response from us. If forgiveness is unlimited, then only God can forgive. To such an answer Jesus would have surely replied, "Now you're beginning to get the point." Indeed, only God can limitlessly forgive, because forgiveness is the work of God. We miss the point when we begin to think about forgiveness as a duty that is ours alone to do. When we conceive of forgiveness as a commodity to be given or withheld, we do not understand forgiveness. Forgiveness is not a right that belongs to the offended party to give or refuse. Forgiveness is not a human activity. Forgiveness is the work of God.

Eugene O'Neill tells the story of a man who killed his wife on the grounds of excessive forgiveness. Every night he would come home drunk, and every night she would tell him that he was the scurviest, most good-for-nothing scum ever to crawl out of the cracks of life. Then, she would say, "But, I forgive you."[2] He heard her words, but he also got the message. If the truth were known, there are lots of folk for whom the absolving utterance, "You are forgiven," is belied by the accompanying word of self-righteous judgment. The Gospel reading, however, confronts us with the unwelcome fact that we cannot forgive. It is humanly impossible. The call to forgive our sisters and brothers an unlimited number of times is something we cannot do, yet it is precisely what we must do. When we grasp both our duty and our inability to forgive, we are in a position to give God the glory. Only then are we capable of understanding that forgiveness is God's work, not ours. And only when we recognize that forgiveness is the work of God will we be ready to ask what it might mean to practice forgiveness. Until we recognize forgiveness as the work of God, we cannot practice forgiveness.

II.

We are on the way to practicing forgiveness when we discover what it means to be forgiven. The second part of the Gospel reading is a parable. It seems that a certain king wanted to clear his accounts payable, but a particular servant owed him an unpayable debt. Ten thousand talents represents more than the earnings that a day laborer could expect for one hundred and fifty thousand years. It was so vast a sum as to be almost unimaginable (like the examples that present-day economists give to explain the national debt by comparing it to a stack of hundred dollar bills stretching to the moon and back). Once you get past a certain point, ordinary minds cannot grasp what it means. We cannot begin to conceive how much he owed, let alone how he might repay it.

The king called in the debt. At first the servant stalled. When that didn't work he begged and pleaded. Then the unimaginable happened. The king forgave the debt. No sooner had he left the king, however, than the forgiven servant met a man who owed him one hundred denarii, mere pocket change by comparison. The second servant begged and pleaded, but the first servant demanded immediate payment. When the debtor could not pay what he owed, the forgiven man had him thrown into debtors prison. When the king heard this, he revoked his forgiveness and threw the first man into prison forever.

Jesus ends the story with these troubling words, "So my heavenly Father will also do to every one of you, if you do not forgive your brother or sister from your heart" (v. 35). Being forgiven is bound together with practicing forgiveness. Why are the two so linked? Surely it is not that forgiveness is *quid pro quo*. Rather, Jesus suggests that it has something to do with discovering forgiveness. The first servant never grasped what it meant to experience God's limitless forgiveness. Seventy-seven times cannot express it, and neither can ten thousand talents. Only when we begin to discover what it means to be truly forgiven, can we begin to practice forgiveness.

One of the simplest and most wonderful expressions of what it means to be forgiven is contained in a hymn that we know and love:

> I hear the Savior say,
> Thy strength indeed is small,
> Child of weakness watch and pray,
> Find in me thine all in all.

> Jesus paid it all,
> All to him I owe,
> Sin had left a crimson stain,
> He washed it white as snow.[3]

When we realize that we are much more like than unlike the people who have wronged or hurt us, we can begin to imagine what it might mean to practice forgiveness. When we realize that we are in no position to forgive others, we can begin to grasp how we might go about practicing forgiveness. My suspicion is that most of us who find it impossible to practice forgiveness at some point cannot accept God's forgiveness in Jesus Christ. We may even pray "forgive us our debts" (Matt. 6:12), and we may claim the promise that "if we confess our sins, [God] who is faithful and just will forgive us our sins" (1 John 1:9). Yet to be forgiven is too radical. So we try to be good enough and we judge others who are not good enough by our standards. The Gospel lesson today helps us see that we are on the way to practicing forgiveness when we discover what it means to be forgiven.

III.

We are on the way to practicing forgiveness when we embody the pattern of God's gracious, forgiving love. Forgiveness not only *takes* practice but, more importantly, forgiveness *is* a practice. Forgiveness is not so much a spoken word or a performed act or a felt feeling. Forgiveness is the embodiment of the pattern of God's forgiveness revealed in Jesus Christ through the Holy Spirit. To practice forgiveness requires learning the disciplines and habits that make us more like God. To practice forgiveness we must unlearn the sinful habits that cause us to be alienated from God and God's creation. To practice forgiveness we must learn the disciplines that enable us to be reconciled to God and God's creation. If to forgive our sister or brother "seventy-seven times" really means "one more time," only the habits and skills of God's kingdom can make that "one more time" possible.

In his book, *Letters to Malcolm*, C. S. Lewis observes, "Last week, while at prayer, I suddenly discovered—or felt as if I did—that I had forgiven someone I have been trying to forgive for over thirty years. Trying and praying that I might."[4] Lewis understood that without the hard work of prayer the words "I forgive you" are empty. Only through such disciplines as prayer can we hope to practice forgiveness by embodying the pattern of God's gracious and forgiving love in Jesus Christ.

The movie *Dead Man Walking* tells a true story of how an unsuspecting Catholic nun became the spiritual director of a death row inmate. Convicted for the brutal murder of a young couple, the prisoner maintains his innocence. Throughout the movie, the murderer does little to make us identify with him as a human being. He is sickening and repulsive. Yet Sister Prejean continues to guide him, hoping somehow to touch his soul. Finally she leads him to an act of contrition and penance. In a final gesture, he declares to the parents of his victims, "I hope that my death gives you some peace."

For the parents of the young girl, however, there is no peace even in retribution. They have only their hate. Their reaction is understandable, even natural. The father of the young man is not so hardened. At the graveside services for the murderer, the murdered boy's father stands at a distance. Sister Prejean goes to him. He tells her, "Sister, I wish I had your faith." She replies, "It's not faith. It's a lot of work." In the final scene, we see the two of them together in prayer, busy in the hard work of embodying forgiveness.

Whose forgiveness is it anyway? It is God's forgiveness, not ours. The act that today's Gospel reading calls for is quite simply impossible to perform by human standards. Only God can forgive. But we can begin to imagine what it might mean to practice forgiveness when we contemplate the fact that "God proves his love for us in that while we still were sinners Christ died for us" (Rom. 5:8). That is forgiveness. God refused to allow sin to determine the relationship between the Creator and the creation, so God forgave us in Christ. Learning to practice forgiveness, then, is not a question of wondering if we can forgive; it is asking whether we can embody God's forgiveness. Bertrand Russell once observed that "we have, in fact, two kinds of morality side by side; one which we preach but do not practice, and another which we practice but seldom preach."[5] The gospel not only calls for a church that preaches forgiveness, but it calls forth a community that practices forgiveness. May God make us into a people who practice what we preach and preach what we practice.[6]

Notes

1. Simon Wiesenthal, *The Sunflower* (New York:Schocken Books, 1976), pp. 32–58.
2. Eugene O'Neill, *The Iceman Cometh*, Act IV.
3. Elvina M. Hall, "Jesus Paid It All," 1865.
4. C. S. Lewis, *Letters to Malcolm: Chiefly on Prayer* (London: Geoffrey Bles, 1964), p. 137 (chap. 20).
5. Bertrand Russell, "Skeptical Essays", cited in *The Macmillan Dictionary of Quotations* (New York: Macmillan Publishing Company, 1989).
6. I want to acknowledge my deep appreciation for and dependence on the wonderful book by L. Gregory Jones, *Embodying Forgiveness* (Grand Rapids: Eerdmans, 1995). Although I have not quoted from it, much of the thought of this sermon reflects his insightful theological analysis of the practice of forgiveness.

COMMENT

Many writers have observed that preaching is a form of pastoral care for the congregation. It is also a means of spiritual guidance. This is a far cry from the shallow "how-to" sermons that are so pervasive today. The point of spiritual guidance is not to provide a shortcut for busy people. Good spiritual guidance may make their lives more and not less difficult. It will lead them to face crucial decisions and assume new priorities. Spiritual guidance means inviting people into the life of the spirit.

Curtis Freeman gives us a wonderful example of a sermon that treats a common topic in Christian churches—forgiveness—and helps us as listeners to confront the deeper reality this subject evokes.

A NOT-SO-SIMPLE QUESTION

We ought to practice forgiveness. Who could disagree? Listeners might as well yawn and go to sleep, except for one thing: forgiveness is the most overaffirmed and underpracticed reality in the church. It is not because we do not need it. It's because we do not know where to begin. Every Sunday, dozens of parishioners come in the doors with ancient grudges, racial resentments, buried angers and primal rages from incidents where they have been (or felt themselves to be) wronged, abused, neglected or mistreated by others. The question Freeman treats is powerful: How can we really practice forgiveness?

WHAT DOES THE BIBLE SAY?

Every sermon starts with some kind of basic idea or outline. It may be about one subject that we wish to address in a variety of ways. Perhaps we will deal with a subject in a logical order, or look at three particular aspects of a subject. One of the crucial dimensions of a sermon has to do with its having a point (at least one!) and having something to say. Equally important is the way in which we develop the progression of the sermon.

An outline is not simply a matter of coming up with three points. An outline must have dynamism (from the Greek word *dunamis* which means "power"). Power in an outline means an energy that will attract and keep a listener's or reader's attention for the journey. Boring sermons commonly make two dreadful mistakes. They are usually far too long, and by the end they have not taken the listener anywhere. It's acceptable to wind up where we started, as long as we go somewhere in the interim! Only by helping us "make a journey" can a sermon change our perspective on the original thought.

How does a sermon have "dynamic"? In a dynamic sermon the ideas actually "move" logically from one thing to the next. Unconsciously the hearer goes with the preacher. There is curiosity or anticipation about the next development, or agreement about the force of logic ("that's right, that's it!").

Notice how Freeman develops his points. He begins with a very simple question: "Can we practice forgiveness?" This is the question of the sermon. It is no academic matter. It is one of the most troubling personal and pastoral issues we face, day in and day out. So the question has personal relevance and interest for virtually anyone listening.

The outline must, however, retain that relevance and the interest of the listener, and at the same time remain faithful to the biblical text. A lifeless outline might say something like: "We need to forgive. We ought to forgive whenever someone asks for it. If we don't forgive, we won't be forgiven." Such a sermon would certainly capture the surface points of the texts, but would miss their deeper significance.

WHAT, THEN, SHALL WE DO?

It is one thing to describe a journey, something else entirely to help other people enter into it. When Freeman tells us that forgiveness is a practice, he does not primarily mean that it is a behavioral technique. Rather, it is a pathway to transformation whereby we encounter, then walk with God, toward new life.

Freeman's story of the drunken man whose wife killed him with forgiveness is a good one to illustrate the treacherous deceptions into which we can fall on this subject. A moralistic command, "You ought to forgive," can lead to superficiality and self-righteousness. Most pastors encounter people who declare, "I forgave him," while listening to an angry retelling of the sin. Too often our preaching about this has caused such misunderstandings. To tell people simplistically, "You'd better forgive, or else!" is to invite precisely the kinds of hypocrisy and trivialization that we so often see. Forgiveness is not a simple declaration or a behavioral technique. Forgiveness is a profound and wrenching journey.

Notice Freeman's outline in this sermon:

1. Forgiveness is God's work, not ours.
2. We are on the way to practicing forgiveness when we know what it means to be forgiven.
3. Forgiveness becomes possible when we embody God's gracious, forgiving love.

The outline moves naturally from one point to the next. It clarifies a misunderstanding ("It's not something you do alone; you need God's help"). Then we see forgiveness as something made possible by genuine encounter with God's gracious forgiveness of us ("Until you have experienced it on the other end, it will be difficult for you to empathize with the one you need to forgive"). Finally, forgiveness must become something that moves from words and external actions to a place deep within us. It must finally be an expression of who we have become in our Christian journey.

Freeman closes with the wonderful illustration from *Dead Man Walking* in which the nun who is the main character in the story says of forgiveness, "It's not faith. It's a lot of work." In a church cheapened by superficial notions of grace, this is shocking. Forgiveness is something that we must work at!

C O M M E N T

COMMENT

SUGGESTIONS

- Not only is it important to develop a dynamism within a sermon outline, but this dynamism must be a development from our own thinking and reading. After a few years in the parish, ministers start to receive mail about sermon outlines available through subscription. There are books that offer outlines for texts as time-savers. These resources often say something like, "The busy pastor does not always have time to do the study for a sermon. These helps can insure that you deliver a dynamic and life-changing message to your church without that laborious search for ideas!"

- My response is that without the laborious search, the sermon will be as interesting to the congregation as it is to you! It is someone else's idea. That is a completely different notion than to take a book that one has read as part of the ongoing discipline of study, and make its message comprehensible to a congregation. When we do that, we have wrestled with its contents, and we then reveal that engagement to our listeners.

- Freeman is a scholar and professor, so this is a natural part of his work. But he is also a pastor in a small, inner-city congregation. He brings the teaching dimension into his preaching quite effectively. He has obviously been influenced in this sermon by a book by Gregory Jones. That is an appropriate use of outside resources. When a preacher has read a serious treatment of a subject and has critically reflected upon it, then seeks to convey the results of his or her own reflection on the subject, the sermon can offer powerful depth and wrestling with biblical texts.

- When you plan your preaching, do you also plan a course of challenging reading that parallels the texts and subjects you will treat? Don't always go for the "easy adaptation," like books full of illustrations or stories. Our reading should include books with which we disagree, books that challenge us, books that reward us only after wrestling with them!

- Pick out several old sermon outlines you have used. Is there any "movement" in them? How might you rework them to create a more dynamic tension and development within them?

Gary A. Furr

LOST AND FOUND: CLIMBING THE WRONG LADDER

LUKE 19:1–10

REV. JOHN F. CROSBY
CHRIST PRESBYTERIAN CHURCH
EDINA, MINNESOTA

REV. JOHN F. CROSBY

LOST AND FOUND: CLIMBING THE WRONG LADDER

LUKE 19:1–10, NIV

I was working on a paper this summer for a doctoral program that I'm in. One of the things I found fascinating was that right along with the church fathers and modern church pastors, the required reading for the course included the works of Peter Drucker. Peter Drucker is, in many ways, the father of modern management theory. He is one of those who took all the chaotic, artful impulses of leadership and tried to say, "How do we become effective leaders?"

Drucker has had one basic message for decades:

If you would succeed as an organization, you need to do two things. You need to decide what business you're in. So go back and look at the very beginnings of your life together. As an organization, say what business you are in. Decide that. Second, you need a vibrant mission statement that gives a vision for who you are and where you're going. The leaders need to have memorized it, so it's a part of who they are and they need to talk about that vision, so that throughout the organization people capture the urgency of the mission. The job of the leader is to constantly examine and promote that vision for understanding, buy-in, and evaluation.[1]

Last week we looked at our foundations as a church. We talked about the difference between building our lives and this church on sand, and building them on the Word of God. Today, and for the next four weeks, I'd like to follow Drucker's advice and talk about what it is exactly that we're about at Christ Presbyterian Church. Drucker says that our "mission" is all that keeps us from becoming yet another sterile bureaucratic organization which spends all of its energy just keeping the machinery going before it finally falls apart.

Drucker points us to the people who made candles but didn't see that they were really in the lighting industry—and so went out of business. He highlights watchmakers who made "tick, tock, tick, tock" famous. When quartz watches came along, they could not adjust to the fact that they were in the time business, not just the watch business. He points to empty churches downtown, out in rural areas, or in the suburbs. They may be huge edifices with wonderful stained glass windows, but they are boarded up because they are empty buildings, no longer filled with people. They have forgotten their mission and their purpose.

In thinking about our mission as a church, I'd like to read today from a story in Luke chapter 19, because I think it says who we are and what our mission is. The setting is the last week of Jesus' life on earth. He's heading to Jerusalem for the final week of his life and the events that lead to the crucifixion and resurrection. His heart is heavy and he wants to spend time with his friends, Mary, Martha and Lazarus, who live at Bethany on the other side of Jericho.

Jesus entered Jericho and was passing through. [Important: he wasn't planning on staying there, he was passing through.] A man was there by the name of Zacchaeus; he was a chief tax collector and was wealthy. He wanted to see who Jesus was, but being a short man he could not, because of the crowd. So he ran ahead and climbed a sycamore-fig tree to see him, since Jesus was coming that way.

When Jesus reached the spot, he looked up and said to him, "Zacchaeus, come down immediately. I must stay at your house today." So he came down at once and welcomed him gladly.

All the people saw this and began to mutter....

This last sentence is important. In the Gospels, there are times when Jesus talks to the crowds, and the Pharisees get angry and mutter against Jesus. There are other times when Jesus interacts with the disciples or the Pharisees, and the crowds are upset and angry, so they mutter. There are also times when the disciples are confused and mutter. But this is the only time in all the Gospels where we are told that *all* the people muttered. All parties were upset. "He has gone to be the guest of a 'sinner'," they said.

Then in Luke's account between verse 7 and verse 8, some time passes. If this is typical Middle Eastern hospitality, Zacchaeus invites Jesus to stay overnight at his palatial home. The next day, at the most convenient hour of the day, he throws a feast for Jesus. The people get to watch through the gates or from the walls. That might put a different slant on why they murmured.

But Zacchaeus stood up and said to the Lord, "Look, Lord! Here and now I give half of my possessions to the poor, and if I have cheated anybody out of anything [Like, "If the Pope is Catholic"], I will pay back four times the amount."

Jesus said to him and to the crowd, "Today salvation has come to this house, because this man, too, is a son of Abraham. For the Son of Man [that's Jesus' name in the Gospels] came to seek and save what was lost."

I would say that was Salvation with a capital "S." Jesus is Salvation, and Salvation has come to Zacchaeus in the form of Jesus.

The Son of Man came to seek and save what was lost. If I had to distill the mission of Christ Presbyterian Church into five words, it would be: *Seek and save the lost.*

We follow the example and mandate of Jesus Christ, who said, "Go and make disciples of all nations, baptizing them in the name of the Father and of the Son and of the Holy Spirit.... And surely I will be with you always" (Matt. 28:19–20). That's our mission.

For the next four weeks, I'd like to talk about *seeking and saving the lost.* We will look at the various places in the Bible where that happens. I have two very explicit hopes for this series. First, I hope that we will come to understand the mission of Jesus Christ in a personal way. I want us to understand in a fresh way that lost people matter to God. By the end of that time, I hope you'll know whether you're lost or you've been found, and if you're lost, that you'll know how to get home.

Second, I hope that if you've discovered the love of God, you'll have a renewed passion for sharing that love with lost people around you. If we don't believe that people who surround us are spiritually lost and need salvation, then we've missed what Jesus says is the whole reason for his coming in the first place—to "seek the lost."

What does that mean? The first time Jesus said to the crowd, "I've come to seek and save the lost," they probably thought they understood what he meant. We lose things all the time, don't we? You may not know this, but in our church we have a "Lost-and-Found" box. This box is always overflowing with the usual things: my hat! several gloves, none of which match; a crucial part of baby paraphernalia—the all-important pacifier. If some of you ladies are missing a purse, check the box—we may just have it. The box also contains vital things such as prescription eyeglasses and Bibles.

The church takes all these lost things and throws them in the box. If you lose something, you call the office, or you come to the office and report it: "I lost my wallet," "I lost my Bible." We try to keep track of what we find.

But other lost things are not so ordinary. "I lost my job." Or we speak of a "lost marriage." Somebody once wrote, "I lost my way in life."[2] Many of us know people—both men and women—who lose their direction in life.

A lost child is a tragedy. I play basketball with a guy named John. Monday, I went to the funeral of John's fourteen-year-old son, who committed suicide. He lost meaning, purpose. Kids often lose their innocence. Some feel so guilty, they can't go back home, even if nobody knows they've lost their innocence.

Sometimes people lose faith. Sadly that happens even in a church. We want to believe, but we are mouthing mere religious words and going through the motions of church. We have lost touch with God and have lost our way.

We lose things all the time. Is there anything of yours in our Lost-and-Found box? Or have you lost something else, something bigger? How do we find our lost possessions? What does it mean to be lost spiritually? Lost people usually don't look lost. They dress the same as other folk. They talk the same; they may even be the life of the party. Being lost means that we're missing something, whether we feel it or not. Being lost means that we're going in the wrong direction. Being lost means that we need help. We need to be found. Being lost is not a feeling, it's a condition. Many people are lost and don't have a clue that they're lost.

What does it mean to be lost *spiritually?* Paul told the Colossian church that at one time they were separated from God, alienated because of the way they behaved, unable to be reconciled to God (Col. 1:21). And Paul wrote to the Romans, "For all have sinned and fall short of the glory of God." The wages of that kind of life, he told them, "is death," (Rom. 3:23, 6:23).

To be lost means to be separated from God, alienated and condemned to an eternity without God's love. The Old Testament speaks of the lost as sheep who have wandered away and can't get back. Spiritually speaking, "lostness" means that the person who may be the life of the party is in reality missing the party in the kingdom of God. God is calling. Lostness is living for today rather than for eternity. Do you live just for today? Maybe you're lost. We're created to live forever. People are lost who don't see that putting anything else in the center of their life than the living God will result in their going where they will never be found. Lost people are all around us. They sit among us.

It is also possible to feel lost because we don't realize how much God is for us. We don't understand that God wants to save us and make us whole. God wants to know us personally.

Even church people often think that they're okay with God if they have just learned the right language, the right behaviors, the right songs. But they may still be totally lost. Church people often come across as judgmental. They boast, "We found the secret." Remember that bumper sticker several years ago? "I found IT!" "It" can express a very valid spiritual experience if someone has found the love of God. But often, those of us on the inside come across as exclusive and judgmental, as if finding "it" makes us better than other people.

Sometimes our society is much more aware of what being lost is like than we are. We live in a culture that offers people so many choices they're swamped. Still, the tabloids are filled with people searching for something more in their lives. In our society today, many people have a sense that something is wrong. They are hungering for meaning and purpose. They know that there must be more to life than material existence. There are people like Zacchaeus all around us climbing trees to see who might be out there, because they're lost.

Some of us are up that tree, along with many of those closest to us. What does God do about that? How does God seek and save the lost? First, *God puts on skin.* In the person of Jesus Christ, God walks around noticing people stuck up a tree. He says, "I know I can't help those of you who are so religious you think you've got everything together. You go your way, maybe we'll see you in heaven." But to those who are hurting, to those who have lost their children or their innocence, or their job, or their way, or their faith, Jesus walks up and stands at the bottom of the tree and says, "Hey, Zack, here I am. Come on down."

Do you know the only thing that God cannot see? The only thing God cannot see in this church is a crowd. God doesn't see crowds. He sees Mark, Judie, Nora—he sees you. He comes and calls us by name, "Come on down. I want to spend time just with you. I want to go home with you."

God comes to Zacchaeus and takes him home. For the first time in his palatial house, Zacchaeus is really at home. Jesus warms his heart and says, "Zack, I know you. Zack, you're a child of God." (That's what it means to be a son of Abraham.) "You're a child of God, and you can act like a child of God." Zacchaeus jumps up from the table and says, "That's it! I don't need all this money anymore. I'll give half of it to the poor. If I've cheated anybody, I'm so sorry, let me pay it back." God says, "Today, you've been saved because you're a child of God."

If you don't hear anything else this morning, hear this: *Lost people matter to God.* God will go anywhere and do just about anything to find lost people. Lost people matter to God. Do lost people matter to you? Do lost people break your heart the way they break God's heart?

What did God do to find Zacchaeus? He sent Jesus. What does God do today? He sends us. He sends people just like you and me. He tells us, "I want you to go get 'em." That takes a special kind of person. It takes a hero.

What do you think of when you think of a hero? I used to think of the movie characters played by John Wayne or Charlton Heston. But real heroes are *ordinary people who make extraordinary choices* in the middle of life.

Heroes are people who save what's lost. They don't always do it by taking the lost out of the mouths of lions. But every time we leave this sanctuary, we are going into the middle of a life-and-death struggle that calls for heroes. We have choices. Will we seek to save the lost? Will we be "heroes," ordinary persons who choose what God wants us to do?

What does an ordinary person do? In this setting, they do just what Jesus did.

1) They interrupt themselves. They allow themselves to be inconvenienced. Remember, our passage says that Jesus was passing through and he stopped. Do we stop?

2) After they have stopped, people who are willing to be heroes invest time in others. Jesus stopped and told Zacchaeus, "I have to spend time with you today." Do we spend time with people when they don't serve some purpose in our life?

3) If we want to be a hero, used by God, then we have to be ready to be misunderstood. The Bible says that all the people murmured at Jesus' action with Zacchaeus. What's he doing with him? He's a cheat. Be ready to be misunderstood, even opposed. Sharing God's love gets messy.

4) We need eyes to see lost people. Jesus couldn't just go on through a crowd, because he kept seeing people up a tree and people around him in need. God wants to give us the same kind of eyes.

5) Do you know that 83 percent of the people who are not in church today would come if somebody they knew would just ask them? They would come and perhaps hear a message that would change their lives. Do you know that the love of God will not stop until God talks to each of the lost?

I want to close by asking you to do a little homework. First, think who the lost people are in your life. Is it you? Have you lost your way, your faith? Are you spiritually lost? Or is it somebody in your family, at work, school, or in your circle of friends? If you don't know anybody who is lost, think again. There is probably someone. That's the first thing, to identify one lost person.

Second, pray for that lost person once or twice this week. That's all. Just pray for them, that God might send someone who will say to them, "Come home."

Let's begin by praying now: Lord Jesus, we're all in the crowd together. Some of us are spectators just wanting to see what's going on. Some of us have been following you, trying to figure out who you are and how we can be like you. Some of us are curious, some of us are lost, like Zacchaeus. But we're all here together. Don't walk on by, Jesus. Help us today, so that what is lost may be found. And teach us what it means to find the lost and welcome them home, in your name. Amen.

Notes

1. Peter Drucker, *Managing the Non-Profit Organization: Practices and Principles* (New York: Harper Collins, 1994), p. 47.

2. "Midway in our life's journey I went astray," Dante, *The Inferno*, trans. John Ciardi, Canto 1, line 1 (New York: Mentor Books, 1954), p. 28.

COMMENT

If Plato could quote Socrates defending his life with the words, "the unexamined life is not worth living,"[1] and the writer of Ecclesiastes could observe that "everything is meaningless, a chasing after the wind" (Eccles. 2:11), then John Crosby's sermon focuses on a topic which any pastor needs to address time and time again: purpose. *Why* do we do *what* we do? But instead of quoting Qoholeth or Socrates, Crosby refers to a writer his congregation is much more likely to recognize and respect. The phrase "management guru" often accompanies Peter Drucker's name in print. Crosby's congregation drawn from the affluent suburbs of the Twin Cities area, likely includes many people in business and management who look to Drucker the way many pastors interested in church growth look to Lyle Schaller or George Barna.

Drawing references from the real life of our congregation can help communicate the relevance of our message. The testimony of a respected authority from *their world* can help us connect with our listeners and bring them into *our world* of biblical faith and theology. We must involve our listeners in each sermon through the demonstrated importance of the topic to them, as well as through the clarity and artistry of our presentation.

PROBLEM

Crosby seeks to convince his congregation that their mission is to "Seek and Save the Lost." No doubt some people heard this sermon as being about identifying their mission, while most heard it as a sermon about human lostness. Crosby says that people lose their "way in life," lose their "innocence," and lose their "faith." His effectiveness in presenting this problem depends on expressing it in terms they can understand. His sentence: "We lose our faith; we want to believe, but we are mouthing mere words, religious words that don't make sense anymore"—develops a rapport between him and the congregation. It says that it is all right to express doubt, and that faith is born out of the darkness.

Crosby uses Drucker to assert that in order to be effective, a church, like any organization, needs to know its mission, and tell it. That is not only the problem addressed in this one congregation by this one sermon, but it is a problem that most churches face. Much congregational strife arises out of differing assumptions about why a congregation exists. Why are we here? To worship God? To train for ministry? To give our children a moral grounding? To provide a network of social contacts? To be inspired, reassured and encouraged? To support one another through struggles? These and many other purposes describe the reasons people come to church. Conflict within a congregation is often the result of the clash of two of more differing assumptions about the purposes of the church. A unified purpose puts everyone on the same page.

Within the larger problem of congregational purpose or mission lies the task of explaining what it means to "Seek and Save the Lost." Here Crosby asks two questions: (1) What does it mean to seek the lost? (2) How does God seek and save the lost? He approaches this problem by stating those questions as the purpose of the sermon series he is inaugurating: (1) "I want us to understand...that lost people matter to God." (2) "I hope...you'll have a renewed passion for sharing [the love of God] with lost people around you."

Crosby first describes what it is like to be *spiritually* lost by using traditional theological language: "To be lost means to be separated from God, alienated and condemned to an eternity without God's love." His skill as a preacher shows in his interpretation of that in language his people can grasp, and recognize as affirming, not condemning: "Do you live just for today? Maybe you're lost. We're created to live forever.... In our society today, many people have a sense that something is wrong. They are hungering for meaning and purpose. They know that there must be more to life than material existence. There are people like Zacchaeus all around us climbing trees to see who might be out there, because they're lost." Here Crosby taps into the materialism and consumerism of our day that leaves us hungering for meaning and purpose. He has interpreted the terms "lost" and "alienated" for a modern audience.

C O M M E N T

TEXT

The early New England Puritans despised the "dumb reading" of biblical texts, and were always ready to comment on the text as they read it to the congregation. Although they did it apart from their lengthy sermons, Crosby has incorporated the text into this sermon, and comments on it as he proceeds. For listeners who are becoming less and less biblically literate, such interpretation helps them understand these ancient texts from another time and place.

Crosby presents Jesus as someone who, in Luke 19:1–10, knows, tells, and lives by his mission, "to seek and save the lost." Jesus' seeking out Zacchaeus is an object lesson in the meaning of that mission. It is also a demonstration of what happens when we go against our *perceived* mission in favor of our actual one ("He has gone to be the guest of a 'sinner'"). Jealousy, grumbling and opposition are often the result.

Crosby provides some quick but insightful background in this sermon. He observes that Jesus intended to pass through Jericho, not to stay. This adds considerable weight to his argument that in order to seek and save the lost, those who follow the way of Christ must be willing to have their personal agendas interrupted. The preacher also describes "typical Middle Eastern hospitality" and leads us to a better understanding of the crowd's murmuring.

PROCLAMATION

In answering the questions, "How does God seek and save the lost?" Crosby proclaims the Incarnation and God's saving power through Jesus Christ. He says that in the person of Jesus Christ *"God puts on skin."* Referring back to his image about modern-day Zacchaeus, he says that in Jesus, God could—and did—notice people who were "up a tree." This is the power and the particularity of God in human flesh. From the vantage point of the Incarnation, Crosby says, God can come to lost people and take them home, "really home." Salvation comes to Zacchaeus. He comes to understand his identity as a "child of God." Zack's newborn faith in Jesus finds expression and authentication in a heart freed from greed.

Jesus names him as God's own. The good news proclaimed in this sermon is simply that lost people matter to God, and God acts to save them.

RESPONSE

From the proclamation of God's salvation through Jesus Christ in the Zacchaeus story Crosby moves on to ask, "What does God do today?" How does God save the lost today? We listen carefully, only to hear an answer which may threaten us: "God sends us." The response this sermon invites is for each hearer to commit to the common agenda of seeking and saving the lost. Those who do so, Crosby identifies as "heroes."

Bringing the sermon full circle, Crosby asks the congregation to own the mission of seeking and saving the lost. He concludes by identifying five characteristics of "heroes." The first four are named explicitly:

1. Heroes interrupt themselves.
2. Heroes invest time in others.
3. Heroes are ready to be misunderstood.
4. Heroes have eyes to see lost people.

Note that the fifth characteristic is stated in the form of questions: Do we know that what stands between many lost people and the love of God is an invitation to church? Who are the lost people in your life? Would you pray for them? The preacher asks people to respond by recognizing, reaching out to, and addressing the needs of lost people around them, particularly by giving them an invitation to join in worship.

SUGGESTIONS

- Who does your congregation listen to? Who are the Peter Druckers among the people you serve? Knowing the common interests and occupations of your congregation can lead to a better understanding of your listeners. Is there a radio personality, a sports figure, a scholar whose wisdom in a field of expertise, who provides a parallel application to the life of discipleship? Knowing who your people respect can add to the persuasive power of your preaching.

• Does your congregation need a mission statement? For some congregations, joint ownership of a mission comes only after joint participation in the creation of such a statement. While much of the work of creating a mission statement must come from study, discussion, and prayer, the pulpit ministry has an important role to play. People need to be persuaded that: (1) a mission statement is important; (2) their participation is important; and (3) certain theological guidelines need to be upheld.

• Mission statements are not "one size fits all." A congregation's mission is related to its location, membership characteristics, and size. Many congregations have assumed that they know their purpose for generations, only to discover in times of crisis the existence of many differing assumptions about purpose. A sermon calling a congregation to journey toward hearing God's call in their life together can be a decisive turning point in a church's history.

• Many preachers would rather give ten traditional sermons than one children's message. One idea for a children's talk that comes to mind from Crosby's sermon is the Lost-and-Found Box. Such a box could be brought in for children to see. After a discussion of the various items in it (some funny ones could be planted), one could make the transition to the church being God's "Lost and Found." "I was lost, and I came here, where Jesus found me."

Peter J. Smith

Note

1. Plato, *Apology*, from *The Dialogues of Plato*, trans. Benjamin Jowett.

A Dangerous Disturbance

AMOS 8:1–12

REV. DR. ROBERT T. SNELL
THE BRICK PRESBYTERIAN CHURCH
NEW YORK, NEW YORK

REV. DR. ROBERT T. SNELL

A DANGEROUS DISTURBANCE

AMOS 8:1–12, NRSV

Y ou will no doubt be greatly relieved to hear the good news: I am not a twenty-five-year-old, wild-eyed zealot fresh out of seminary. I am not going to thunder at you with the voice of Amos, speaking as the voice of God, judging you, condemning you and threatening you with the wrath of God because of your tepid, if not evil, response to the God of Abraham and Sarah.

But if I do not bring you God's message in that way, where is God's strong prophetic voice and how is it heard in our time and place?

I first visited New York City in 1986. That was before my seminary days and my subsequent ordination to the ministry of Word and sacrament. During that two-day business trip, I stayed in one of the Sheraton Hotels on Seventh Avenue. When some free time developed, I decided to explore midtown, although I did not have the itinerary or preparation of a well-informed tourist. I simply headed off eastward hoping to find Rockefeller Center and Fifth Avenue.

The overwhelming landscape of architecture and inhabitants, of energy and motion, of sights and smells, was strange and wondrous to this visitor from Lynchburg, Virginia. I was enthralled. Walking along first one street and then another, I eventually discovered the canyons of

Rockefeller Center. The most powerful of the many impressions of my first visit was soon to follow.

When 50th Street dumped me out onto Fifth Avenue, I was stunned by the sight of St. Patrick's Cathedral. In a powerful and evocative way, St. Patrick's Cathedral jerked me out of my awe and admiration of the gods of New York City, and reminded me that the Lord is God, the Lord alone. In glory and majesty the cathedral stood as monument and testimony to other priorities and commitments. It stood, it stands, as a bold, aggressive, even subversive retort to an environment that fairly screams, "The highest and best use of that land is not for a house of worship."

In the late seventies and early eighties I was a real estate salesman. Although primarily concerned with sales and marketing, I naturally and necessarily learned something about appraising real estate. "Highest and best use" is a critical factor in assessing the value of real property. "Highest and best use" is related to "Location, location, location." The value of any piece of improved real property is determined by adding the "highest and best use" value of the land to the "highest and best use" value of any improvements on the land—unless the improvements do not represent or allow the highest and best use of the land. In that case, the value of the land is depreciated. It is depressed. It is penalized.

In our society's system of valuation, the block of Fifth Avenue on which St. Patrick's stands is devalued because the cathedral is on it. In the same way, the value of one corner of Park Avenue and 91st Street is severely depressed because we are here. In the judgment of our society, we are foolishly and irresponsibly misusing a valuable asset.

Reinhold Niebuhr once wrote, "The modern ministry is in no easy position; for it is committed to the espousal of ideals which are in direct conflict with the dominant interests and prejudices of contemporary civilization."[1]

As we heard in our lectionary text this morning, the prophet Amos was called by God to proclaim a message in direct conflict with the dominant interests and prejudices of his contemporary civilization. In the eighth century B.C., during the period of the divided kingdom, God's word came to Amos of Tekoa, a shepherd and dresser of sycamore trees. God instructed Amos to leave the southern kingdom of Judah and go to the northern kingdom of Israel. There he was to proclaim a terrible word of judgment on God's people.

Amos proclaimed God's terrible word of judgment at a time of Israel's exceptional strength, vigor, and prosperity. Syria, Israel's perennial enemy, had been subjugated by Assyria; and Assyria, weakened and preoccupied by internal problems, was temporarily stalled in its drive for supremacy. Under Kings Joash and Jeroboam II, Israel exploited the weakness of its neighbors by expanding its borders and taking full advantage of its strategic location astride the principal trade routes of the Middle East. The resulting prosperity is thoroughly documented by Amos's many references to food, drink, clothes, great houses, winter and summer homes, and extensive profitable commercial activity.

The word Amos proclaimed was one of unrelenting judgment and terrible punishment. A special relationship between God and Israel was presupposed. "You only have I known of all the families of the earth" (Amos 3:2). But far from being the basis for privilege and exemption, the special relationship entailed responsibility and obligation. "You only have I known of all the families of the earth; therefore I will punish you for all your iniquities." God delivered Israel out of bondage in Egypt. God protected and sustained Israel in the wilderness. God gave the law and the prophets to Israel for guidance and correction. But Israel was faithless in this special relationship, and the consequences, Amos said, would be awful.

What was the evidence of Israel's failure as God's people? The condition and treatment of the poor. Repeatedly, when the complaints against Israel become specific, they are concerned with the conditions of the poor and dependent, the weak and the needy.

They…trample the head of the poor into the dust of the earth,
    and push the afflicted out of the way;…
they lay themselves down beside every altar

on garments taken in pledge;
and in the house of their God they drink
    wine bought with fines they imposed" (2:7–8).

The poor and weak were denied justice "in the gate" (5:12). Courts served up justice that was the best money could buy. The prosperity and luxury that Israel so self-indulgently enjoyed were built and sustained at the expense of the poor.

Hear this, you that trample on the needy,
    and bring to ruin the poor of the land,
saying, "When will the new moon be over
    so that we may sell grain;
and the sabbath,
    so that we may offer wheat for sale?
We will make the ephah small and the shekel great,
    and practice deceit with false balances,
buying the poor for silver
    and the needy for a pair of sandals,
    and selling the sweepings of the wheat" (8:4–6).

God does not blame the victim. The conditions of the poor are not the fault of the weak and needy. They are the fault of the strong and prosperous. So God promises:

I will tear down the winter house as well as the summer house;
    and the houses of ivory shall perish,
and the great houses shall come to an end,
    says the Lord (3:15).

And again:

Alas for those who lie on beds of ivory,
    and lounge on their couches,

and eat lambs from the flock,
 and calves from the stall;
who sing idle songs to the sound of the harp,
 and like David improvise on instruments of music;
who drink wine from bowls,
 and anoint themselves with the finest oils,
  but are not grieved over the ruin of Joseph!
Therefore they shall now be the first to go into exile,
 and the revelry of the loungers shall pass away (6:4–7).

Amos declared that God had rejected Israel's worship, even though it was decent and in order. It was regular, beautiful, even full of zeal. But poverty and injustice for the weak in the presence of privilege and affluence for the strong made the community's worship an abomination before God.

I hate, I despise your festivals,
 and I take no delight in your solemn assemblies.
Even though you offer me your burnt offerings and grain
 offerings,
 I will not accept them;
and the offerings of well-being of your fatted animals
 I will not look upon.
Take away from me the noise of your songs;
 I will not listen to the melody of your harps.
But let justice roll down like waters,
 and righteousness like an everflowing stream (5:21–24).

God's anger was kindled by and directed against the social, political, and economic order, the community as a whole, not just against isolated individuals. It was the community that stood condemned because poverty and injustice for the weak was tolerated in the presence of affluence and privilege for the strong. It was the social order that God vowed to destroy.

The eyes of the Lord God are upon the sinful kingdom,
and I will destroy it from the face of the earth...(9:8).

None of this was a message Israel wanted to hear. It was a bold,
aggressive, even subversive retort to the dominant interests and prejudices of the day. Sent by God, Amos was a dangerous disturbance in the
land of Israel.

Karl Barth, one of the greatest Protestant theologians of this century,
said in a sermon he delivered while still serving as pastor of a small village in Switzerland, "To have a Christian pastor in their village is to have
always a disturbance in their life. The Bible cannot come open without
creating a dangerous disturbance."[2]

Our text should be a dangerous disturbance in our midst. Even
today, God judges communities by their treatment of the poor and weak.

The coincidence of three front page articles in Friday's *New York
Times* (July 21, 1995) should give us pause. The *Times* reported, first,
the rejection of affirmative action in hiring and admissions at the
University of California. A second article reported the decision of the
House appropriations committee to dismantle family planning assis-
tance to the poor. Third, the *Times* reported that Congress was poised to
grant cattle ranchers like William Hewlett and David Packard, of
Hewlett-Packard fame and fortune, a virtual lock on public lands at fees
75 percent below market rates—affirmative action for the strong at the
expense of the weak.

That same day, the front page of the *Wall Street Journal* (July 21,
1995) reported that the House appropriations committee had approved
an overhaul of public housing that would raise the rent of two and one-
half million of the poorest households in our country by one thousand
dollars per year. What would Amos say?

They lay themselves down beside every altar
    on garments taken in pledge;

and in the house of their God they drink
   wine bought with fines they imposed (2:8).

If the care and administration of our community needs another thousand dollars per household, far better for households like mine to give it, than for me to take it from the poorest of the poor simply because I am strong enough to get away with it.

Can you imagine how Amos would respond to the suggestion that an appropriate solution to crime in our city is a wall of private security officers around the upper east side?

Where is God's strong prophetic voice and how is it heard in our time and place? God's strong prophetic voice has been given to you and to me. It is to be heard from us.

One Princeton theologian and ethicist has written, "If it is not possible to articulate, defend, and embody a public theology in personal and social existence, the churches ought to close their doors, or admit that they have nothing substantive to offer the world beyond what modernity already offers the affluent, and simply become centers for cheap therapy and self-help techniques, probably on a fee-for-service basis."[3] A more damning prospect cannot possibly be imagined.

God has called us and placed us here to be more than a therapeutic community, more than a lifestyle enclave of wholesome recreation and fellowship. Like our real estate, we espouse ideals which are in direct conflict with the dominant interests and prejudices of our contemporary civilization. Yes, God has called us to comfort the afflicted, but also to afflict the comfortable. God has called us to create a dangerous disturbance in a world that serves other gods. If we are not the center of a dangerous disturbance, but merely an innocuous, anachronistic presence, a benign eccentricity, then we deserve and can expect God's judgment.

I said at the beginning that the good news is that I am not a twenty-five-year-old, wild-eyed zealot fresh out of seminary. I am not going to thunder at you with the voice of Amos, speaking as the voice of God, judging you, condemning you, and threatening you with the wrath of God because of your tepid, if not evil, response to the God of Abraham and Sarah. The bad news is that I don't have the guts to do it. Amen.

Notes
1. Reinhold Niebuhr, *Leaves from the Notebook of a Tamed Cynic,* Reprint ed. (Louisville, KY: Westminster/John Knox Press, 1990), p. 4.
2. Karl Barth, "The Pastor Who Pleases the People" (sermon preached in 1916).
3. Max L. Stackhouse, *Public Theology and Political Economy* (Lanham, MD: University Press of America, 1991), p. 161.

COMMENT

I could probably count on one hand the number of times I've read from the book of Amos—and I'd be willing to bet that I'm not alone. The book of Amos is not one to inspire comfort and hope.

Amos has never been a very popular fellow. Few prophets are. The Israelites didn't like what Amos had to say; modern listeners like his words even less. Amos has been making people uncomfortable for centuries.

Nearly every preacher struggles with what it means to be "prophetic." When faced with texts filled with judgment, condemnation, and very little hope, how does one proclaim the good news, or for that matter, what is the good news? What does it mean to challenge the status quo? How can one be both effectively prophetic and compassionately pastoral? Quite simply, how does one proclaim a message that few, if any, members of the congregation want to hear?

Not surprisingly, when lectionary readings direct our attention to this Old Testament doomsayer, most ministers choose an epistle or Gospel reading for their sermon text. But not Robert Snell. In his sermon, "A Dangerous Disturbance," he meets the prophetic challenge head-on. This sermon is worthy of note for that reason, if nothing else. But much more can be gained from a closer look at Snell's sermon than simply honoring his effort to tackle the difficult.

THE CALL TO BE PROPHETIC

Snell recognizes the inherent contradictions in preaching from a prophetic text. He recognizes that "proclaiming a message in direct conflict with the dominant interests and prejudices" of the contemporary culture is a perfect set-up for eyes to glaze over, ears to tune out, and heads to nod off. But he also recognizes that Christian ministry is about more than telling his listeners simply what they want to hear.

So how do you get people to listen to what they don't want to hear?

Begin with the unexpected. Snell begins with the good news. He begins with what he's *not*. By reassuring us that he's not a twenty-five-year-old, wild-eyed zealot, nor one who will thunder with the voice of Amos, he immediately makes us wonder what he *is* going to do with the text.

We don't have to wonder long. He immediately gets to the point. In the second paragraph, he sets the dilemma before us:

> But if I do not bring you God's message in that way, where is God's strong prophetic voice and how is it heard in our time and place?

In the opening illustration of this sermon, Snell challenges the status quo in an acceptable arena for most of his listeners. Drawing our attention to the real estate term, "highest and best use of the land," he points out the incongruence between Christian values and the culture's values with a nonthreatening example. Few listeners sitting in a church would dispute the value of the cathedrals and churches in the city. He's got our attention. We think we're on the "right" side. We're allowed to think, briefly, that Amos's railings are directed at "them" out there, that is, the culture and not at "us" safely seated within the walls of a house of worship.

But Snell quickly breaks through our safe detachment. The parallels between the affluence of the Israelites at the time of Amos and twentieth-century America are hard to miss. "Amos proclaimed God's terrible word of judgment at a time of Israel's exceptional strength, vigor, and prosperity." That prosperity was "thoroughly documented by Amos's many references to food, drink, clothes, great houses, winter and summer homes, and extensive profitable commercial activity."

Just think. Snell preached this sermon in New York City. Home of Wall Street. The Big Apple. Manhattan. Amos's references to "food, drink, clothes, great houses, winter and summer homes, and extensive profitable commercial activity" are an apt description of almost any major city in the United States. But in New York City the words take on particular significance considering the number of advertising agencies, brokerage houses, and mega-media broadcasting operations. These words from an eighth-century B.C. prophet aren't irrelevant; these words are descriptive of the here and now. All of a sudden this sermon is hitting a little too close to home. Are *we* the ones who allow our lives to be consumed by food, drink, clothes, great houses, winter and summer homes, and extensive profitable commercial activity? Are *we* the ones whose failure as God's people will be judged by the condition and treatment of the poor?

This is the point in the sermon at which we can close our eyes and almost hear the nervous coughing and clearing of throats. We can almost see the restless shifting in the pews, the crossing and uncrossing of legs. If the good news was what Snell is *not,* the bad news found in the words of Amos is pretty grim. This sermon is becoming increasingly uncomfortable.

THE VALUE OF STRUCTURAL SIMPLICITY

Snell was preaching from a text nobody wants to hear, dealing with a subject few want to consider, offering a word of judgment most prefer to ignore. With that much working against him, he needed a few things working for him. What he uses to his advantage is threefold: he keeps the sermon simple, he allows the text to speak for itself, and he preaches with an honest humility.

Structurally, Snell opens with a story of his first visit to New York City. Then he tells just enough of the historical context of Amos to make the parallels with his own story obvious. He then allows the words of Amos to create a "disturbance" within his listeners. The essential message of this sermon is stated quite simply in two lines:

> "Yes, God has called us to comfort the afflicted, but also to afflict the comfortable. God has called us to create a dangerous disturbance in a world that serves other gods."

What makes this sermon effective, what makes it possible to move beyond the stinging words of the prophet, is Snell's choice to convert the judgment of Amos into a call for us. Therein lies the hope. Therein lies the good news.

But Snell doesn't stop there. He humbly comes back to where he began, reassuring his listeners that he is not going to thunder at them with the voice of Amos. The good news/bad news structure of his opening and closing comments is more than an attention-getting ploy. By closing with the words, "The bad news is that I don't have the guts to do it," Snell allows the judgment of the text to be directed at himself. He models an openness to self-examination. He places himself under the text. In these closing words, he's no longer voicing the indictment; he's receiving the judgment—for it's only in hearing the judgment that we can humbly follow the call.

SUGGESTIONS

- Snell uses three front-page articles from major news publications to illustrate the timeliness of the prophet's words. Daily headlines frequently offer illustrative material appropriate for theological interpretation. Do you allow current events to inform your preaching? How?

- Amos is known as a prophet of social justice. Look back through your sermons for the last six months. Is this an area of minimal attention in your preaching? Is a sermon dealing with social justice a timely consideration in your ministry?

- The quotes by Reinhold Niebuhr and Karl Barth are pointed, direct, and disquieting—or at least they *should* be. Reflect on these quotes. Listen to your thoughts. Does reflection on the words of these great theologians spark a few sermon possibilities? Why not work Barth's phrase, "a dangerous disturbance," into your preaching? And how do you experience Niebuhr's word about the conflict between Christianity and culture?

Debra K. Klingsporn

PRAYING IN THE DARKNESS AT NOON

MARK 15:33–34

REV. DR. STEPHEN BRACHLOW
PROFESSOR OF CHURCH HISTORY
AND CHRISTIAN SPIRITUALITY
NORTH AMERICAN BAPTIST SEMINARY
SIOUX FALLS, SOUTH DAKOTA

REV. DR. STEPHEN BRACHLOW

PRAYING IN THE DARKNESS AT NOON

MARK 15:33–34, NRSV

W e have come down the long road of Lent, a road that began on Ash Wednesday back in February and now brings us here to Good Friday. The day of the cross. The day of Golgotha. The day that darkness covered the land at noon. And it was there, in the darkness of that day, that Jesus cried out with a loud voice: "My God, my God, why have you forsaken me?"

In this great cry of absence, this prayer from the opening lines of Psalm 22 that arose out of the depths of his experience of forsakenness on the cross, the Gospel writers identify the suffering of Jesus with the suffering righteous in psalms of lament. But that identification runs in more than one direction. Indeed, on this Good Friday we may find ourselves identifying with the lament of Jesus in the prayers that at times arise out of the darkness of our own lives.

We recognize in his prayer on the cross something of our own experience: that the prayer of Jesus in the darkness that covered the land at noon is at times very painfully like our own; that his experience of God's absence is something of our experience; that his loneliness is also our loneliness; that in him we indeed find one who "hath borne our griefs and carried our sorrows," one who can sympathize with us in our fears, in our distress, in our pain, in our emptiness, and in our loneliness—one who knows what it is to cry out, "Why have I been forsaken?"

In a recent book about prayer and Christian faith entitled *When the Heart Waits,* Sue Monk Kidd makes the following observation about the spiritual journey, an observation that we know from our own experience of life is simply true. "Soul making," she writes, "is not necessarily a happy thing. Crucial parts of it are not. It almost always involves a painful excursion into pathos wherein the anguish is enormous."[1]

How different her picture of prayer is from the one we so often get in books on spirituality these days that portray prayer either as a means of self-fulfillment or as a spiritual resource for managing our stressed-out, time-pressed modern lives. In a therapeutic culture like ours, prayer easily becomes one more therapeutic tool, a spiritual technology for enhancing our quality of life or calming our frazzled nerves.

But in Scripture and in classical Christian tradition, prayer has little to do with self-improvement or making life comfortable. Rather, authentic, Christ-centered prayer is always about encountering God as God is and ourselves as we actually are. "True prayer," P. T. Forsyth wrote near the end of the last century, "does not allow us to deceive ourselves."[2] When we are willing to enter those empty, lonely, and sometimes painful places of our lives in faith—instead of trying to avoid them, or even to get beyond them—we may discover that those very same places of human brokenness also offer some of the deepest well springs within us from which to draw the clear, refreshing water of authentic prayer. The American-born English poet T. S. Eliot understood this, I think, when he wrote,

I said to my soul, be still and let the dark come upon you,
Which shall be the darkness of God.[3]

In Scripture there are many examples of people who pray, but their experience of prayer is clearly not always an easy one. We often find them praying in great personal turmoil or in deep despair. "Why are you cast down, O my soul," Psalm 42 asks repeatedly, "why are you disquieted within me?" The psalm then asks that question we have all asked: "Why, God, have you forgotten me?"

What does this say to us about our experience of God in prayer? The picture we have from the Gospels of Jesus praying on the cross in the darkness at noon reminds us that the way to God through prayer is not to be found by avoiding the shadows that descend upon our lives. Nor is it to be found by keeping our distance from the pain and turmoil of the world around us. Rather, authentic Christian prayer invites us to live in the often painful realities of life with Christ in faith. It invites us to be willing to walk into the dark places, vulnerable as we may be there, knowing that somehow, by the mystery of God's grace to us in Christ, the road to Golgotha which passes through the darkness that covered the land at noon is also the same road that leads to the inevitably surprising dawn of Easter morning.

Augustine realized this so profoundly when his fifth-century world fell apart with the collapse of the Roman Empire and all the chaos that ensued in the unraveling of his society. He came to recognize that God may be found at work not only in the world's order and beauty, but also in its "darkness, declaring God's mercy at night in the middle of the world's chaos and wretchedness."4

Good Friday—this day of Christ's cross, this day when darkness covered the land at noon—reminds us that life is serious business. It is not some Carnival Cruise Caribbean holiday we are on as people of faith, where life sails tranquilly over calm, clear, luminous, turquoise waters, or into those perpetually golden, tropical sunsets we see on television. Neither is our experience of God in prayer a journey into some religious fantasy land. As the prayer of Jesus on the cross reminds us, the life of true prayer can at times be full of painful realities. Christ calls us in this season of the cross to face with him all the darkness of our own lives—the fears we have, the pain of living, the brokenness of our world—to face it with him in faith and in trust, assuring us by his own death on the cross that the way to true life, and so the path of true prayer, leads through the cross of Good Friday.

If we heed his call, we will find that we can pray in "the darkness at noon" of our own lives, as Christ did on that day at Golgotha, knowing that God, through this very same crucified One, is an ever-present help in times of trouble, our refuge and our strength in the day of our distress. Amen.

Notes

1. Sue Monk Kidd, *When the Heart Waits: Spiritual Direction for Life's Sacred Questions* (San Francisco: Harper San Francisco, 1990), p. 98.
2. P. T. Forsyth, *The Soul of Prayer,* (London: Independent Press, Ltd., 1960), p. 20.
3. T. S. Eliot, "East Coker," *Collected Poems 1909–1962* (New York: Harcourt, Brace & World, Inc., 1963), p. 186.
4. Augustine, as quoted in Rowan Williams, *Christian Spirituality: A Theological History from the New Testament to Luther and St. John of the Cross* (Atlanta: John Knox Press, 1979), p. 81.

COMMENT

THE SERMON AS MEDITATION

There are sermons. There are meditations. There are teachings. And there are words of comfort and consolation. Stephen Brachlow's message is a bit of each. It is a meditative sermon that teaches with comforting words. Not a bad blend, considering the occasion on which it was preached, Good Friday. Even a cursory reading of his message conveys a contemplative mood as Brachlow leads us to the foot of the cross and allows us the privilege of an audience with the dying Savior. It is a sermon which must have been delivered in a calm and steady voice, by one who has known sorrow and endured the loneliness of unanswered prayer.

Brachlow brings us close enough to the tortured Christ to hear the tremor in his breathless cry of abandonment. Close enough we can taste his sweat, smell his blood, and shiver in the cold wave of death that sweeps over Golgotha at that moment. Sometimes the best measure of a message is the mood it conveys rather than the content it presents. Brachlow understands this often overlooked subtlety of preaching, and he crafts his message to envelope his audience with the pathos of the cross. This is a fine example of a sermon designed for a specific occasion—a simple but powerful variation on the familiar crucifixion theme.

SIMPLICITY OF CONTENT

There is a remarkable efficiency to this message. Two verses from Mark's passion narrative provide the context. Brachlow focuses on only one of Christ's seven last words from the cross, "My God, my God, why have you forsaken me?" He uses these words as a point of entry into the wider subject of prayer. Jesus, in his moment of isolation and agony, cries out for all of us, lamenting the dreadful condition sin has brought upon us. In his prayerful cry, he calls upon God to occupy the space of suffering and death through which we all must pass on our way to redemption.

Notice how Brachlow uses Christ's words as a personal plea for his listeners, inviting them to attach their own personal sufferings to those endured by Jesus on the cross. "We recognize in his prayer on the cross something of our own experience: that the prayer of Jesus…is at times very painfully like our own; that his experience of God's absence is something of our experience; that his loneliness is also our loneliness; that in him we indeed find one who 'hath borne our griefs and carried our sorrows,' one who can sympathize with us in our fears, in our distress, in our pain, in our emptiness, and in our loneliness—one who knows what it is to cry out, 'Why have I been forsaken?'" There's no denying this is a long sentence, but it is also a mouthful of sound Christology, prompting us to make the transition from being objective observers to identifying personally with the death of our divine advocate.

Throughout the rest of the message, Brachlow considers the deeper aspects of prayer, especially as it flows out of our own desperation. How do we pray when we sense God is absent? Good-time prayers are one thing, but how are we to address God when the hurt is so deep that it smothers all hope? Of what use is this kind of woeful plea? This is a profound question, one which is relevant to all our lives. Brachlow knows this and sets his sights on bringing us counsel. With the aid of such thinkers as P. T. Forsyth, T. S. Eliot, and Augustine, Brachlow draws a stark contrast between the faddish tendencies of today's feel-good prayers and the profound prayers of the broken-hearted…from "those empty, lonely, and sometimes painful places of our lives in faith." His conclusion? Our most authentic prayer experiences may emerge from those wrenching times when the very act of prayer itself seems nearly impossible.

Is this conclusion theologically sound and biblically tenable? Absolutely. Brachlow cites the Psalms to support his thesis. Again and again in the Scriptures, there is a direct relationship between human despair and authentic prayer. The accounts of God's people demonstrate that prayer is often born of the darkness and that the life of faith involves pain, disequilibrium and struggle.

WHAT DIFFERENCE DOES IT MAKE?

Brachlow himself poses the "so what?" question for his listeners. "What does this say to us about our experience of God in prayer?" Here we find the preacher's exhortation, calling the believer to be willing to "walk into dark places" by refusing to avoid the "pain and turmoil of the world around us." This is the invitation to "authentic Christian prayer." The contrast between the horrid events of Good Friday and the bright celebration of Easter Sunday speaks of the larger paradox that is the Christian life. God is present in the peaceful and beautiful places of life, but God is equally present in our darkness and suffering...perhaps even *more* present.

"Life is serious business," Brachlow tells us, "...not some Carnival Cruise Caribbean holiday." Our prayers are not a sojourn in the realm of wishful thinking. True prayer and painful reality go hand-in-hand for the sincere believer, as witnessed in Christ's suffering on the cross. Consequently, when we most feel the sting of alienation from God, the dying Savior assures us God is at hand, and our suffering is an opportunity for authentic communion with God.

SUGGESTIONS

- Brachlow gives us a cherished glimpse of the preacher as a pastor. This is a pastoral message, presented with the same sincerity one might bring to the hospital bedside of a suffering patient. It might be a housecall to a shut-in or a counseling session with an estranged spouse. The sermon becomes a means for conveying God's strength to those who feel their own weakness.

- Competent preaching depends on the preacher's sensitivity to the congregational environment: recent events impacting the people, the ever-shifting economic climate, and even the weather itself. Any one or all of these can affect the disposition of the congregation, resulting in intangible but very real shifts in their spiritual/ emotional psyche. The sensitive pastor is aware of these shifts and ready to respond by using the pulpit as a vehicle for pastoral care.

C
O
M
M
E
N
T

- There is a time for biblical exposition and instruction from the pulpit. There is a time for rousing exhortation. But there is also a time when as preachers we need to gather our flock around us and embrace them with the strong and comforting assurance of God's grace. Study this sermon as an example of pastoral care given at an opportune moment.

Richard A. Davis

THE LOVE THAT LIES BENEATH THE WOE

GENESIS 45:1–15a

REV. DR. JOHN MARK JONES
TRINITY UNITED METHODIST CHURCH
WEST COLUMBIA, SOUTH CAROLINA

THE LOVE THAT LIES
BENEATH THE WOE[1]

GENESIS 45:1–15a, REB

J oseph and his brothers are at it again. Treachery. Deceit. Power-
plays. The same old junk the family was dealing with years ago is
still at play. Do families ever change? The wounds we gave and
received years ago never quite heal, do they? Year after year we ache with
the same old compulsions that make us sick and that finally drive us into
the grave. So it is with Joseph and his brothers. So it is with our families.

You remember what this family was doing when we saw them last
(Gen. 37)? Joseph, Jacob's next-to-youngest and favorite son, had ratted
on his brothers for some inconsequential naughtiness. So some time later
Jacob sends Joseph to look for the older brothers, who are tending sheep
in Shechem, and report back to him. When the brothers see the favored
one coming, they decide at first to kill him. But Reuben, the eldest, talks
them out of that, so they throw Joseph into a pit instead. Reuben goes
off, and when he gets back to the pit, Joseph is nowhere to be found.
Unbeknownst to him, Joseph has been sold to Midianite traders who are
on their way to Egypt. There he will be sold as a slave. When the brothers concoct a lie for their father about Joseph's being killed by wild beasts,
Jacob plummets into the dark hell of grief, refusing to be consoled by his
other children. To sum it up, when we saw the family last, they were
enmeshed in so much tragic despair, it seemed nothing could save them.

This family has been terribly wounded. Wounded by the father's great love for one child to the disregard of others. Wounded by jealousy, resentment, abuse, rage. Wounded by deceit and treachery. How is it possible to recover from so many deep and lasting wounds?

When we have been wounded by our family's tragic history, what can we do to recover? If you or I were to go to a family therapist, he or she would say to us, "We have to reconstruct your past. We've got to talk about your family, and your place in it. Are you the oldest son who feels responsible for his mother's feelings? Are you the daughter who is always trying to please Dad, yet never really succeeding? Are you the youngest who thinks he's let down the family, never quite able to measure up to their expectations? Are you the favored child, loved by your parents, resented by your brothers and sisters? Let's look into your past, reconstruct that family history, and see if there is any hope at all of recovering from the wounds that bind you."

What do Joseph and his brothers do with their wounds? For the most part, the brothers wallow in guilt and despair. Mind you, some of that guilt is appropriate. What they did was wrong. They abused and abandoned their brother. Of course, it doesn't take much depth psychology to understand why they did it. The flaws in this family are painfully obvious. The father prefers one child over all the others, loves that child more than the others, and overtly displays his preference. Jacob, the father, set this tragedy in motion long ago. At the same time, it is the brothers themselves who chose to react to their sick father's agenda. They made the choice to abuse and abandon Joseph, and they are suffering the consequences.

The brothers do something else with their wounds. They not only view themselves as guilty; they also view themselves as God's victims. Or more to the point, they view God as the avenger of their evil. Here's how it works. The brothers have come to Egypt looking for grain. There is a drought in the whole area, but Egypt has been storing grain for seven years in anticipation of the drought. Everybody is coming to Egypt for grain. And who dispenses grain? Joseph, the king's right-hand man.

Joseph, sold into slavery years ago, has used his God-given wits to gain power.

When his brothers come to Egypt to buy grain from Joseph, they do not recognize him. Now thirteen years older, Joseph is so heavily clothed in regal robes and heavily bearded as to be incognito. Oh, but Joseph recognizes them. Yes, he knows them all by sight. And knowing his brothers, Joseph decides to trick them. He accuses them of spying on Egypt. They profess their innocence, but to no avail. So Joseph has them thrown into prison. And what do the brothers say of their punishment?

> "No doubt we are being punished because of our brother [Joseph, whom we abused and abandoned years ago]. We saw his distress when he pleaded with us and we refused to listen. That is why this distress has come on us." Reuben [the oldest brother] said, "…Now his blood is on our heads, and we must pay" (Gen. 42:21–22).

Later all the brothers say in response to their calamity, "What is this that God has done to us?" (42:28).

I wonder how many of us see our plight as the brothers saw theirs. "God is punishing me for some offense committed years ago." Or, "God is holding me to the fire because of my sin." If we have this view of God, we see our failures as punishment for our sins.

I'd like to believe it's all that simple. You do wrong, God gets you. Do right, God rewards you. But I can't. And the reason I can't believe it is that quite often the wicked prosper and the good suffer. Rabbi Kushner was right when he said that bad things sometimes do happen to good people. And sometimes good things happen to bad people. Neither the human family nor God does a "good" job of meting out justice in this world. As Jesus says, God makes the rain fall on the just and the unjust alike. If God is going to work out an equitable system of reward and punishment, it will be in the next world, not in this one.

Another thing. In this story we're talking about family. Jacob's family.

Israel's family. Your family. My family. The family's wounds are not caused by God. Each family has to claim responsibility for its own wounds. But after claiming responsibility, what do we do with them? What do we do with the wounds that bind us? The brothers succumb to guilt and despair. Some of that guilt is appropriate. They are responsible for what they've done. But guilt that leads to despair is fatal, whereas guilt that leads to repentance and change can be healthy.

We do see some change in these brothers later in the story (44:30–33). But here the writer of Genesis is more interested in the change that takes place in Joseph. What does Joseph do with those wounds from the past? The writer says unashamedly that "he wept" (45:2; see also vv. 14–15). In fact the writer says that Joseph "wept so loudly that the Egyptians heard him."

What do you reckon is in those tears? Memory? Memory often conjures tears. Maybe Joseph is remembering all the harm he and his brothers did to each other. Remembering the betrayals, the deceit, the hostility, the breaches of trust. Remembering all the wounds they inflicted on each other. I bet Joseph is even weeping in acknowledgment of all the wrong he did.

Our memory of all the past hurts we've felt and all the hurts we've inflicted on others is painful. Memory haunts us. It brings up fear, remorse, guilt and confusion over the tragedy of the past.

I have a friend who used to live near me. For many years I was close to every member of his family. About twenty years ago he and his first wife divorced. Would you believe that his sister, blaming only him for the failure of the marriage, didn't talk to her brother for more than twenty years? Not long before my friend's father died, I said to him, "Bill, reckon Sarah and Clark will ever reconnect? It's hard to believe this is all about his divorce twenty years ago."

The old father told me something I'd never heard before. "It's not just about the divorce," he said. "It's about something that happened forty years ago. Clark and his youngest brother, Tim, whom you never knew, were skiing on Lake Hartwell. Clark was pulling Tim, who was an expert skier and swimmer. But Tim went down and never came back up. He drowned in Lake Hartwell. He was Sarah's closest brother. They were inseparable growing up. I think Sarah has always blamed Clark for Tim's death."

Yes, memory haunts us. Memory brings up demons from the past that we never completely conquer. I am happy to say that Sarah and Clark have reconnected. But of course that family still wrestles with demons.

What do we do with those demons? What do we do with memories that haunt us? Let go of them? It's not possible. We never forget. Forgive maybe, but never forget. Eudora Welty is right: "The memory can be hurt, time and again. But in that may lie its final mercy. As long as it is vulnerable to the present moment, it lives for us."[2]

How do we make memory live for us? By being honest about the past—its hurts, pains, wounds—and then by mustering all the courage we can find to redeem the present. Notice what Joseph says about the past. Weeping, he says to his brothers, "Do not be distressed or blame yourselves for selling me into slavery here; it was to save lives that God sent me ahead of you.... God sent me on ahead of you to ensure that you will have descendants on earth, and to preserve for you a host of survivors. It is clear that it was not you who sent me here, but God, and he has made me Pharaoh's chief counselor, lord over his whole household and ruler of all Egypt" (vv. 5–8).

Do you think God was behind it all? Behind the deceit, the treachery, the abuse, the abandonment? Was God behind all that? I don't think so. I don't think God causes that in families. But we might as well be honest: all of that junk is in families. In all families. I wouldn't say God is behind all of that. But I do believe God somehow finds a way to get down in the middle of it. And maybe by getting down in the middle of all our junk, God is able to use our sordid past in such a way as to redeem our present.

But you know, Joseph's take on events is downright daring. It takes guts to look for God in our wounded past. Joseph's interpretation is that

God has been there all along. And with that kind of daring faith, Joseph can treat those wounds from the past with the balm of forgiveness and begin a process of healing for a new future. A new future for him and his family.

What do we do with memory? What do we do with those wounds from our tragic family history? According to this story, the first thing we must do is identify the wounds. There's no sense in pretending they don't exist. They are in everybody's family. But then, after identifying the wounds that bind us, we muster the courage to forgive, as Joseph did, and thereby bind those wounds.

Being honest about the family's wounds is no easy matter. It wasn't easy for Joseph and his brothers. It's not easy for us. Some of the past is not easy to forgive. Some of it is not easy to love. But understand, we're not called to be any more perfect than this tragically flawed family whose story is somehow like our own. And as Carlyle Marney once said, "We do not let our failure to love perfectly keep us from loving as best we can. To be responsible means to face all that makes us shamed and uncomfortable, and to continue to press for the love that lies beneath the woe."[3]

In the face of hurt and despair invoked by the past, Joseph and his brothers find the courage to press for the love that lies beneath the woe. When all is said and done, searching for this love may well be the last good hope available to the family. The family of Jacob. The family of Israel. Maybe even your family. And mine. All of us together pressing for the love that lies beneath the woe, together binding the family wounds.

Notes

1. This line, "the love that lies beneath the woe," was adapted from Melville's *Moby Dick* by Carlyle Marney, who made use of it in a sermon preached more than thirty years ago. Reference to the sermon, "When Wisdom Flirts with Madness," is found in John Carey, *Carlyle Marney: A Pilgrim's Progress* (Macon, GA: Mercer University Press, 1980), p. 125.

2. *U.S. News and World Report*, 15 February 1993, p. 81.

3. Quoted in Carey, *Carlyle Marney*, p. 125.

COMMENT

Family therapists have long called attention to the fact that families oper-
ate as complex systems. Over time, families develop their own ways for
managing crises, settling arguments, and relating in general. Family
members pass these attitudes and behaviors along from one generation
to the next. Small wonder, then, that a young parent acknowledges the
terrible truth, "I've become my father!" or "I'm just like my mother!" We
almost automatically fall into the same patterns of relating to each other
and rearing children that we experienced in our family of origin.
Changing the pattern requires sustained and intentional effort. Even
then, the patterns are so ingrained that change is exceedingly difficult.

John Mark Jones draws on this aspect of the Joseph story to proclaim
his message. He focuses on the relationships within Joseph's family and
the ways in which they sought to deal with their shared wounds.

PROBLEM

"You only hurt the ones you love." So the saying goes. That's the crux of
Jones's sermon. At the very beginning he raises the question he seeks to
address: "Do families ever change? The wounds we gave and received
years ago never quite heal, do they?" All families wrestle with that issue.
Some of the wounds we inflict on those nearest us are minor. They sting
for a while, but we move on. We are also capable, however, of inflicting
enormous pain on those closest to us. Living with the pain, getting
beyond it, and healing it require much from everyone involved. And certainly, for the person or the family of faith, another question arises:
Where is God in all of this?

Most of us are accustomed to hearing the story of Joseph's reunion
with his brothers as an affirmation of God's hidden ways in this world. In
Genesis 45:7–8 Joseph gives a ringing declaration of God's providence:
"God sent me before you to preserve for you a remnant on earth, and to
keep alive for you many survivors. So it was not you who sent me here,

COMMENT

but God." Jones shifts the focus from Joseph's understanding of what God has done to what has happened in this twisted family. God has preserved the family by working in Joseph's life, to be sure. But the wounds are still there. The good ending to a terrible story does not mean that everything is automatically all right. No matter what God has done—what will this family do? How will they live out together the gracious act of God that enabled their very survival?

TEXT

Before getting into the text for the sermon, Jones devotes a great deal of time establishing the context. The reunion between Joseph and his brothers only makes sense if one understands all that has transpired. The point Jones wishes to elaborate in the sermon itself makes sense only if the family history is unpacked. So, throughout the first half of the sermon, he draws on previous portions of the Joseph story, relating key incidents that highlight the problems within this family.

For example, in Genesis 37 Joseph's brothers are very intentional in selling Joseph to the Midianite traders. Their action in the story underscores the point Jones wants to make. This family operates by treachery and deceit.

By relating such episodes from the family's earlier history, Jones sets the stage for the text. Both Joseph and his brothers have a lot at stake in this meeting. By choosing to reveal his identity, Joseph takes a tremendous risk. He will not only bring himself into the open, but he will bring all the hurts into the open as well. For the brothers, this is a terrifying prospect. Will the past be used against them, or will Joseph work with them to create a new and different future? As Jones relates Joseph's bold moves, he appeals to Genesis 45 and Joseph's actions there to suggest some ways families might move to heal some of their self-inflicted wounds.

PROCLAMATION

Near the close of the sermon, Jones announces the good news in the story. Joseph declares that God was able to work and do something good with all the deceit and treachery. God used the brothers' evil intent to spare the entire family. Jones is careful to say that God is not the cause of all ill-will and double-dealing. He does, however, declare that nothing is beyond God's power to use, not even a dysfunctional family: "I do believe God somehow finds a way to get down in the middle of it. And maybe by getting down in the middle of all our junk, God finds a way to use our sordid past in such a way as to redeem our present."

That's the gospel for all of us. God is present, not as the cause of all the junk families dish out. God is present not to inflict some harsh penalty. No, God is present to redeem. God puts himself right in the middle of all our bad stuff to do something good with it. In making this affirmation, Jones highlights the Incarnation and gives it center stage in his sermon. His title can thus be read on two different levels. Despite all the ways in which we hurt each other in families, we still love one another. We are always working to uncover and bring to light the love we have for one another that lies just beneath the surface of some of the hurtful things we do. But Jones also reminds us that there is an even greater love beneath our woe—the love of God. God is in the middle of all our junk. If we work alongside God, our junk can be redeemed through God's love. God's love is just beneath the surface of all our woes. Certainly this affirmation lies at the heart of all genuinely Christian preaching.

The other good news this sermon brings is an honest admission that all families are flawed. In this day and age perfection is peddled as the norm for everything. Nothing is any good unless it is the absolute best—not even marriages and families. Consequently, we wrestle with unreasonable expectations about how well we should manage family life. The truth is none of us gets it right all the time. We need to own that. In doing so, we open ourselves to the love that lies beneath our own woe and the redemptive possibilities that love brings.

RESPONSE

Without a doubt, this is a very pastoral sermon. A very passionate one, too. I get the impression that Jones is addressing a particular situation that has developed within his congregation. Within this framework, he calls on everyone "to muster all the courage we can find to redeem the present." He encourages families to keep working at loving one another, even if they don't do it perfectly. He wants his hearers to keep their eyes open for signs of God's presence in the midst of their imperfection.

SUGGESTIONS

- Researchers tells us that most people today have opted out of church not because of hostility but out of the sense that the church has nothing to say to them. This sermon is a good example of how the church's proclamation can touch real life. It is a very practical sermon that doesn't resort to an oversimplified outline of the "five steps you can take to fix your family." The sermon does, however, utilize a biblical story to illuminate the difficulties modern families face while affirming the nearness of God. Review your preaching from the last six months. How many sermons have been directed at the needs faced by your parishioners? Reread the stories of the Old Testament patriarchs in terms of their family relationships. Such a reading will no doubt provide a wealth of relevant preaching material.
- Have you ever preached a sermon directed primarily at an individual or a family? Although such sermons must be delivered with a great deal of tact and sensitivity, I am convinced that when we do seek to preach to "somebody," we wind up speaking to everybody.
- Listen for the ways in which your people speak of how God has been present, even in the messiest and most difficult situations of their lives. Their testimonies will enable you to put more flesh on your proclamation of the gospel.
- The text of this sermon uncovers the hard truth that even when God acts, not everything is resolved. Not everything is made right. Old wounds may lie beneath the surface. Difficult challenges often remain. We still have to live with others. We still have to do our part. Too often our preaching gives the impression that God will

take care of everything, and we fail to address questions of responsibility. We don't always make clear God's part and our part. Examine your own preaching to see if you have emphasized one aspect at the expense of the other.

William J. Ireland, Jr.

C O M M E N T

A SURPRISING UNCONVENTIONAL FRIEND

LUKE 19:1–10

REV. DR. DAVID L. WILLIAMSON
FIRST PRESBYTERIAN CHURCH OF HOLLYWOOD
HOLLYWOOD, CALIFORNIA

A SURPRISING UNCONVENTIONAL FRIEND

LUKE 19:1–10

Today we come to the end of our series, "Face to Face with Jesus: Life-Changing Encounters." The wonderful hymn we have just sung, "O the Deep, Deep Love of Jesus," is a summary of what we have observed and experienced in these readings from Luke, the book which one author calls "the Gospel of contagious joy."[1]

Last week I asked you the question, Is it possible to keep all of the commandments and miss the kingdom? This week I want to ask you, Is it possible to keep none of the commandments and enter the kingdom? To ask the question another way: Who do you think of as the most unlikely candidate for church membership? Who is the most unlikely person to get into the kingdom of God, to receive eternal life? Last week, we talked about the most likely candidate who missed out! This week, we look at the least likely candidate and what happens to him in his face-to-face encounter with Jesus.

When I was a child, my mother warned me about the friends that I might make. I have passed that kind of encouragement and instruction on to my children. She also taught me the Sunday school song,

Zacchaeus was a wee little man,

A wee little man was he.

He climbed up in a sycamore tree,

For the Lord he wanted to see.

And as the Savior passed that way,

He looked up in the tree,

And said, "Zacchaeus, you come down,

For I'm going to your house for tea.

(That must have been a British translation!)

There was some incongruity between my mother's teaching about friends and her encouraging me to learn and sing that song. She would lovingly approve whenever I sang that song in her presence. But if I had actually brought a Zacchaeus home with me to be my friend, she definitely would not have approved.

In this series of sermons, we have been looking at the surprising friends Jesus made, and also at the people he let slip away—like the Pharisees and the rich young ruler. Jesus' friends include this rag-tag collection of disciples, a leper, a pagan army officer, a woman of the street—and now Zacchaeus. Frederick Buechner says, "Zacchaeus makes a good one to end with because in a way he can stand for all the rest. He's a sawed-off little social disaster with a big bank account and a crooked job, but Jesus welcomes him aboard anyway, and that's why he reminds [us] of all the others too."[2] And perhaps he reminds us of ourselves. This strange group all became friends—surprising, unconventional friends with one who was himself a surprising unconventional friend. That friendship transformed Zacchaeus's life.

Let us put ourselves back into the scene. Jesus is on his way from Galilee to Jerusalem. His route follows the Jordan Valley south until it intersects in Jericho with a road heading west, up the Wadi Kelt to Jerusalem. Jericho is an extraordinary place—a luxurious resort town, an oasis, a garden city much like our Palm Springs and Coachella Valley, La Quinta or, for some of you, PGA West. The stately palms can be seen from a great distance, and as you get close, notice the fig and citrus groves and the beautiful rose gardens.

Jericho was such a delightful resort city that Herod made it his winter capital, and officials from Rome visited it for winter vacations. Today, Jericho is still a beautiful oasis, but it is a poor West Bank town which happens to be the capital of the Palestinian state. And there is just one sycamore tree left in Jericho.

On the way into the city, Jesus meets the rich young ruler, our disappointed hero from last week. After that encounter, recorded in Luke 18:18–30, he meets a blind man begging by the side of the road, whom he instantly heals. There is a growing excitement around Jesus as he comes into Jericho and keeps going on his way towards Jerusalem. Enthusiasm builds into a paradelike atmosphere—crowds praising God and cheering for Jesus. You would think he was running for office or something—which is exactly what the people around him wanted him to do.

A notorious, wealthy resident of Jericho wants to get in on the action, to see Jesus for himself. But there is a problem. He is a very short person, "vertically challenged," we might say. He can't see a thing except the backs of other people's shoulders. But he is resourceful and determined. He acts like a kid again and climbs up into a sycamore tree, where he crawls way out on a limb to catch a bird's-eye view of the approaching entourage. What a funny, strange sight that must have been. This short scoundrel, the richest man in town, all dressed up in his Armani suit, hanging on a limb for dear life, eyes squinting, looking down the road.

Then it happens. Just as Jesus passes under the tree, he suddenly stops and looks up. There is Zacchaeus! I imagine that as their eyes met, that limb started to shake like crazy, until Zack gained his composure long enough to hear Jesus invite himself to Zacchaeus' home for dinner.

"'Get down out of there in a hurry,'" Jesus says. "'I am spending tonight with you,'" Buechner describes the scene, "whereupon all Jericho snickered up their sleeves to think he didn't have better sense than to invite himself to the house of a man that nobody else would touch with a ten-foot pole."[3] Zack climbed out of that tree hardly believing his good luck, delighted to take Jesus home with him. (I imagine that as they head off, the word back at his home among his servants is, "Guess who's coming for dinner?") Meanwhile those who remained behind are startled and dumbfounded, shaking their heads indignantly and grumping to themselves. "What business does Jesus have getting cozy with this crook? Such association is highly indecent. It is politically incorrect."

The Scripture says that Zacchaeus stands in front of Jesus, a little stunned, and stammers out his generous, spontaneous response, "Master I will give away half of what I possess to the poor, and if I have cheated anyone I will give back four hundred percent." (The law only required a 20 percent interest on gain acquired improperly. Zacchaeus promised 400 percent!) Talk about a surprise. Talk about impact. Talk about change. I like to think it happened immediately, right there on a street corner in a resort city, under a big sycamore tree. A life was changed. Zacchaeus found reordered values, new direction, and a friendship that would last for eternity. "Today is Zack's salvation day," Jesus said. And turning to the startled, grumping crowd, he announced, "I have come to seek out, to find and to restore the lost."

Unlike the image suggested by the little Sunday school song, Zacchaeus is a scoundrel. He is a bad dude, a sinner, a chief of sinners. He was considered a traitor to his nation, to his people and to his faith, because he victimized his own people. We know that he was the chief tax collector, not just another agent. Rome gave him a certain fee to collect from the people, but he and his agents would keep whatever additional money they could extort. He was robbing the people blind and everyone knew it, but nobody could stop him. Zacchaeus had to be the least popular, most despised man in Jericho, the last person ever to be invited to a social gathering.

He is interesting as well. Whatever made Zacchaeus take this kind of drastic action, we don't know. Perhaps there was a deep hunger, a longing and yearning in his heart to meet the Savior. Maybe he desired friendship, more meaning for his life. Perhaps he sensed a need for forgiveness.

Or perhaps he simply wanted to find something more. He certainly had a tremendous amount of curiosity. He heard about this itinerant preacher that some thought to be the Messiah, and his curiosity pushed him up a tree, out on a limb!

Whatever the reason, Zacchaeus takes the initiative. He seeks Jesus, who says, "Seek and you shall find." There is a determination and resourcefulness that leads Zacchaeus to go to great lengths, to take risks, to get way out on a limb, out in full view of all the people who hated him. He is so eager to see Jesus that he doesn't care what happens or what other people think. His action reveals a profound humility, openness and authenticity.

In his humility, in his openness to God and God's grace, Zacchaeus allows God to change him instantly, thoroughly, head-to-toe—and to checkbook! Zack is a contrast with the rich young ruler. Whereas the rich young ruler was a good, righteous and acceptable person who met Jesus and went away sad, clutching his wealth, Zacchaeus (also rich) is an unrighteous, unacceptable sinner who met Jesus and went away rejoicing with his hands empty but his heart full. The rich young ruler clung to his wealth, trying to protect his reputation and save himself. He was full of pretense. Zacchaeus had no pretense whatsoever. He risked his reputation, gave his wealth away, and allowed Christ to save him. The rich young ruler missed the kingdom of God by an inch; Zacchaeus makes it by a mile.

What are some of the lessons for us in Zacchaeus's face-to-face meeting with Jesus? First, there is hope for us, for each of us. God loves scoundrels. He loves sinners. We have seen it before. We have observed it in other face-to-face encounters with Jesus, and we see it again here. Jesus—what a friend for sinners! So, there is hope for me, a sinner. There is hope for all of us who recognize our need. "For the Son of Man came to find and to restore, to seek and to save the lost." Take heart, dear friends. No one, not a one of you, is too bad, too far away. It's never too late. We can claim that for ourselves. "Just as I am, without one plea./O Lamb of God, I come."

Second, notice the importance of anticipation, of taking initiative, of taking risks, of being resourceful. Anticipation is always crucial. Look at athletics. A batter needs to anticipate where the pitch is coming. Fielders anticipate where a ball is going to be hit. Skiers anticipate where they are going to carve their next turn. Runners anticipate the starter's pistol so that they can explode off the starting block. A football linebacker has to anticipate where the hole is going to open so he can fill it.

In the spiritual realm, anticipation puts us in the place where Jesus can meet us and surprise us. Are you anticipating God's speaking to you in a new and different way, in the life of our church, in your own relationship with God? Are you ready for God to do something new in your life? Be an initiator, a risk-taker, a resourceful Christian seeking the Lord who wants to give us the kingdom. Reach out for the living Christ, the one who himself reaches out and seeks us.

Third, we discover in this passage the importance of welcoming Jesus into our homes and into our hearts with gladness and celebration. I am called to make my home a place where Jesus can be a welcome guest for each member of my family. God also calls me to have a welcoming attitude toward all, for God welcomes everyone into a relationship with him. God calls me to make my home a place where all can feel at home, and no one is excluded because of social standing, race, ethnicity or political persuasion. God calls me to have a house, a home, a relationship that is open to sinners and saints alike.

We also learn from Zacchaeus not only to let God love us, but to let God change us. Zacchaeus encountered Jesus face-to-face and it turned his world upside down. We, too, need to encounter Jesus and allow ourselves to be changed, to be transformed from caterpillars to butterflies, from scoundrels to servants. In fact, we are called to change not just once, but again and again. How does God want you to change today?

It's football season again, and we have the annual wish for change that the *Peanuts* character Charlie Brown goes through in his relationship with Lucy. Charlie hopes that this year Lucy will not be her scoundrel self by pulling the football away as he comes running down the field to kick it. In one of those comic strip episodes, Lucy says, "Ecclesiastes chapter three, 'To everything there is a season, a time to be born, a time to die, a time to plant, a time to pluck up, a time to weep, a time to laugh, a time to mourn, a time to dance, a time to love, a time to hate, a time for war, a time for peace.'" Charlie Brown is convinced that this time Lucy really has changed her heart and her life. So he comes charging down the field to kick the football—and Lucy pulls the football back! Splat goes Charlie Brown—again! In the last frame, unrepentant Lucy says, "and a time to pull the football away." Charlie Brown asks, "How long, O Lord?"

I wonder if the Lord sometimes says that to us as he looks at our hesitation to allow him into our lives to change us the way he intends.

As much as we can learn from Zacchaeus, I invite you, dear friends, to take a look at the other person in the story, the key and central person. Take a look at Jesus. "Turn your eyes upon Jesus./Look full in his wonderful face." I invite you to see, to hear, to feel his presence, to experience your own face-to-face encounter with him, to discover who Jesus is. I invite you right now to do just that. If you will, close your eyes, and allow the picture of Jesus' coming to Zacchaeus to be the picture of Jesus coming to you. Allow that scene to develop before you in your mind's eye. If it's more comfortable to look up at the cross, do so, but allow God to speak to you in a new and special way as you put yourself into this scene. Keep your attention there for as long as you want, to see, hear and encounter Jesus now.

As you focus on this scene, you will notice Jesus' tremendous popularity. There is something naturally attractive about this One. People are drawn to Jesus, attracted to him. And so a crowd gathers.

Then notice that Jesus is a friend of sinners. The Lord of surprises continues to surprise us with his choice of friends—questionable, even despicable persons. Jesus is the friend of the friendless. And in a few days he will be betrayed and denied by the respectable ones!

Abraham Lincoln once received a letter appealing for a pardon, but it was not accompanied by any letter of recommendation. He asked his assistant, "Has this man no friends?"

The assistant said, "No, sir, he hasn't."

Lincoln replied, "Then I will be his friend."

For us, Jesus is our friend, even when we have no one to commend us to God.

As you watch Jesus come to meet you, recognize that he has not come to condemn. Jesus doesn't use his face-to-face encounters to scold. You see, there is something far more important to Jesus. What is important to Jesus is the relationship that he wants to have with Zacchaeus, with every individual, with each of us.

Remember what Jesus asked the woman caught in the act of adultery after her accusers left: "Is there no one left to condemn you?"

"No one, sir," she answered.

"Well, then," Jesus said, "I do not condemn you either. Go, but do not sin again" (John 8:10–11, TEV).

"In Christ," Paul tells us, "God was reconciling the world to himself, not counting their trespasses against them" (2 Cor. 5:19, RSV).

Notice how Jesus pays attention to the individual. Jesus spots Zacchaeus in the midst of the crowd. In the midst of the crowd, Jesus responds to one woman with a hemorrhage (Mark 5:24–34). Someone has said that Jesus did not die for *us*—the world as the conglomerate mass—but for *each of us* as individuals. In the midst of our world, Jesus spots us. Listen as he calls that one out of the crowd by name! "Zacchaeus, come down." Jesus knows us by name! Jesus knows and cares for our individual uniqueness. He invites us to a relationship with him on a first-name basis.

When Jesus invites us to dinner, to fellowship around the table, to a close and intimate friendship, he says, "I no longer call you servants.… Instead, I have called you friends.… Greater love has no one than this, that he lay down his life for his friends. You are my friends" (John 15:15, 13, 14, NIV).

Jesus is also the One who produces change. Contrary to modern pessimism, people can and do change. Even though psychology tells us that we are resistant, and Scripture reminds us that it is difficult to change,

God can produce genuine and lasting change. And God does! In the individuals Jesus met, he produced change, sometimes instant and spontaneous, sometimes gradual and sustained, but change nevertheless.

So, turn your eyes upon Jesus and look full in his wonderful face. Let the Jesus who came to Zacchaeus come to you. Jesus and Zacchaeus find in each other a surprising, unconventional friend. Zacchaeus finds Jesus the friend of the friendless and the friend of saints alike. Can you find Jesus to be the friend who sticks closer than a brother, who lays down his life for his friends? Can you see him come to you today? Can you hear him call you by name? Can you hear him ask to be a guest at your home today, for the rest of your life and for eternity? Can you and I allow that friendship with him to change and continually transform us? The Son of Man came to seek and to save, to befriend and to change each of us.

Notes

1. John Killinger, *A Devotional Guide to Luke: The Gospel of Contagious Joy* (Waco, TX: Word Books, 1980).

2. Frederick Buechner, *Peculiar Treasures: A Biblical Who's Who* (San Francisco: Harper & Row, 1979), p. 180.

3. Ibid.

COMMENT

I love the tune and lyrics of Carole King's hit song of the early 1970s, "You've Got a Friend." When I hear the James Taylor recording played on the radio, my ears perk up and I'm nostalgic. We all need friends. God created us to find fulfillment in relationships. It's energizing and comforting to be able to assure another person with the words, "You've got a friend." In this sermon, David Williamson invites his listeners to claim a deep and abiding relationship with a surprising unconventional friend. He makes this proclamation with creativity, clarity and understanding.

PROBLEM

The problem addressed by this sermon is implied but not directly stated. It is the problem of establishing a meaningful, intimate, lasting relationship. The final sentence of the sermon proclaims God's solution to this problem encountered by every human being. "The Son of Man came to seek and to save, to befriend and to change each of us." In this sentence, the preacher offers his listeners a compelling invitation to form a relationship with a surprising unconventional friend, Jesus Christ.

During the opening of the sermon, Williamson asks an interesting question: "Is it possible to keep none of the commandments and enter the kingdom?" In a way, this question also presents the problem which the sermon addresses. However, the preacher does not choose in the body of the sermon to follow the thread suggested by this question. Instead, he implies an answer as he develops the gospel truths from Luke's story of Zacchaeus, the little man up in the tree. It would be interesting for one to follow through on this thread as a subtheme. Is it possible to keep none of the commandments and enter the kingdom? The answer to this question would ultimately be "Yes." Life in the kingdom is not predicated on following the commandments, but on faith in the forgiving power of Jesus.

TEXT

Williamson does an excellent job of developing the text. He spends some important time placing the text into the context of Jesus' ministry. He emphasizes that the event is preceded by Jesus' encounter with the rich young ruler who could not follow Jesus because he loved his possessions too much. Bringing into play the surrounding events of a biblical text is an important way of leading listeners to see the truth of a text and fit it into the context of their own life situation. Williamson skillfully retells the story of Jesus' encounter with Zacchaeus. This helps us see points in the text with which we can identify. In some way, everyone is like Zacchaeus—seeking and searching for a more fulfilling and purposeful life. The beautiful part is that if Jesus can be so open as to accept a scoundrel like Zacchaeus, how much more will he be open to accept and love the listener.

The whole notion of "You've got a friend" permeates the retelling of this story. Like Zacchaeus, many hear about Jesus, but they seek to see and hear him within the safety of "tree branches" that mask their identity and minimize any personal risk. However, like Zacchaeus, some may discover that the tree limb is in reality the growing edge of life as Jesus saws off the limb and invites himself home to dinner. To faithful insiders, this may sound preposterous. The truth that Jesus dines with and befriends sinners is repelling to some of the stuffy faithful. The thought that the kingdom could be open to commandment breakers is offensive and heretical. But this is the core of the gospel proclaimed by Jesus in his treatment of Zacchaeus. Williamson brings this out beautifully in his treatment of the story.

In this sermon the preacher also treats the entire text. Not only does he tell of Jesus going to the home of Zacchaeus, but he relates Zacchaeus's contrite behavior. The tax collector is willing to make extraordinary retribution for his past acts of unfairness. The unconventional friendship of Jesus with Zacchaeus transforms his life. Jesus proclaims this renewal by saying, "Today salvation has come to the home of Zacchaeus." At the same time Jesus senses the shock and grumbling of the crowd. He uses this opportunity to teach when he says, "I have come to seek out, to find and restore the lost."

The preacher now offers a helpful summary: "Zacchaeus was changed thoroughly—from head-to-toe, and to checkbook." The transformation of Zacchaeus is a direct contrast to the rich young ruler in the preceding story. He was a commandment follower. But he could not part with his possessions. He loved them too much. Zacchaeus, on the other hand, was willing to sell out everything to invest in Jesus and his ministry.

PROCLAMATION

After retelling the Zacchaeus story, Williamson asks: "What are some of the lessons for us in this encounter?" The preacher proceeds to explore the event through two windows—the window of Zacchaeus' experience, and the window of Jesus' ministry and teaching in this situation.

One of the inspiring ways of viewing the gospel message in Scripture is by considering its impact on the lives of those who are touched by it. Zacchaeus' experience with Jesus is one of the most dramatic encounters recorded in the Gospels. Jesus' friendship prompts a complete turnaround in the life of a callous and devious tax-collector. This is indeed good news.

As Williamson explores the event from the perspective of Zacchaeus, he uncovers four lessons for us. First, Zacchaeus' story gives the listener hope. Jesus does not hate sinners. He comes "to seek and to save the lost." As the preacher puts it: "No one, not a one of you, is too bad, too far away." Our hope is that Jesus is "a surprising unconventional friend." The second thing the Zacchaeus narrative teaches is the importance of anticipation, taking the initiative—even in the face of risk. We are encouraged to place ourselves where Jesus can meet us and surprise us, even if it is up in a tree. Third, we learn from Zacchaeus the importance of welcoming God into our lives with gladness, and extending that welcome to other people. Finally, Zacchaeus teaches that God will turn our world upside down if we let him. Our hesitation may slow God down, but God is relentless in the pursuit to befriend us and change us.

C O M M E N T

RESPONSE

Williamson continues the sermon by inviting the listener to consider some lessons that emerge from looking at Jesus. He cleverly develops this concluding section of the sermon by taking the listener on a mind's-eye journey. "If you will, close your eyes and allow the picture of Jesus' coming to Zacchaeus to be the picture of Jesus coming to you." The preacher then colors in the picture of Jesus who stands before the listener. Jesus "is a friend of sinners and the friendless." He comes to establish a relationship. He is a friend who pays attention to the individuals and their needs, struggles and joys. He calls each person by their familiar first name and invites them to dine with him. Jesus is a friend who produces change and newness.

Williamson concludes with the familiar words of that wonderful hymn: "So, turn your eyes upon Jesus and look in his wonderful face...The Son of Man came to seek and to save, to befriend and to change each of us." In short, Jesus is a surprising unconventional friend. In this sermon, Williamson offers a gentle, attractive and easily understood invitation to life and the kingdom. There is an easy flow and natural continuity in the sermon. The preacher directs us on a journey in which we are able to befriend and be changed by Jesus. The good news to which we are invited to respond is: "You've got a friend."

The kingdom is ours not because we follow the commandments, but by the grace of God as we know it through our friendship with Jesus. And to go one step further, our friendship with Jesus leads us to live and behave in new ways—even to the extent of paying back multifold those whom we have offended. Friendship with Jesus leads us to live a step beyond the commandments.

SUGGESTIONS

- Use familiar stories and songs as points of connection with the listener. Williamson's use of the Sunday school song, "Zacchaeus was a wee little man," delightfully illustrates this suggestion.

- Retelling a Scripture story in a sermon helps bring the story and its truth to life. Work at creative ways to retell biblical narratives in language and images with which modern listeners can identify.
- When appropriate and useful, consider the "mind's-eye journey" approach. It is helpful to color in some of the images and actions for the listener. Note Williamson's use of this technique toward the end of his sermon.
- Use items from the popular media as familiar points of contact with listeners. "Peanuts" is used in this manner here, for example.
- In sermon preparation, it is always critical to consider the biblical context of the text. Many ideas flow from contextual insight. Additionally, identify the similarities between biblical times and the contemporary context of listeners.
- In a sermon like this, consider providing a real-life illustration of a modern-day Zacchaeus. Although Williamson did not do this in this sermon, such illustrations offer the listener helpful insight for real-life application.

Donald K. Adickes

LIFE AS IT IS SUPPOSED TO BE LIVED

PSALMS 1 & 2

REV. DR. GARY DENNIS
LA CANADA PRESBYTERIAN CHURCH
LA CANADA FLINTRIDGE, CALIFORNIA

LIFE AS IT IS
SUPPOSED TO BE
LIVED

PSALMS 1 & 2, NRSV

L ife as it is supposed to be lived. Isn't that what we all want? But
what is the key ingredient in finding that purpose and meaning?
How do we find it?

The wonderful children's books that C. S. Lewis wrote revolve
around that essential ingredient needed for life as it is supposed to be
lived. Take, for instance, the first book *The Lion, the Witch and the
Wardrobe.*[1] Four children, Peter, Edmund, Susan and Lucy, in 1940 go to
stay with their uncle to get away from the bombings of London.

As the children play in their uncle's huge country home, they acci-
dentally find a way into the magical land of Narnia. In Narnia it is always
winter and never Christmas because of the evil reign of the White Witch.
But the animals of Narnia, who can talk, explain to the children that the
Great Lion, the true ruler of Narnia, has returned and is once again on
the move. The reign of the White Witch is near its end.

The children react in different ways to hearing the name of Aslan, the
Great Lion. Peter, Susan and Lucy decide to find him as soon as possible.
But Edmund quietly slips off to find the witch who enslaves him and

threatens to kill him if he doesn't tell her where his brothers and sisters are, and about Aslan's return.

The other children find Aslan in time to fight in a great battle with the White Witch and her followers. Edmund is rescued. He asks for forgiveness, but according to the deep magic of Narnia he must be killed as a traitor. The breathtaking part of the story happens when Aslan offers to be sacrificed instead. Lucy and Susan then watch as the lion willingly surrenders to the White Witch who kills him with a stone knife on a great stone table.

But Aslan knew that according to a deeper magic, if a willing and perfect victim were sacrificed in a traitor's stead, the witch would not only lose her claim on the individual, but death would start working backwards. The Great Lion returns to life and leads the children and the others in a final victorious battle against the witch and her forces.

As the central reality in Narnia, Aslan creates life as it is supposed to be lived. But who is Aslan for you and me?

For the writers of the psalms, God is the central reality of life. To begin to live life as it is supposed to be lived, we must draw near to God. The psalms answer the question of how we do that in creative ways, particularly in one group of psalms which have been called psalms of orientation. Two of these are Psalms 1 and 2. Let us consider them together.

Look first at verse 3 of Psalm 1. Here the psalmist gives us an important suggestion for discovering more about life's meaning. The writer is describing people who live life as it is meant to be. He says,

> They are like trees
>   planted by streams of water,
> which yield their fruit in its season,
>   and their leaves do not wither.

I am fascinated by the image of the tree. It is as though the psalmist is telling us that our first step should be to find ourselves a tree, sit down in front of it, and look at it long and thoughtfully. Such contemplation can become a kind of prayer, moving us toward God, the central reality, and focusing us on life as it is meant to be lived.

The image of the tree also suggests to me that prayer, which is one way to move toward God, begins not with what we don't see, but with what we do see. That is, prayer begins in the senses. Prayer begins in the body and in our experience of the world around us. And that may mean that prayer, and our movement toward God, begins when we stub our toe or get slapped in the face by an enemy.

We make a big mistake in our relationship with God, one that will make us miss much of life's meaning, when we try to avoid pain and difficulty, or when we try to hide from God because things are going wrong or we are angry. The psalms show us that we need to face the tough circumstances of our life, confront them head on, and allow them to direct our attention to God.

Psalms 1 and 2 picture for us the two ways of dealing with life's problems. Psalm 1 suggests that we meditate on God's word in order to discover God's intention for our life. For those who live life as it was meant to be,

> their delight is in the law of the Lord,
> and on his law they meditate day and night (v. 2).

Psalm 2 describes the opposing way. The word translated "meditate" in Psalm 1:2 is the same Hebrew word translated "plot" in the first verse of Psalm 2:

> Why do the nations conspire,
> and the peoples plot in vain?

The Hebrew word means to murmur (aloud), to ponder, to study (in ancient times meditation often involved speaking aloud). Both *meditate* and *plot* describe the same action: an absorbed interest in and focus on the word of God. Psalm 1 directs us to meditate on the word of God with delight, receiving it as life-giving. Psalm 2 says there are a lot of people who do just the opposite. They plot against the same word.

One of the things we regularly have to decide is whether we are going to meditate or plot. I often have to make this decision in the middle of the night. Someone has done something to me that I think is unfair or spiteful. I wake up at two or three in the morning, and the first thing that comes to my mind is that person and what he or she has said or done. Usually, this thought is followed by a groan, because I know that if I let myself focus on what happened, I will begin to *plot*. I will begin to think about what I wish I had said or done. Then, I will become more and more agitated and will not go back to sleep for hours. The next day I will be grumpy at best. That's what plotting always does to me. It pushes me further from God.

Yet I can make another choice when that unfair something wakes me in the middle of the night. Rather than plotting, I can choose to meditate on God's word. I can say to myself, "I am not going to let myself think right now about what happened. There will be a better time for process-ing that." Instead, I can follow the suggestion of Psalm 1, so I often *medi-tate* by saying the Lord's Prayer over and over again.

Sometimes when I am really upset, I might have to say the Lord's Prayer for an hour before I can fall asleep again. But what a difference it makes to fall asleep after saying, "Our Father, who art in heaven," instead of plotting the hurt I want to do to another person.

Plotting moves us away from God. Meditating moves us toward God.

Interestingly, Psalm 2 takes us one step further in answering the question as to how life is supposed to be lived. The psalmist writes (in vv. 4–7) that God

who sits in the heavens laughs;
　　the Lord has them in derision.
Then he will speak to them in his wrath,
　　and terrify them in his fury, saying,
"I have set my king on Zion, my holy hill."

I will tell of the decree of the Lord:
He said to me, "You are my son;
    today I have begotten you."

Among many Jews by the time of Jesus, Psalm 2 was read as a "messianic" psalm. For them the psalm expressed the hope of the coming of an ideal king—a Messiah—in the tradition of King David of old. The early Christians in the New Testament believed that Jesus Christ was the fulfillment of Psalm 2 and other Old Testament expressions of messianic hopes and ideals. First-century Christians, and Christians throughout the ages, have proclaimed that words like these in Psalm 2 point to Jesus as the One who ultimately brought fulfillment of God's salvation and purpose. And so today, the words of this psalm point us to Jesus. Jesus is the one who is begotten by God, God's Son. Life as it is supposed to be is a life that is always moving toward Jesus our example, our Savior, "the pioneer and perfecter of our faith" (Heb. 12:2).

In Greek mythology, when Hercules wrestled with the giant Antaeus, he was not able to defeat him. Every time he threw him to the ground Antaeus arose stronger than before. But then he discovered that Gaea, the earth, was the mother of the giant, and that whenever her son fell back upon her bosom she gave him renewed strength. So Hercules changed his tactics. Lifting Antaeus high in the air, away from the source of his strength, Hercules held him there and crushed him.

In a way, this story is a parable of life as it is supposed to be lived. As children of God, when we let troubles cast us back upon the bosom of God, we too can rise with renewed strength. The day we realize that troubles, misfortunes, disappointments and handicaps are the stuff that throw us back upon Jesus where we can renew our strength, that is the day we will have discovered the key ingredient in life as it is supposed to be lived. Isn't that what we all want—to let everything that happens to us move us toward Jesus Christ?

You remember the Great Lion, Aslan—the ruler of Narnia. He offered himself to be sacrificed. He died. But in doing so, death itself started working backwards. Aslan returned to life and led the final battle against evil. In Narnia, Aslan created life as it is supposed to be lived.

In our real world of time, space and human history, God became flesh in Jesus Christ, dwelt among us, and became a servant obedient even to death on a cross. But God raised him from the dead and has highly exalted him as Lord of all. In Jesus Christ, God has not only shown us how life is supposed to be lived; he has made it possible to live that life. Jesus Christ makes it possible for us to live a new life each day. So let us look to Jesus. Let us come to him. Let all that happens in our lives move us toward Jesus Christ. Can we? Will we?

Note
1. C. S. Lewis, *The Lion, the Witch and the Wardrobe* (New York: Macmillan, 1950).

COMMENT

Life as it is supposed to be lived. Wouldn't we all like to know the secret behind that phrase? The sermon title alone implies a promise—not only that an ideal is possible, but that in a few short moments, we are going to find out *how.* If Gary Dennis wasn't in ministry, he might have found his calling in marketing. Who *doesn't* want to know the secret behind "life as it is supposed to be lived"?

Dennis begins with a simple question, but one that strikes at a universal longing within us all. For those who've known heartbreak, uncertainty, confusion—and who hasn't—that simple statement, "life as it is supposed to be lived," hooks us immediately. And where better to go to find an illustration of life as it is supposed to be lived than within the pages of a children's story? The stories of Aslan and the *Chronicles of Narnia* have captivated readers for nearly fifty years.

BE SIMPLE. BE ACTIVE. BE IMAGINATIVE.

Nearly every minister has heard parishioners comment, "I get more out of the children's sermon than I do the *real* sermon!" Those comments are humbling for the person filling the pulpit week after week. For a story to hold a child's attention or for a sermon to speak to adults, the storyteller or preacher must do three things: Be simple, be active, be imaginative. Gary Dennis does all three in this sermon.

Dennis uses a very simple structure: an introduction that sets up the problem; a biblical text that addresses the problem; a practical application drawn from the text; and the solution to the question he initially raised. Simple, active, imaginative.

After raising a question that hooks our interest and illustrating it from a children's story, Dennis walks us through Psalms 1 and 2. This is an unusual pairing of biblical passages which the preacher uses to identify the problem and proclaim a good-news solution. He moves quickly through these texts, keeping the listener focused with frequent questions, and offering pragmatic theological observations along the way. We don't even get past verse 3 of the first psalm before Dennis states with sound-byte brevity four observations about prayer that could easily form the basis for a book, seminar or six-week class:

> Prayer...begins not with what we don't see, but with what we
>   do see.
> Prayer begins in the senses.
> Prayer begins in...our experience of the world around us.
> Prayer...begins when we stub our toe....

I'm not sure I've heard a better primer on prayer from the pulpit than these four observations. Dennis is following a carefully crafted progression in this sermon, one that the reader finds as easy to follow as counting 1-2-3. The strength of this "light" expository style is the simplicity, the pragmatic applications, and the clarity of the points made.

A common shortcoming in preaching is the lack of self-disclosure. Any preaching which lacks an appropriate use of self-revelation places the preacher above the text, and too many listeners simply "tune out" the words spoken from the pulpit. Dennis avoids this pitfall by including the honest, engaging distinction between "meditating" and "plotting." Again, he *actively* demonstrates the point he wants the reader to understand: "Plotting moves us away from God. Meditating moves us toward God.... Life as it is supposed to be lived is a life that is always moving toward Jesus."

With these words, Dennis has brought us to the punchline of the sermon. The point is made. The question is answered. Dennis doesn't over-conclude. He doesn't belabor the point. Again, he allows simplicity and clarity to work for him. Direct mail studies have shown that the average person has to see direct mail advertising at least three times before making a purchase. Educators say that learning takes place when we hear the same information with repetition. This sermon exemplifies what marketers and educators have long known: we don't get a message by hearing or seeing it only once. Dennis makes the point, clarifies the point, then allows the text to substantiate the point. He gives no more than four paragraphs to his conclusion—and we don't have to wonder what the "take-away" is: "The day we realize that troubles, misfortunes, disappointments and handicaps are the stuff that throw us back upon Jesus where we can renew our strength, that is the day we will have discovered the key ingredient in life as it is supposed to be lived."

C O M M E N T

SUGGESTIONS

- If you haven't read the *Chronicles of Narnia,* indulge yourself and do so. You owe it to yourself. You'll find them wonderfully entertaining, theologically stimulating, and tirelessly captivating.
- The four observations about prayer Dennis draws from Psalm 1 could easily form the basis for a sermon or a series of sermons. No matter how long we have been people of faith, we still long for helpful specifics when it comes to prayer.
- What is *your* favorite children's story? *The Velveteen Rabbit? The Hobbit? Robinson Crusoe?* Let it inform your preaching. If you can't think of some good children's stories, start asking the experts—the kids around you.
- "Plotting moves us away from God. Meditating moves us toward God." Take this key point from Dennis' sermon and develop your own sermon or series of sermons on prayer. What biblical texts might form the basis for such a sermon or series on prayer?

Debra K. Klingsporn

WHAT REALLY CHANGES PEOPLE?

LUKE 19:1–10

REV. RONALD W. HIGDON
BROADWAY BAPTIST CHURCH
LOUISVILLE, KENTUCKY

REV. RONALD W. HIGDON

WHAT REALLY CHANGES PEOPLE?

LUKE 19:1–10, NRSV

O n the outskirts of Jericho Jesus heals a blind man and, Luke tells us, all the people who saw it praised God. Jesus then enters Jericho and invites himself to Zacchaeus's home for lunch, and all the people who saw it grumbled.

We like to see God working in ways we expect. We are taken aback when our religious presuppositions are challenged. That is exactly what Luke does in what we call chapter 19 of his Gospel, which is really part and parcel of his continuing story of Jesus told in one whole piece.

If Fred Sanford of the 1970s *Sanford and Son* television program had been in the crowd in Jericho that day, he would have said, "Elizabeth, this is the big one." Unfortunately, we have removed the story of Zacchaeus from its context and it has lost much of its punch. Punch it has. It literally knocks the stuffing out of a safe and predictable religion. Of course, that is what Jesus keeps doing in the Gospels. That is what he keeps doing today.

Luke uses only a few words to set the stage for what his readers think is coming.

"He [Jesus] entered Jericho and was passing through it. A man was there named Zacchaeus; he was a chief tax collector and was rich" (vv. 1–2).

That's all early hearers of this Gospel had to know. For someone to be working for Rome collecting taxes was bad enough, but the taxation system was known for its abuses. Jericho was a wealthy town, a major trade center, and therefore one of the greatest taxation centers in Palestine.

Rome had what might be called the original flat tax system—there was a flat-out tax on everything! There were stated taxes of fixed amounts: a poll tax, a ground tax (one-tenth of all grain grown and one-fifth of wine and oil), and an income tax. These taxes were levied at set amounts. The real problem lay with the second group of taxes: duties on almost everything. The Roman government put these taxes out to bid; the highest bidder had the privilege of collecting them. He simply paid Rome the agreed amount and kept everything above what he collected. Zacchaeus is called a chief tax collector which means he had subordinate collectors working for him.

And they were a busy group of people. A tax was payable for using the main roads, the harbors, and the markets. A tax was payable on a cart, on each wheel of the cart, and on the animal which drew it. There was a purchase tax on certain articles, and there were import and export duties. A tax collector could stop a man on the road, make him unpack his bundles and charge him just about whatever he wanted to. If the man could not pay, sometimes the tax collector would offer to lend him money at an exorbitant rate of interest.[1]

When Luke tells us that Zacchaeus was a chief tax collector and was rich, it is obvious what Zacchaeus had been up to. In first-century Palestine, robbers, murderers, and tax collectors were classified together.[2] Zacchaeus was hated and rightly so!

There was a movie some years ago called *Waiting for the Light*. The story centers on two children who encounter a truly unhappy and angry man whose yard contains apple trees which no one is allowed to pick. In attempting to pick some of the apples, the children have a combative encounter with the owner. They decide to get even by rigging a ghostly experience in his yard. Their trick backfires and the man thinks he has seen an angel. His apple orchard makes the national news and people come from everywhere to see the site of a modern miracle. In the course of the movie there is a transformation. The final scene depicts this man smiling and lovingly giving a basket of apples to the children. One of the family members utters the clincher of the movie, "Now, that's a real miracle!"

When I compare the healing of the blind man on the outskirts of Jericho with what happened to Zacchaeus, I look at Zacchaeus and say, "Now, that's a real miracle!" I think that's really what Luke wants us to see. He tells us that Zacchaeus is a chief tax collector after the disciples hear Jesus say, "Indeed, it is easier for a camel to go through the eye of a needle than for someone who is rich to enter the kingdom of God" (Luke 18:25). Surely we have an impossible situation when Jesus and Zacchaeus meet. We know what the outcome is going to be; at least that is what Luke wants us to think.

Many have pointed out that the hero of the story is Jesus. That is true, but I don't want you to forget what a brave man Zacchaeus was for even being in the crowd that day.

Zacchaeus so wanted to see Jesus that he risked mingling with the crowd, a very large crowd on its way to Jerusalem for the Passover Feast, a crowd that would take every opportunity to get in a few kicks—verbal and physical—at this hated tax collector. One author is certain that at the end of the day Zacchaeus was black and blue with bruises.[3] Zacchaeus may have climbed into a tree so that he could get a better view, but surely it was also one of the safest places he could be.

Because Zacchaeus was a tax collector, he was barred from the synagogue. It took real courage for such an outcast to mingle with those who truly felt he was unworthy of any kindness whatsoever.

Think, too, what courage it took for Jesus to do what he did. What Jesus did was shocking, bold, courageous, and unthinkable. He invited himself to the home of this outcast. And when he did, we are told that "all who saw it began to grumble," or you could say that "there was a general murmur of disapproval" (REB). The crowd plainly said, "He has gone to be the guest of one who is a sinner" (v. 7).

One writer gives this modern paraphrase, "When Jesus got to the tree, he looked up and said, 'Zacchaeus, hurry down. Today is my day to be a guest in your home.' Zacchaeus scrambled out of the tree, hardly believing his good luck, delighted to take Jesus home with him. Everyone who saw the incident was indignant and grumped, 'What business does he have getting cozy with this crook?'"[4]

Of course, that is always the business of Jesus. Getting cozy with those people whom others wouldn't touch with a ten-foot pole. Just think of all the respectable, deserving, safe people with whom Jesus could have gone home. Just think of how his approval rating in Jericho would have soared if on top of healing a blind man Jesus had followed the religious protocol of his day. But he had not come to play it safe. He had come to be about his Father's business. The Father's business had to do with sinners.

We must also note that Jesus never seemed to worry if people thought he was condoning sin because he ate with sinners. That's just the price you pay for helping people who really need help.

What is important in our story is that in the midst of the grumbling crowd a miracle happens—Zacchaeus is changed! Yes, I will admit, he was ready to be changed. Luke lets us know that by picturing Zacchaeus as a man so anxious to see Jesus that he runs ahead of the crowd and climbs up into a fig-mulberry tree. When Jesus tells him to hurry down so that he can go to his home, Zacchaeus hurries down, happy to welcome Jesus to his home.

Some commentators suggest that when Zacchaeus got to his house with Jesus, the murmur of the crowd became such a roar that Zacchaeus turned around and faced the crowd and made his startling announcement: "Look, half of my possessions, Lord, I will give to the poor; and if I have defrauded anyone of anything, I will pay back four times as much" (v. 8).

The crowd must have been awestruck. To give away half was one thing but to restore fourfold was indeed extraordinary. The law stated that if a person voluntarily confessed to wrongdoing, only the value of the original goods plus one-fifth had to be paid (Lev. 6:4–5). Zacchaeus was determined to do far more than the law demanded.[5]

The big question is: What changed Zacchaeus?

A *Peanuts* comic strip featuring Charlie Brown and Lucy have them standing behind a wall. Lucy, with elbows on the wall, says to Charlie Brown, "Are you interested in having me tell you something for your own good?"

"I'm not sure," replies Charlie Brown.

Lucy continues, "Well, if it will help you to make up your mind...I'd enjoy it, too!"

We rightly suspect that Lucy has more of her own good in mind than what is good for Charlie Brown. She is about to lay another word of condemnation on him which will make her feel better but which will not help Charlie Brown at all. Has Lucy ever helped Charlie Brown? It may seem a trivial question until we frame it in the light of our text: Did those who murmured and grumbled that day help Zacchaeus? Did their condemnation, even though true and justly deserved, produce a change in his life?

Condemnation is never a liberating word. But grace is. Grace offers possibilities that condemnation never offers. Condemnation only drives a person farther down. "You rotten, no-good sinner" is not a therapeutic word. This was never the technique Jesus used with sinners. Grace is the word which enables people to change.

I cannot imagine how Zacchaeus felt that day when Jesus stopped and looked up into the tree where he was literally out on a limb. Surely, many in the crowd thought, "Boy, is Jesus going to let him have it!" They could hardly wait to hear the words of condemnation, and were ready to cheer Jesus on. But instead of hearing what they expected, they heard words of grace: "Zacchaeus, hurry and come down; for I must stay at your house today."

I can imagine that for the first time in years Zacchaeus felt included. He felt he was a son of Abraham. He felt a sense of much-needed pride because Jesus, the great teacher and healer from Nazareth, had chosen him. Zacchaeus felt once more that he was a part of the human race. He was no longer an outcast.

One of the most insightful lines I have ever read is this one: "Giving advice is one thing; empowering a person to change is another."[6] Jesus empowered Zacchaeus to change by grace, acceptance and affirmation. Grace and acceptance and affirmation which came to Zacchaeus just as he was—a sinner.

The episode ends with Jesus' announcement, "Today salvation has come to this house, because he too is a son of Abraham. For the Son of Man came to seek out and to save the lost" (vv. 9–10).

I'm glad that as Jesus was entering Jericho he stopped and healed a blind man. In order to make it "understandable," many have tried to explain just how Jesus performed that kind of miracle. I'm especially glad that Jesus stopped and wrought a miracle in the life of Zacchaeus. That one is not so easy to explain.

Not many people thought Zacchaeus would ever change. We know people we don't think will ever change. Jesus stopped on his way to Jerusalem and offered the possibility for change through grace and acceptance. When people grumble and murmur today about a gospel of grace for those they feel are undeserving, I simply say, "Hey, why not give Jesus a chance? Nothing else has brought a change, why not give grace a try?"

I fear that a statement written years ago is still true today, "The Church has always been afraid of being as loving as its Master. We just cannot really believe that 'this Man receives sinners.' Still less can we really believe that he is the 'friend of sinners,' and on his own word, loves them as much as he loves the saints."[7]

Why not try love and grace and acceptance? Who knows what changes and miracles will happen? Maybe even in our own lives.

Notes

1. William Barclay, *The Gospel of Luke* (Philadelphia: Westminster Press, 1956), p. 61.
2. Ibid.
3. Ibid., p. 244.
4. Eugene H. Peterson, *The Message* (Colorado Springs: Navpress, 1993).
5. Barclay, p. 244.
6. Lowell D. Streiker, *Family, Friends, and Strangers* (Nashville: Abingdon Press, 1967), p. 63.
7. Leslie D. Weatherhead, *Time for God* (Nashville: Abingdon, 1967), p. 37.

COMMENT

The message of Jesus that is most conveniently forgotten or ignored by those who profess to follow him is that we must love our enemies and work to help sinners rather than just the people we like. It's hard to put that message into practice. It's much easier to sit in the same pew every week and talk to the same people. By addressing the topic of Jesus' tendency to make people uncomfortable, Ronald Higdon shows he knows the importance of reiterating the message that Jesus came to save sinners. That's not an easy or comfortable calling.

In the modern world, centuries removed from the Jesus of the Gospels, it's easy to become complacent and comfortable in our Christianity. But ease and comfort are not what Christianity is about. Nor is that what preaching is about. Part of the preacher's job is to pick up where Jesus left off and make the followers of Christ as uncomfortable as those who grumbled when Jesus embraced the sinning tax collector Zacchaeus. By inviting himself to the house of this wealthy man who was loathed by the people, Jesus incurred the criticism of the "righteous" ones of his day. It was a messy undertaking. Loving the unloved and the unlovable always is.

SAVING SINNERS, NOT JUST SAINTS

Proclaiming Jesus' affinity for sinners helps Christians recognize that sinners need an opportunity for salvation. That is what Jesus saw as his mission—welcoming home prodigal sons and daughters, not congratulating good people on their goodness. Higdon makes this point well with his insight that the healing of the blind man on the outskirts of Jericho, which is most impressive to the crowd, is not nearly so spectacular in proper context as Jesus' miracle of transforming the life of Zacchaeus. The problem is to make people see that they too need to extend forgiveness and grace to those who may seem undeserving.

UP A TREE AND OUT ON A LIMB

Higdon fully explores the imagery in the Zacchaeus story: Zacchaeus is up a tree and out on a limb. There is a tendency in retrospect to see Zacchaeus as a bland and kindly figure in need only of a mild nudge. But with his review of how tax collectors and the tax system of first-century Palestine operated, Higdon paints a grim picture of Zacchaeus and his actual standing in the community. The point is easy for modern-day readers to gloss over, even those who have an apocalyptic view of the Internal Revenue Service. Tax collectors in the Roman Empire were often unsavory characters and, among devout Jews in Palestine, they were regarded as outcasts and unprincipled collaborators with the godless Gentile Romans. Though Higdon briefly dips into a historical mode to recapture this context of civic mistrust in tax collectors, it is a very breezy treatment, not heavy-handed.

Think about the style and tone of this sermon and how it fits the story of Zacchaeus as told in the Gospel of Luke. Higdon does not cite heavy historical and sociological references from New Testament scholarship in his description of the tax system in Jericho. Most of his references in this sermon come from the medium of modern popular culture. He alludes to Fred Sanford, a television character, and to Charlie Brown, a cartoon character. He alludes to a line from an inspirational book and a movie with a syrupy plot. He makes sparse use of literary allusions, except to recite the text of a light poem he has used for wedding ceremonies. What's going on here? It seems to me that Higdon has chosen a sermon style that is easy on the ears, soft on the mind, and familiar to his audience. The sermon is not erudite or stuffy. It is down-to-earth and simple in its language, point and presentation. Yet it carries an important theological message that can touch the heart of listeners. The style and tone may not fit every preaching context. But the message is clearly present.

EXTENDING GRACE

Higdon calls on us as Christians to do for each other as Jesus did for Zacchaeus. That provides a concrete and pure example of how to apply the gospel in our everyday lives. By offering grace to the seemingly undeserving Zacchaeus, Jesus performed a miracle that all of us can perform. We may not be able to heal the blind, but the sharing of grace with others may be a more spectacular and spiritually useful miracle. Higdon writes that "people grumble and murmur today about a gospel of grace for those they feel are undeserving." The point of this sermon is that the story of Zacchaeus challenges us whenever we are tempted, for whatever reasons, to be stingy with the gospel. God's grace is an extravagant, free gift. Free to us, and free to others. It is to be shared freely.

SUGGESTIONS

- The preacher must know his or her audience as well as possible and know what approaches work best for that audience. Decisions about style, tone and presentation must be based on an awareness of the culture, demographics and proclivities of the congregation. An analysis of an issue that shows a familiarity with the works of the theologians of Yale, Oxford and Tubingen may work in some settings more effectively than allusions to Fred Sanford and Charlie Brown. It all depends. How would you describe your preaching context in sociological terms? Who are your people? How does this awareness influence the way you preach?

- In your preaching, provide background and context from the Scripture, but keep it simple. In this sermon, a few details on the penurious nature of the Roman tax collecting system restore a zing to the story that may be lost on modern readers. But these details do not sidetrack or derail the point of the story for the sake of biblical background information. How do you provide background and context for a text in your preaching? Do you tend to provide too much background, or not enough?

Greg Garrison

THE BEGETTING
OF JESUS

MATTHEW 1:1–17

REV. DR. MARTIN B. COPENHAVER
THE WELLESLEY CONGREGATIONAL CHURCH
WELLESLEY, MASSACHUSETTS

REV. DR. MARTIN B. COPENHAVER

THE BEGETTING
OF JESUS

MATTHEW 1:1–17, NRSV

T his may be the first time you have ever heard a sermon on this particular passage of Scripture. It may, perhaps, be the last. The opening of Matthew's Gospel is not one of those oft-repeated, beloved texts that brightens every Advent season. In fact, if truth be told, the genealogy of Jesus, placed so prominently at the very beginning of the first book of the New Testament, can be a bit of an embarrassment. This long list of "begats" is referred to quite often by those who want to point out the tedium of the Bible—all those names, many of which we have never encountered before and never will again, names without faces or stories, some of them virtually unpronounceable, tumbling one after another in quick succession.

I did hear one musical setting of this passage which delighted me, partly because it was such a surprise that a composer could do anything at all with such unpromising material. But when there is no accompanying music, the passage can seem about as interesting as reading the Manhattan telephone book. Even under the best of circumstances, reading someone's genealogy is like looking at their family slides, but without the benefit of pictures to break up the monotony.

Luke, who was more of a literary artist than Matthew, at least had the sense to write three action-packed chapters of his Gospel before introducing Jesus' genealogy. Luke waited until we were already hooked on the story before interjecting the stuff that might otherwise put us to sleep. Matthew, however, starts right off with the genealogy. He thinks it is that important. It is. The early church fashioned this genealogy so that it would be not only a summary of the history of Israel but also a kind of hologram that captures the whole gospel story. I want to demonstrate what I mean by that statement.

Most people have at least one famous ancestor. According to Matthew's genealogy, Jesus had quite a few. Two in particular stand out. They are two of the most important figures in all of Jewish history. Not wanting us to miss the point, Matthew does not wait for us to get to their names in the genealogy but instead mentions them right off in the very first sentence of the Gospel: "An account of the genealogy of Jesus the Messiah, the son of David, the son of Abraham."

It began with Abraham, as the whole of Jewish history begins there. Abraham was the great patriarch, the father of the Hebrew people. It was through Abraham that God promised to bless all the peoples of the earth. In fact, Abraham's place as father of the Hebrew people was so important that his descendants often referred to him simply as "Father." This is probably why, when Jesus addressed God as "Our Father" in his familiar prayer, he also added "who is in heaven," to make clear that he was not referring to Abraham.

To trace Jesus' ancestry back to Abraham is to say that Jesus' story begins, not with his birth, but long before. The story of Jesus begins where the story of Israel begins, with Abraham. According to Hebrew tradition, God promised Abraham that he would father a nation, a promise that seemed more improbable with each passing year because, far from being able to parent a nation, Abraham and his wife Sarah could not give birth to a single child. But, as the story goes, when they had almost given up, sure enough, along came their son Isaac, a name which means "he laughs"—a fitting name, indeed, for someone born of parents who were both in their nineties.

In every subsequent generation, the Hebrews held up Abraham as a great example of faith. They saw Abraham as the one who never lost faith that God would somehow make good on his promises, even when everything else seemed to point to the contrary. This old man, his face lined from so many years in the desert that it almost looked like a desert landscape itself, this man believed that God would fulfill his promises. Abraham could imagine a genealogy—as yet without names—that would begin with him and stretch through the centuries. It would be both the history of his lineage and the tracing of the fulfillment of God's promises through the generations.

Later in the genealogy, there is David. Throughout his Gospel Matthew finds various ways to remind us that Jesus is from the lineage of David. It is always nice to be able to claim a little royal blood in your background, but that is not why Matthew makes such a point of the familial connection between David and Jesus. Of course it makes sense that the King of kings would descend from the most beloved of all kings in the history of Israel, but there is more to it than that. The Hebrew people always believed that the promised savior, the Messiah, would come from David's bloodline. When Matthew says that Jesus descended from David, he is entering that as evidence that Jesus is in fact the Messiah.

Many people of Jesus' day did not see in him the promised Messiah. After all, Jesus did not look as though he had descended from the greatest of kings. He was born in a small, dark corner of the world without fanfare. He had no wealth and little education. He spoke with the uncultured accents of the country. And now they are expected to believe that this is a descendant of the great king David, that this is the Messiah?

Even if the people around Jesus doubted that such could be possible, I don't think David himself would have doubted it. Those who revered David as the great and powerful king might forget what David himself could never forget, that he, too, came from a very humble background, that he, too, was an unlikely one to play a special role in God's plan. According to Hebrew tradition, God chose David to be a king when David was but a country boy himself, still with peach fuzz on his face, a shepherd, of all things! What an unlikely beginning for so great a king! But, as David's descendant, Jesus, would even more dramatically demonstrate, God always appears in unlikely places through the most unlikely of people.

If most people have at least one famous ancestor, I also feel quite sure that everyone has at least one notorious ancestor. According to Matthew's genealogy, Jesus is no exception. There are four women mentioned in Jesus' lineage—a fact worth noting in itself. Though I am sure that Jewish genealogists recognized that women had some role in the perpetuation of the family, the women are not usually mentioned in genealogies. But there is also something striking about these four women whom Matthew includes in Jesus' genealogy, because all of them were party to famous scandals.

Tamar is the first. She married Judah's eldest son. When he died, Tamar married Judah's next eldest son, as was the custom. When he died, Judah began to see a disturbing pattern evolving, so he refused to let her marry his third and only remaining son. Tamar wasn't too pleased about this because she very much wanted to have a child. So one day she got dressed up like a prostitute and waited by the side of the road. Her first customer, who could not recognize her with the prostitute's veil over her face, was none other than her former father-in-law Judah. Judah was deceived and a child was conceived. That child was an ancestor of Jesus.

Rahab was a prostitute who lived in Jericho. Unlike Tamar, Rahab was not an amateur prostitute, but a true professional. When Joshua sent some Hebrew spies into Jericho to help case the city before the invasion, they stayed at Rahab's house, or should we say, establishment. When the king of Jericho got word that these spies were staying there, he sent some of his men to capture them. Rahab told the king's men that, yes, some customers answering the description had been there that evening, but they had just left. When the king's men gave up their search, Rahab went up to the roof of her house where the spies were hiding and gave them the all-clear, allowing them to escape. The result was that the Hebrews eventually captured the city. This is the only story told about Rahab. Her name is not mentioned again until the genealogy of Jesus. She had a child named Boaz. That child was an ancestor of Jesus.

Ruth, a Moabite girl—a Gentile—married into a family of Hebrew transplants living in Moab because there was famine going on at home. When Ruth's young husband died, her mother-in-law, Naomi—a widow herself—decided to pull up stakes and head back to Israel because the famine had ended. Although Naomi urged Ruth to remain in Moab among her own people, Ruth insisted that her home was wherever Naomi was. "Where you go, I will go, and where you live, I will live," Ruth told her, "and if your God is Yahweh, then my God is Yahweh too" (Ruth 1:16). When the two widows arrived in Israel they encountered a relative, Boaz, a well-heeled farmer, who helped Ruth when she went to work in his fields. Everything was on the up and up, but Naomi became jealous over all the attention that Boaz lavished on the young Ruth. One night, when Boaz had eaten a big dinner and had tossed down more than a few nightcaps, Naomi suggested that Ruth should lie at the foot of his bed and warm his feet. Naomi knew that Boaz's mother was none other than Rahab and she probably assumed that Rahab's professional activities would have left scars on her young son. In any case, Naomi was sure that when Boaz woke to find Ruth at his feet that he would be so put off that he would reject Ruth. Naomi had also spent enough time with Ruth to conclude that the young woman would be too naïve to anticipate Boaz's reaction. It didn't exactly work out the way Naomi planned. Not only did Ruth warm Boaz's feet, she also warmed his heart and he married her. They had a son named Obed. In time Obed had a son of his own named Jesse, and Jesse in turn had seven sons, the seventh of whom was David, the great king, and an ancestor of Jesus.

Bathsheba, who is referred to in the genealogy as "the wife of Uriah" conceived a son with David. This would have been a joyous occasion, except that Bathsheba happened to be married to someone else at the time. That child eventually died. When Bathsheba's husband died, she had another child with David. That child was an ancestor of Jesus.

Contrary to what we might conclude at first, the stories about these people are not out of keeping with the Christmas story. Rather, Matthew is making an important point by including them in his account of the birth of Jesus. Jesus was born of great patriarchs and kings, to be sure, but Jesus also descended from very real people, with real problems and real flaws. Some were Jews and others were Gentiles. They were not all pious and good people, either. They were, in their own ways, flagrantly human. They were, to put it another way, sinners. Such were Jesus' ancestors, a very human lot, and such were the kinds of individuals Jesus sought out during his life. His genealogy reminds us that even before Jesus was born he had a special kinship with sinners.

Beyond the famous and the scandalous there are many names in Jesus' lineage about whom we know nothing. They are not mentioned elsewhere in the Bible. They had their hour upon the stage of history and slipped silently away. We can imagine a few things about them though: they worked, had hopes and dreams, wept, laughed and struggled. Along the way, they had occasion to wonder what it was all about.

We know they had children. Those children had children. One of those children was Jesus of Nazareth, God's anointed one, the Savior of the world. And so these names: Abiud, Eliakim, Azor, Zadok, Achim, Eliud, Eleazar, and all the rest—have come to mean a great deal to me. Behind these names I have come to see people who contributed no memorable words, amassed no great power, achieved no great fame—which is to say, they were people very much like you and me. Yet, wild miracle that it is, they too played an important role in God's plan from the very beginning. They remind me that we are often the last to sense how God might be at work in and through our lives. God's design is hidden from us who live as just one small part of that design. Jesus' ancestors remind me that we are often the last to know how our seemingly random and restless lives might in some way contribute to God's plan. These people, now just names to us, but so much more to God, also remind me that there is no such thing as an anonymous person in the sight of God.

When I read this list of names bridging the centuries between Abraham and Jesus, I am struck by something else. Advent is a time of expectant waiting for the birth of Jesus. In this waiting we join, not only with all of our Christian brothers and sisters of every tongue and race, but also with those named in Jesus' genealogy, and with all others who anticipated his birth for generations, awaiting the fulfillment of the promise.

This Advent, as we wait for the coming of the Lord, we join Abraham, David, Tamar, Azor and all the others in history who waited. Together we wait for the light that is to come into the world. We wait together for Jesus, who casts his light centuries into the future, to our lives, and centuries into the past, to their lives as well.

COMMENT

Martin Copenhaver is right. In forty years, this is the first time I've read a sermon on the "begats." I wasn't sure it could be done. The preacher must have felt as much of a challenge as the composer who set the text to music. How well Copenhaver does this sermon is an indication of what we can learn from him about preaching.

HOW THIS SERMON ILLUSTRATES GOOD PREACHING

Biblical stories. Copenhaver includes important characters from the genealogy using contemporary words in succinct paragraphs to tell six stories. If a congregation is biblically literate, what stories a single name can carry! This connects the lineage and helps us see the unfolding process of God's revelation.

Analogy and choice descriptions. Copenhaver preaches with pictures, not just words. He helps us see, not just hear. Comparing the text with the Manhattan telephone book and a hologram works beautifully. Describing Abraham's lined face as a desert landscape, and David's youthful beard as "peach fuzz," enables us to see them in our imagination. The mention of famous scandals peaks our interest. Reminding us that Jesus' ancestors were flagrantly human is a way some might describe Jesus' Incarnation. Referring to Naomi's family as Israeli transplants makes the story more contemporary. These choice descriptive words bring life to the sermon.

Women's stories. In earlier times these stories probably would not have been used in a sermon. As a result of the women's movement, and our resulting awareness, it's essential we review the stories of women in the Bible and recognize their wisdom, contributions and significance in our faith history. These stories are good illustrations of how women contributed, often in spite of, rather than because of, their circumstances.

Pulling the hearer into the sermon. A friend who read the Gospels for the first time after her midlife conversion said she found herself on every page except that of the "begats." Copenhaver helps us find ourselves even there.

Telling stories with which the hearer can identify, whether by sexual or character traits, is one way of getting the listener involved. Copenhaver also "hooks" his hearers by mentioning those in the genealogy about whom we know nothing, who "slipped silently away." Many of us feel this way about ourselves at times. But then the preacher turns this to a positive feeling near the end of the sermon when he says that in waiting through advent "we also join...with those named in Jesus' genealogy." Meaning is cast into the future as well as the past.

What a wonderful touch to remind us we are part of God's plan.

Humor. The humor in the sermon is almost subliminal, coming out consciously in the references to the absence of children in the service and the Christian Coalition. Yet there are other places humor is felt: the reference to the "begats" set to music, Luke's placement of the genealogy, the reference to one famous and one notorious ancestor, and to Rahab's house as an "establishment." Levity brings balance to preaching and heightens the impact of more serious aspects in communicating the gospel.

Style. The paragraph about those we don't know in Jesus' genealogy illustrates the skill of the preacher. "They worked. They had hopes and dreams. They wept. They laughed. They struggled. Along the way, they had occasion to wonder what it was all about." The pace and timing are like poetry.

THEOLOGICAL CONSIDERATIONS AND PASTORAL CARE

This sermon is strong theologically because it reminds us of essential Christian truth. The way Copenhaver proclaims this truth reveals his pastoral heart. We all need to be reassured that God makes good on God's promises, especially when everything seems to point to the contrary. We all need to recognize that God appears in unlikely places through unlikely people. We all need to be reminded that we are sometimes the last to see how God is at work in our lives and yet are a part of

God's design, however small or large that might be. In our day of impersonal living we want to know that God is not impersonal and we are not
anonymous in God's sight. In keeping with the Advent season in which
the sermon was preached, Copenhaver reminds us that expectant waiting is part of our spiritual journey. Making these truths relevant is pastoral care at its best.

The way in which the preacher handles each biblical story is also an
expression of his pastoral concerns. If one can discuss sex, prostitutes, a
king's adultery, notorious ancestors, and a man who sees immortality in
his descendants—and do it all with a pastoral heart—then no person
should be afraid to open his or her own heart to such a pastor.

Overall, this is an excellent sermon in both style and content. In it
we see the fine art of preaching.

SUGGESTIONS

- Titles can stimulate our imagination and increase our interest in
  hearing a sermon. I wonder if this one could be more appealing.
  "Begat" and "beget" are archaic words. Young people and baby
  boomers may never have read the King James Version. Current
  popular translations use "was the father of." Would "Jesus' Family
  Tree" be better, or some allusion to Jesus' socially mixed background?

- Have you ever tried preaching from the genealogies of Jesus in
  Matthew and Luke? Compare and contrast these two genealogies
  (Matthew 1:1–17; Luke 3:23–28) and do a sermon focusing on
  how these genealogies serve the purposes of each Gospel.

- As interesting as Copenhaver's interpretation of Naomi's and Ruth's
  relationship is, I could find no biblical justification for it. Is Naomi's
  jealousy and assumption about Boaz's relationship with his mother
  just an interesting conjecture, or was it employed to make us go
  back and read the story again? It certainly made me reread the
  story. In a sophisticated congregation, this might be a good educa-
  tional technique, just as I reread the story of Tamar to be sure she

had twins instead of just the one child mentioned in the sermon. If we use assumption or conjecture, it's helpful to make that clear to our listeners.

- Do a sermon or series on Copenhaver's theme, "We join all the others in history who waited." Consider, for example, using Hebrews 10:35–11:40 as a text. How might you draw on your own family history to illustrate the sermon(s)?

Paul D. Lowder

C O M M E N T

TOPICAL INDEX

Advent

The Begetting of Jesus 291

The Visit of the Magi 151

Blindness

Sight for Sore Eyes 33

Change

A Surprising Unconventional Friend 251

What Really Changes People? 279

Church

Sight for Sore Eyes 33

Cross

Praying in the Darkness at Noon 227

Death

Ellipsis and Eternity 111

Elijah

What Are You Doing Here? 167

Eternity

Ellipsis and Eternity 111

Failure

What Are You Doing Here? 167

Family

The Love that Lies Beneath the Woe 237

Forgiveness

A Surprising Unconventional Friend 251

Bruised Reeds and Dimly Burning Wicks 17

Practicing Forgiveness 183

Fulfillment

Temple Crossing 49

God

    Bruised Reeds and Dimly Burning Wicks 17

    The Man Jesus 63

Good Friday

    Praying in the Darkness at Noon .227

Grace

    On Taking Pain Seriously 99

    What Are You Doing Here? 167

    What Really Changes People? 279

Hiddenness of God

    Meanwhile 127

Idolatry

    Bruised Reeds and Dimly Burning Wicks 17

Injustice

    A Dangerous Disturbance 213

    The Love that Lies Beneath the Woe 237

Intersection

    Temple Crossing 49

Jesus

    Risky Business 139

    The Begetting of Jesus 291

    The Man Jesus 63

Joseph

    Meanwhile 127

    The Love that Lies Beneath the Woe 237

Light

    Sight for Sore Eyes 33

Listening to God

    The Visit of the Magi 151

    What Are You Doing Here? 167

Lostness

    Lost and Found: Climbing the Wrong Ladder 197

Love

    The Love that Lies Beneath the Woe 237

    What Really Changes People? 279

Meaning

    Life As It Is Supposed to Be Lived 267

Meditation

    Life As It Is Supposed to Be Lived 267

Memories

    The Love that Lies Beneath the Woe 237

Mentors

    Blessed by Mentors 83

Mission

    Lost and Found: Climbing the Wrong Ladder 197

Moral Vision

    Sight for Sore Eyes 33

Pain

    On Taking Pain Seriously 99

    The Love that Lies Beneath the Woe 237

Prayer

    Life As It Is Supposed to Be Lived 267

    Praying in the Darkness at Noon 227

Prophetic Voice

    A Dangerous Disturbance 213

Risk

    Risky Business 139

Salvation

    Temple Crossing 49

    The Man Jesus 63

Servanthood

    Risky Business 139

Social Justice

    A Dangerous Disturbance 213

Suffering

   Bruised Reeds and Dimly Burning Wicks 17

Waiting

   Temple Crossing 49

Wisdom

   The Visit of the Magi 151

Zacchaeus

   A Surprising Unconventional Friend 251

   Lost and Found: Climbing the Wrong Ladder 197

   What Really Changes People? 279

Scripture Index

Genesis 37:1–4, 29–36 127

Genesis 45:1–15a 237

1 Samuel 3:1–10 83

1 Kings 19:1–18 167

2 Kings 20:1–21 111

Psalm 1 267

Psalm 2 267

Isaiah 42:1–9 17

Amos 8:1–12 213

Matthew 1:1–17 291

Matthew 2:1–12 ....17, 151

Matthew 18:21–35 183

Matthew 25:14–30 139

Mark 15:33–34 227

Luke 2:22–32 49

Luke 9:49–56 63

Luke 19:1–10 ....197, 251, 279

John 6:1–15 63

John 9:1–41 33

2 Corinthians 12:7–10 99

Colossians 1:15–20 63